The Iran-Iraq War

The Iran-Iraq War

The Politics of Aggression

Edited by

Farhang Rajaee

University Press of Florida

Gainesville / Tallahassee / Tampa / Boca Raton

Pensacola / Orlando / Miami / Jacksonville

The University Press of Florida is the scholarly publishing agency for the State University System of Florida, comprised of Florida A & M University, Florida Atlantic University, Florida International University, Florida State University, University of Central Florida, University of Florida, University of North Florida, University of South Florida, and University of West Florida.

Library of Congress Cataloging in Publication data appear on the last printed page of the book.

University Press of Florida
15 Northwest 15th Street
Gainesville, FL 32611

Contents

Acknowledgments

In 1988, a number of Iranian universities and research centers sponsored The International Conference on Aggression and Defense. I owe a great deal to many people who contributed both in organizing the conference and later in preparing the book. Dr. Kamal Kharazi, a professor at Tehran University and the conference chair, maintained his enthusiasm and encouragement throughout the book's preparation. Walda Metcalf and the staff at the University Press of Florida deserve special thanks not only for their competent work but for keeping the lines of communication open with me overseas. The contributors were thoughtful, generous, and forthcoming. The staff who helped translate some of the papers from Persian into English and those who helped in typing were kind and helpful. The comments of the anonymous readers of the manuscript were welcomed and are hereby acknowledged.

Farhang Rajaee

1

Introduction

FARHANG RAJAEE

The Iraqi army crossed the border of Kuwait on August 2, 1990, and occupied the capital city of this small oil-rich state on the southern edge of the Persian Gulf. The occupation lasted a few months and ended on February 28, 1991, after an offensive launched by a conglomeration of forces basically from Western powers and in accordance with the general guidelines of United Nations resolutions.

This event was not the first in recent years in which the Iraqi army had committed an act of aggression, one not only against the principle of good neighborly relations but also against the principles of international law. The same army crossed the border of Iran on September 22, 1980, and started a war with the newly established revolutionary regime in that country. For social, economic, political, and historical reasons, and specifically as a reaction to the revived Islamic revolutionary ideology, this war lasted almost a decade with both sides spending about $350 billion. It ended in August 1987 when Iran formally accepted Security Council Resolution 598 on July 18, 1988, which called for a cease-fire. Neither side could claim victory—although, interestingly, Saddam Hussein did so in a speech on the anniversary of the Ba'ath party's accession to power on July 17, 1991—but the war left its mark on relations between the two countries, on the region's political configuration, and on international political alignments.

Considering Clausewitz's famous maxim that "war is a mere continuation of policy by other means," exactly what type of policy has the Iraqi government been pursuing?[1] And considering that the strategists of any war argue that they are pursuing peace and that the war is "to end all wars,"[2] and granting that the Iraqi regime had a clear policy objective in mind, what kind of "desired order" had they intended for the region? It seems that these questions lie at the heart of the wars that have occurred in the Middle East during the last decade. This collection of essays addresses these questions in a detailed, thorough, and comprehensive way, but within the context of the Iraqi war with Iran.

Since Iraq emerged as a relatively powerful state in the Middle East after the Ba'ath party seized power in 1968, the Iraqis have dreamed about assuming the leadership of the Arab world and becoming the dominant power in the region. During the rule of the monarchy, set up in Iraq by the British in 1920, the central government was involved in maintaining order and pursuing economic development but with little success. The repressive and violent nature of the Ba'ath regime notwithstanding, its ruling elite has not only been successful in establishing security and order; with the phenomenal rise in oil prices between 1973 and 1980, it has been able to implement impressive economic development to a point that seems to have made its repression bearable. Iraq also instituted an active regional policy and, coming out of a long period of isolation, established strong ties with the Soviet Union. In terms of its broader political objective of becoming a leading nation in the area, Iraq cast itself as the defender of the Arab cause. During the 1970s, it utilized "anti-Western" and "anti-Zionist" postures and, during the 1980s, took one of "rejectionist front, anti-Iran, and antirevolution."

Two regional developments gave new impetus to the leaders of the Iraqi regime. The first relates to internal Arab politics. While Nasser of Egypt was alive, the new elite in Iraq did not think of competing with him for leadership of the Arab world. But his death, coupled with the emergence of Saddam Hussein as the powerful deputy in charge of internal security during the presidency of his relative, Ahmad Hussan al-Bakr, marked a new beginning in Iraq's foreign policy. Second, the British withdrawal from the region in 1971 provided an opportunity for the Iraqis to think of themselves as a major regional power. The "golden age of British paramountcy"—in Chubin's words, the period during which domestic disruptions, regional wars, and interference of other outside powers were prevented—disappeared from the region.[3] The policy of regional security had come on the scene, and the political and economic powers of Iran and Saudi Arabia entered into informal cooperation (the "twin pillar" policy) and assumed the responsibility of preserving regional order. In effect, this new arrangement pushed the Iraqi elite's dream for dominance to the background, even though they played on the anti-Western and anticonservative postures. At the same time, as part of their economic development plan, they maintained their military build-up.

The Islamic revolution and the assumption of power by an Islamic elite which had been trying to establish an Islamic order not only took everyone by surprise but drastically affected the region's political configuration. The departure of the shah from Iran on January 17, 1979, removed the greatest hindrance for the Baghdad regime. In fact, Saddam saw himself—in the 1970s as vice-president of Iraq and later as its president when he assumed that responsibility on July 16, 1979—as a competitor of the shah. In late October 1979, Saddam Hussein demanded a revision of the 1975 Algiers agreement. This treaty was intended to put an end to a dispute that had begun centuries before Iraq emerged as a state. None of the treaties or protocols—from the agreements of 1639, the treaty of 1847, the protocol of 1913, to the accord of 1937—were satisfactory for long. And the Iraqis saw the 1975 treaty as imposing the power of the shah on them. When Saddam Hussein tore up the treaty on September 17, 1979, he justified his action by claiming to be the defender of the Arab lands: "We have taken the decision to recover all our territories. The waters of Shatt al-Arab must return to their former Iraqi and Arab rule and be placed entirely under Iraqi sovereignty."[4]

These declarations were only a pretext for the Ba'ath regime in Iraq to follow its objective of becoming the leader of the Arab world and of emerging as the strongest power in the region. Egypt's isolation in the aftermath of the Camp David Accords gave Saddam Hussein the opportunity to lead "the rejectionist front" and cast himself as the champion of the Palestinian cause. The revolutionary situation in Iran and the presumed weakness of the revolutionary state seemed to be the opportunity Saddam had been awaiting. Thus, destruction of the revolutionary regime became a pillar of Iraq's strategy. Months before its actual invasion of Iran, Iraq had shown its disapproval and dislike of the Islamic regime, particularly its strong Shi'i zeal. In April 1979, many Iraqis were forced out of their country for their Shi'i background and, as one scholar puts it, for their roles as "potential revolutionaries."[5] Now it seemed that Baghdad's "rejectionist" and "antirevolutionary" postures would be more effective in Saddam's pursuit of dominance.

Interestingly enough, Saddam's policy converged with a tendency gradually taking shape in the West: to contain the revolution within Iranian boundaries. Washington viewed the revolutionary Iran as the bigger threat to U.S. interests in the region. Politics *do* make strange bedfellows, and gradually the interests of Saddam's Iraq and those of the West—at least their short-term interests—coincided. When Iran cast the United States as "the great Satan" and seized its embassy in Tehran a new element was introduced, a less rational factor, and everyone forgot the real intention of Saddam Hussein and his anti-Western postures and sentiments during the preceding decade. It took Saddam's second invasion, this time of Kuwait, for the world to think more soberly about him.

By then, however, the Iraq-Iran war had taken many turns and had in fact become regional as well as international. Regional politics, the politics of oil, economic competition for cheaper energy, the struggle of status quo versus revolutionary zeal, and family dramas concerning the fate of the U.S. hostages had all intermingled to make it harder to comprehend political developments and trends. What exacerbated the situation was the fact that, on the one hand, the war had gone beyond the bounds of international norms with, for example, the use of chemical warfare and attacks on cities. On the other hand, the usual channels of political and diplomatic discourse were replaced by public media, and the whole political development of the region was undermined by sentiments about the hostage issue. Thus, it became harder to distinguish fact from figure or reality from image. Understanding the reality of the situation not only helps unravel the complex regional politics, if a workable regional order should take effect and be accepted; it also sheds light on more pertinent questions related to human affairs in the course of revolution and war.

To that end, these essays have emerged from among more than fifty papers presented at the International Conference on Aggression and Defense held in Tehran in the summer of 1988. A number of Iranian universities and research centers sponsored the conference, with the aim of studying and evaluating this longest conventional war in recent history. University teachers, lawyers, prominent religious leaders, and scholars from the Islamic world and other faiths and regions participated.

Conference organizers began with a set of questions in mind. What were the underlying issues involved in this war? Who was really the aggressor, and what were the objectives? Was it a border dispute? Were issues related to or rooted in historical difficulties? Or was it a means to stop a revolution that had upset the regional status quo and seemed to be on the verge of upsetting the existing world order and balance of power? Was the war imposed on Iran because, contrary to many people's expectations, the revolution there did not stop at its boundaries? While the conference organizers hoped that such questions would be addressed, greater hope was put on more practical matters such as analyzing the attitudes, intentions, and behaviors of the belligerents, particularly those of Iraq, throughout the various stages of the war.

Many participants dealt with these questions and, by doing so, contributed to our understanding of the nature of war, revolution, order, law, and political behavior. The underlying problems of the Iraq-Iran war that stood out were those of aggression and defense. The Iranians were forced to defend their national integrity and their newly formed revolutionary government. Like other human affairs, the war became complicated and touched on a great number of issues relating to regional and international politics. For example, it had global ramifications for the international oil trade. Relating to Iranian domestic affairs and the unfolding of the revolution, a number of participants addressed ideological justifications or theological exposition for the war, its necessity, continuation, and termination. Each raised many questions and concerns and stimulated intensive debate.

This book, however, cannot include all the papers presented at the conference. Some were too theoretical and academic in nature, and focusing on them here would divert attention from the real problem. The book addresses some concrete issues directly related to the war so as to facilitate our comprehension. For example, because of the proximity of the Persian Gulf to the war zone and because of the strategic and economic import of this international water, the war was bound to affect the region and involve some of the smaller states of the area. Thus, while it was appealing to include papers that dealt with regional issues, this was avoided intentionally. Then the Iraqi invasion of Kuwait outdated some issues altogether. The approach taken here, then, was to concentrate on the more immediate problem, namely the border dispute over Shatt al-Arab. Therefore, only chapters that contribute to the understanding of the conflict—its development, its implications, regional and international involvement, and its significance—were included.

A few words should be added about the revision of the papers and the editorial work. The chapters included reflect the contemporary thoughts of the contributors on the issues related to the war that they were asked to address, as well as the way in which the war was perceived at the time. The changes that have occurred in the region—the peace between Iran and Iraq, the death of the Ayatollah Imam Khomeini in June 1989, the Iraqi invasion of Kuwait, and the impact of the changes in the former Soviet Union—and the amount of information available to scholars, resulting from concerted efforts by all sides to reveal prewar alignments and dealings, no doubt would influence the analysis of the participants had they been asked to revise their papers. Thus, it was decided to preserve them as they were presented, except for turning them into essays for a book.

One important aspect of the statistics presented in some chapters, particularly in chapter 4, must be mentioned. Details of Iraqi attacks on Iranian cities or Iraq's destruction of historical sites, as well as Iraq's use of chemical weapons, were taken from the data bank and publications of what is now called the Center for Documents of the Imposed War. To verify the validity of the assertions in these chapters, I visited the center. Established after the war, it used to be called War Information Headquarters as part of the Joint Chief of Staff of the Iranian armed forces. It is a computerized document center collecting data on all aspects of the war. I was told that this center, on written request, provides information to any scholar or research institute interested in war-related issues. The address given in their bulletin is Center for Documents of the Imposed War, No. 4 Mir-Emad Street, Mutahari Ave., P.O. Box 15875/1615, Tehran. Details of the attacks of the Iraqis from the beginning to the end of the war are being processed and published.

Part I of this book deals with why the war happened, how it began and unfolded, and how it came to a halt. It examines, in detail, the areas in which the Iraqis have inflicted damage not only on Iranian people but on many of their neighbors and allies as well. It analyzes the "war of the cities," chemical warfare, and damage to cultural treasures, in general the way in which the war left its mark on Iran, Iraq, and their respective heritages. Part II looks beyond Iran and Iraq to the effect of the war on the region and on the powers outside the region, analyzing how others saw, interpreted, and reacted to the war. Part III is an attempt to make sense of the war (if sense can be made out of the deaths of tens of thousands on both sides and physical and psychological mass destruction) and what it might mean in terms of international law, Islamic jurisprudence, international relations theory, and historical perspective. It also introduces those aspects of the war that constitute new developments in international laws of war and suggests ways in which these laws could be improved.

Notes

1. Clausewitz wrote, "War is not merely a political act, but also a real political instrument, a continuation of political commerce, a carrying out of the same by other means"; see Claus von Clausewitz, *On War*, ed. Anatole Rapoport (Middlesex, U.K.: Penguin Books, reprint 1974), 119.
2. The general tendency is to cast a war as the means to bring about peace. World War I was always portrayed as "the war to end all wars."
3. Sharam Chubin, "Post-Gulf Security," *Survival* 33, no. 2 (March-April 1991): 142.
4. Cited in John Bulloch and Harvey Morries, *The Gulf War* (London: Methuen London Co., 1989), 38.
5. Ibid., 21.

Part I

Genesis, Development, and Implication

2

Iraqi Attitudes and Interpretation of the 1975 Agreement

IBRAHIM ANVARI TEHRANI

On September 22, 1980, Iraq initiated an all-out premeditated war against Iran, aiming to subvert the Islamic Republic of Iran.[1] Iraqi armed forces managed to bring large areas in western Iran under their occupation. My purpose here is to demonstrate the ill will of Iraqi leaders and the obstructions put in the way of implementing the treaties existing between the two countries.

After Abdol Karim Qasim's coup d'état in July 1958, disputes between Iran and Iraq intensified. From the earliest days of the coup, the Iraqi press published articles against Iran and Radio Baghdad broadcast anti-Iran programs. Iraqi officials began to mistreat Iranians residing in Iraq and to harass Iranian nationals in border regions. The government of Iran showed tolerance and resilience and seized every opportunity to ameliorate the situation. In the latter part of October 1958, Iranian leaders expressed hope that the government of Iraq would participate in the session of the special commission charged with settling boundary problems and questions relating to the Shatt al-Arab waterway by November 6, 1958, so that problems relating to demarcation of frontiers and the arrangements for the administration of the river could be totally settled. The Iraqi government not only showed reluctance to fulfill agreements existing between the two countries but also created new difficulties for Iran in Shatt al-Arab. The rich province of Khuzestan became the target of Iraq's expansionist ambitions. Abdol Karim Qasim declared on December 18, 1959, "We do not wish to refer to the history of Arab tribes residing in Ahwaz and Mohamareh [Khorramshahr]. The Ottoman government of the time handed over Mohamareh, which was part of Iraqi territory, to Iran."

The Iraqi government's dissatisfaction about Khuzestan was not limited to words and rhetorical statements. Iraq started to support secessionist movements in Khuzestan Province and raised the question of Khuzestan in the council of the Arab League, but it was not successful. With the overthrow of Abdol Karim Qasim in 1963 there was a period of relative calm between the two countries for five years. They reached understandings in an OPEC conference on the possibility of equitable and joint exploitation of oil resources and on border problems. When the Ba'ath party came to power in Iraq in 1968, the new government started repeating the old claims for full sovereignty over Shatt al-Arab, thus causing talks between Iran and Iraq to fail.

The expansionist intentions of the new Iraqi government were not confined to its claim over Shatt al-Arab. The deputy prime minister of Iraq declared in 1969, "Iraq has not had serious dispute with Iran over Shatt al-Arab, since this is part of Iraq's territory. The dispute is in connection with Arabistan [Khuzestan] which is part of Iraq's soil and was annexed to Iran during foreign rule." *Al-Jomhuriye*, a newspaper published in Baghdad, declared that a new radio station would begin broadcasting exclusively for "Arabistan" from Basra. At the same time, the Basra television station exhibited a new map of Iraq in which the province of Khuzestan was depicted as "Arabistan" and as part of Iraqi territory. On November 28, 1973, Channel 7 in Baghdad broadcast a program called "Things from History." In this program, the commonly known names of Iranian cities were changed, and even Khorramshahr was shown to be a part of the Iraqi province of Nasserieh. Furthermore, the Arab and Baluchi Iranians were encouraged to rebel against the central government.

The withdrawal of British forces from the Persian Gulf in 1971 helped further the ambitions of the government of Iraq and intensified the old fears and distrust between Iran and Iraq. After Iran restored its sovereignty over the three islands of Greater and Lesser Tonbs and Abu Musa, the Iraqi government severed diplomatic relations with Iran and declared that these islands belong to the Arabs. Iraq complained to the Arab League and the United Nations and proposed in meetings of the Arab League that all Arab states should break relations with Iran. This proposal was rejected. Iraq's complaint to the United Nations was also to no avail, so, in retaliation, Iraq expelled more than 70,000 Iranians.

As a result of the adverse relations between Iran and Iraq, the crisis shifted to the northern borders. During 1972–74 a number of border skirmishes took place. The most important of these, known as "Bloody Sunday," occurred on February 10, 1974. In this incident, heavy equipment was used and a large number of military forces from both sides were killed and wounded. The Iraqi government took the case to the UN Security Council, claiming that Iran had occupied five square kilometers of Iraqi territory and had concentrated large numbers of armed forces along the border and calling for an urgent meeting of the Security Council. The government of Iran asked the secretary-general to send an envoy to prove the invalidity of the Iraqi claims.

After hearing the comments and views of the representatives of both sides, on February 28, 1974, the Security Council did decide to send a special envoy to the region. The council also called on the two parties to refrain from any provocations until the results of the investigation were published. This cease-fire went into effect on March 7, 1974. Secretary-General Kurt Waldheim delegated Vickman Múñez, the representative of Mexico, to travel to Iraq and Iran and to visit border areas.

After hearing the report of the secretary-general's special envoy, the Security Council adopted Resolution 348, according to which the two parties agreed to (1) observe strictly the March 7, 1974, cease-fire; (2) withdraw promptly and simultaneously the forces of the two countries from the border areas; (3) refrain from any hostile action against one another; and (4) resume talks between the two countries without preconditions and with a view to finding a solution for all problems between them.

Disputes over the border and administration of Shatt al-Arab continued, and border clashes intensified. Pursuant to the visit of the UN envoy to the border areas, the cease-fire of March 4, 1974, was instituted; talks between Iran and Iraq began, and the two countries exchanged ambassadors. Saddam Hussein, vice-president of the Revolutionary Command Council of Iraq, summoned the Iranian ambassador and offered a proposal to settle problems relating to Shatt al-Arab and frontiers and security along the border. He emphasized that it would be to the benefit of both Iraq and Iran to reach a comprehensive solution to their disputes.

In keeping with this proposal and to implement Resolution 348 of the UN Security Council, the foreign ministers of Iran and Iraq met in Istanbul on January 16, 1975, but with no results. Following the meeting of OPEC heads of state in Algiers on March 4–6, 1975, Iran and Iraq issued a joint communiqué announcing that an agreement had been reached on the disputes between the two countries. The principles agreed to by the two sides in the Algiers Declaration are

- to effect a definitive demarcation of their land frontiers on the basis of the Protocol of Constantinople, 1913, and the *procès-verbaux* of the Delimitation of Frontiers Commission of 1914;
- to limit their fluvial frontiers according to the Thalweg line;
- accordingly, to restore security and mutual trust along their common boundaries and hence commit themselves to excercising strict and effective control over their common borders with a view to putting a definitive end to all acts of infiltration of a subversive character no matter where they originate;
- to consider the arrangement referred to above as integral elements of a comprehensive solution; hence, any impairment of any of their components shall naturally be contrary to the spirit of the Algiers Agreement.[2]

In order to carry out the principles reached in Algiers, the foreign ministers of Iran, Iraq, and Algeria met alternately a number of times in Tehran, Baghdad, and Algiers to draw up and sign documents envisaged in the Algiers Declaration. In a Tehran meeting held March 15–17, 1975, it was agreed that three committees should be established and that the experts of the two sides should prepare preliminary documents determining the method for posting border marks and report on their progress at the next session in Baghdad. It was also agreed that, if possible, 513 new border marks be posted along the land frontiers, in addition to the 216 old ones. Although Iranian leaders believed that it would be better for the two sides to sit at negotiation tables freely and with their own initiative, Iraqi authorities, particularly Saddam Hussein, insisted on acceptance of the principle of arbitration and on consultation with Algerian arbiters in case of dispute. Hence, it was agreed that Algerian experts would act as arbitrators, subject to the commitment of the two sides to accept arbitration judgment.

In Baghdad, between April 19 and 25, 1975, the decisions of the three committees on land frontiers and control of borders were reviewed and approved. In this session the experts of the three governments agreed that there was no need for positioning more than 380 border marks. But when the matter was raised in the plenary meeting by the foreign ministers, the Iraqi minister declared unexpectedly that previous proposals had been approved by the Revolutionary Command Council and that no modifications to them would be acceptable. Therefore, it was agreed that 513 border marks, as previously proposed, would be positioned along the frontier. Iraqi authorities, however, did not fulfill their obligations and failed to provide necessary facilities to expedite the work.

In meetings in Algiers, held on May 18–20, 1975, the foreign ministers decided on the documents to be signed in Baghdad the next month. The following documents were presented there:

- a treaty concerning the state frontier and neighborly relations, stressing peaceful resolution of disputes, via bilateral talks, the good offices of a friendly third state, or recourse to arbitration;
- a protocol concerning redemarcation of state land frontiers (in Article 1 of this protocol, the two contracting parties confirm and recognize that state land frontiers between Iran and Iraq have been redemarcated by the mixed Iraqi, Iranian, Algerian Committee on the basis of the Constantinople Protocol of 1913, and the proceedings of the Delimitation of Frontiers Commission of 1914);
- a protocol concerning the delimitation of the river frontier between Iran and Iraq (in Article 1 of this protocol, the two contracting parties

> declared and recognized that the stated river frontier between Iran and Iraq in the Shatt al-Arab had been delimited along the Thalweg Line).

Following ratification by the parliaments of the two countries in June 1976, the above treaties came into effect. The land frontiers between Iran and Iraq were redemarcated on the basis of the Constantinople Protocol of 1913 and the minutes of the meetings of the Frontier Delimitation Commission of 1914. In accordance with Article 4 of the protocol concerning redemarcation of state land frontiers and the exchanged letters dated June 22, 1976, between the foreign ministers of Iran and Iraq, it was decided that the transfer of the territories, public and private buildings, and installations whose ownership had been altered by the redemarcation should be officially carried out under the supervision of a mixed Iranian-Iraqi Commission.

The commission began its work in Tehran on May 14, 1978, after a delay of almost one year. Members exchanged views on the joint implementation of the assigned functions and the formation of subcommissions, their terms, and working procedures. The Iraqi delegation, however, disregarded the agenda and announced that, before embarking on such transfers, the location of twenty-one border marks should be changed. Thus, Iraq again disputed issues that were already agreed on and settled by arbitration (as proposed by Saddam Hussein himself), thus delaying the work of the commission. Despite the fact that the Iranian side had declared its full readiness to begin the transfer immediately, the Iraqi side left Tehran before the work was completed.

Later, the Iraqi Embassy sent a note to the Ministry of Foreign Affairs of Iran repeating the views of the Iraqi delegation. In reply, the government of Iran declared that it was prepared to implement immediately the transfer of territories, public and private buildings, and constructions whose national possession had been altered by the redemarcation of land frontiers. But the Iraqi authorities remained silent until September 7, 1980. On September 8, 10, and 17, 1980, the chargé d'affaires of the Islamic Republic of Iran was called to the Foreign Ministry of Iraq, where two notes were handed to him stating that "the Iraqi armed forces are obliged to suppress the aggression of Iran on Zayn al-Qaws and Hose-Meimak."

Iraq was also reluctant to prepare border maps. The revolutionary government of Iran, in accordance with the principle of *pacta sunt servanda*, respected the 1975 treaty and strictly observed its provisions. To implement the protocol concerning state land frontiers, Iran sent the Iraqi Embassy in Tehran eighty maps of frontier lines on the scale of 1:25000 attached to a number of notes, including those of May 17, 1979, No. 1294/18; June 6, 1979, No. 3114/18; June 15, 1979, No. 424/11/11596/18; and February 18, 1980, No. 424/11/12209/18. These maps were prepared in accordance with Article 1 of the said protocol and were sent to the Iraqi Embassy for the Iraqis to indicate the names of villages, towns, and other natural or artificial landmarks. But the Iraqi officials did not reply to even one of these notes and failed to complete and return any of the maps. When two Iraqi bulldozers trespassed on Iranian territory in order to pave the area for drilling oil wells and constructing camping grounds, Iran protested and sent three notes—dated October 24, 1979, January 24, 1980, and February 14, 1980—to the Iraqi Embassy in Tehran. The notes referred to the record relating to the land frontier between Iran and Iraq annexed to the protocol on land frontiers, showing the commitment of the Islamic Republic of Iran to honor the 1975 treaty.

In accordance with the protocol concerning security of the frontier, the army of the Islamic Republic of Iran prepared the Simorgh Plan to prevent infiltration of a subversive element into the territory of the two countries. This plan was not carried out due to heavy snow and was shelved for a long period because of the onset of the Islamic revolution. It was resubmitted to Iraqi authorities at the commencement of revolts in northern Iraq and Iran's Kurdistan Province. Iraqi authorities, however, did not respond. They called back their liaison officers and ordered Iranian liaison officers based in Iraq to leave by March 1979.

The government of the Islamic Republic of Iran adhered firmly to the 1975 treaty. Even after the bombardment of Iranian border villages in the summer of 1979 by Iraqi bombers, the Iranian government dispatched the governor-general of west Azarbaijan to hold talks with his counterpart in Soleimanieh. But the Iraqi regime, claiming to have been forced into the 1975 treaty, considered the period following the victory of the Islamic revolution the best time to revise and possibly annul the treaty. Accordingly, it planned to weaken it gradually. This is evident if we look at the following statements made by Iraqi officials.

(1) The ambassador of Iraq in Beirut, in his interview with An-Nahar (November 3, 1979), said the improvement of relations between Iran and Iraq depended on the realization of the following conditions: (a) revising the 1975 Algiers Agreement with regard to Shatt al-Arab; (b) granting autonomy to Kurd, Baluchi, and Arab minorities in Iran; and (c) withdrawal of the Iranian armed forces from the Tonb and Abu Musa Islands of the Persian Gulf.

(2) Saddam Hussein, in an interview in April 1980, set three conditions for the cessation of hostilities between Iran and Iraq: (a) unconditional withdrawal of Iran from the two Tunbs and Abu Musa Islands; (b) restoration of pre-1975 situation to Shatt al-Arab; (c) recognition by Iran of Khuzistan as an Arab province (using the fictitious name of Arabistan).

(3) In April 1980, at a gathering in north Iraq, in a harsh attack on Iranian leaders, Saddam Hussein declared that Iraq was prepared to settle all of its differences with Iran by resorting to force.

(4) Sadoun Hammadi, who was visiting Finland, said that there was a weak probability for military confrontation between Iran and Iraq but that nothing was impossible.

(5) Naim Haddad, then vice-president of Iraq, stated in an interview reported by Associated Press from Kuwait in April 1980 that "Iraq will endeavor to establish full control over Shatt al-Arab."

Why did the Ba'athist regime of Iraq talk constantly about revising and (later) annulling the 1975 treaty, which, by virtue of its fourth article, was permanent, unalterable, and inviolable? And why did the Iraqis question the Islamic Republic's adherence to it? Is there better proof of Iran's adherence to this treaty than its implementation of it even during the revolution? If the Islamic Republic did not mean to adhere to the treaty, why would it send to Iraq, at a time when it was so preoccupied with the revolution, the useful border maps and the Simorgh Project, which was intended to prevent the penetration of saboteurs into the territory of both countries? And why should the foreign minister of Iran, participating in the Havana Conference, propose to Iraqi officials that they cooperate to implement the protocol concerning frontier security, good neighborly relations, commercial, technical, and economic dealings, pilgrimage tours, and the security of the Persian Gulf?

The ruling regime in Iraq sees things differently. On the principle of Arab nationalism, Iraq has pursued a policy of supremacy, rooted in the ideology of the Ba'ath party. The constitution of the Ba'ath party of Iraq allows the party to wage war to change the unfavorable situation in the Arab world so that Arab-speaking lands could be fully united. With this idea, the Ba'athist regime has exercised an expansionist policy toward Kuwait since that country gained independence. Also in keeping with this policy, Iraq has occupied vast territories along its borders with neighboring countries such as Jordan and Saudi Arabia or has otherwise claimed their possession for Iraq. For instance, in 1970, when civil war broke out in Jordan, Iraqi armed forces entered Jordanian territory under the pretext of helping the Palestinians. Parts of Jordan were kept under occupation by Iraqi forces, who refused to evacuate.

From the very outset of the Islamic revolution it was apparent that Iraqi leaders were following political developments in Iran with special concern and were looking for an opportunity to threaten or wage military action against it. The initial impact of the revolution and its vast popular support discouraged Iraqi Ba'athist officials from immediately adopting an openly hostile strategy against Iran. Two months after the downfall of the monarchy in Iran, Ba'athist leaders in Baghdad held meetings that ended with the issuance of a strictly confidential circular note to party leaders and bosses. News circles in Beirut and the *Christian Science Monitor* published this note, which analyzed the Pahlavi regime, its relations with the United States, and the shah's role in protecting the interests of the West and acting as the policeman of the Persian Gulf. It went on to emphasize that with the collapse of the shah's regime and that of the armed forces, Iran would no longer be able to play the role it had up to that time. Therefore, Iraq would be the only country that could fill the vacuum with respect to matters relating to the security of the Persian Gulf, a task that should be accomplished with planning, precision, speed, and perseverance.

The circular added that the Ba'ath party believed the circumstances were right for Iraq to establish a new geopolitical order. To ensure that the Western world recognized the new circumstances, it was essential to launch a military offensive against Iran so as to bring about the final defeat of the Islamic Republic. In an attempt to subvert the regime in Iran and to divide the country, Iraq organized groups and organizations to carry out overt and covert activities throughout Khuzestan Province, including Ahwaz and Khorramshahr. The "Arab People's Cultural Center," established at the outset of the revolution in Ahwaz, received its instructions directly from the Iraqi Consulate in Khorramshahr. Shadow groups with names like "Arabistan Liberation Front" (Jebhe-al-Tahrir al-Arabistan) were organized, financed, and trained by the Iraqi regime. Scores of spies and terrorists were dispatched to Khuzestan after receiving training and money in Iraq. These agents were later arrested and admitted in court that they had received equipment and assistance from Iraq, that they were directly trained by Iraqi experts in sabotage and terrorist activities, and that they committed such acts as destroying pipelines, refineries, mosques, and even shops and houses. It was also learned that the Iraqi deputy secretary-general of the Common Bureau of Coordination (CBC) of the Shatt al-Arab Affairs and the assistant director-general of the operations section of the bureau were involved in running an espionage network in Khuzestan. Iraqi experts also prepared and printed fictitious maps in which important parts of Iranian territory (Khuzestan, Kurdistan, and even Sistan and Baluchistan) were separated from the motherland.

The following statements by responsible officials of the Ba'ath regime provide clear proof of Iraq's intention to divide Iran:

> Naim Haddad, in an interview in May 1980, said that "Iraq will persist in its claims over the return of strategic islands of Abu Musa and the Greater and Lesser Tunbs that were occupied by Iran in 1970." He further added that "Iraq will endeavor to establish its full control over Shatt al-Arab."
>
> On June 17, 1980, on the occasion of the 12th anniversary of the revolution in Iraq, Saddam Hussein declared: "We praise the struggle of Iranian people against the reactionary and despotic stance and against perverted values hidden under the guise of religion but in reality bordering blaspheming of the true religion of Islam and its noble values and pure and genuine civilization. We send our salutations to the struggle of

> the combatant people of Arabistan who, in their fight for freedom against the racist clique that has deprived them of their basic rights and aspirations, have offered caravans of martyrs."
>
> Later in June 1980, Saddam said, "We now have the military strength to take back three islands in the Persian Gulf occupied by the shah. We have never remained idle since the occupation of these three islands and have constantly prepared ourselves militarily and economically to recapture them."
>
> In an interview on November 12, 1980, that was reported in the Iraqi press, Saddam said: "We are satisfied with our situation and the results of our efforts. Our calculations have so far turned out to be true. The Iraqi forces have advanced along a 550-kilometer front between 20 to 110 kilometers deep inside the Iranian territory." In this same interview, speaking on Iraq's goals in general, he said: "We will not be disturbed at all by the disintegration and destruction of Iran. We openly declare as long as this country remains hostile, each and every Iraqi, and perhaps every Arab will wish to see Iran divided and destroyed."
>
> Addressing a gathering of the people's militia (*Jaish al-Shu'abi*) leaving for the war fronts, Saddam said: "We declare to the Arab people of Arabistan, whose national and ethnic characteristics as a minority are historically well known and to other Iranian people, especially the Kurds and Baluchis and to all true and noble patriots, that we are ready to establish solid relations with them so that they may enjoy their national and ethnic rights and develop neighborly relations in an honorable way. We are ready to offer them assistance including any weapons they may require. This is our decision. Let the Iranian rulers continue the fighting. They will be torn up, while we will be united."

A careful study of the statements by Iraqi officials leaves no doubt as to their intention to divide Iran. Long before waging an all-out invasion against Iran on September 22, 1980, soon after the victory of the Islamic revolution, they were expressing their hostility and dreaming of an opportunity to dismember Iran. In the meantime, the Iraqis were designing plans to carry out their ominous goals at an opportune time.

It should be asked whether the Iraqi attack against Iran was meant to offset a possible Iranian offensive into Iraq and whether it was, in effect, a preventative action. All indications point to the unlikelihood of an attack by the Islamic Republic. Iran was in no position, militarily or economically, to attack another country. A country under economic sanctions, with an army that had had its former structure completely dismantled, could not have contemplated an invasion against another country. It should also be asked to what extent the Iraqi people were opposed to the goals of the Islamic revolution. How could they oppose a movement that had its roots in Islamic beliefs? The animosity came solely from the ruling Ba'athist regime that opposed the Islamic Republic of Iran. Even if the border dispute was the real bone of contention, Iraq should have invoked the agreement to solve the problem peacefully. Article 6 of the protocol stipulates the procedures for such settlement. There is no ambiguity about settling disputes arising from interpretation or implementation of the treaty or its protocols. Further, as emphasized in international law, particularly in the UN Charter, respect for territorial integrity and the unalterability of borders is one of the obligations of the member states of the international community. Iraq, as one of the contracting parties to the 1975 treaty, in conformity with the principle of *pacta sunt servanda*, was bound to fulfill the obligations arising from the treaty with good faith. Instead, without invoking and applying the provisions of the 1975 treaty, the Ba'athist regime unilaterally annulled it. The series of statements by Iraqi officials with respect to Shatt al-Arab, referred to earlier, are clearly indicative of the Iraqi regime's expansionist designs.

Iraq's unilateral action amply demonstrates its intention to launch armed aggression against the territorial integrity and sovereignty of Iran. The Iraqi regime claimed that the revolutionary government of Iran had not fulfilled its obligations. Even if that were true, the bombardment of the cities of Tehran, Isfahan, Kermanshah, Tabriz, Hamadan, Bushehr, Shiraz, and Dezful, extensive invasion, and all-out war were not appropriate responses. Is penetrating ninety kilometers deep inside Iran an appropriate response to a few local clashes claimed by Iraq? If the Iraqi regime, in its own opinion, realized the objective of recapturing the territories that were supposed to be handed over to Iraq, why should it annul the 1975 treaty? Moreover, after annulling and claiming sovereignty over the entire Shatt al-Arab, why did it wage an all-out invasion against the territory of the Islamic Republic of Iran? Can these actions be considered anything other than expansionist?

Were the plots to divide Iran, to destroy and level its border cities, to use chemical weapons in retaliation for the claimed nonobservance of the provisions of treaties by the Islamic Republic of Iran, concentrating on solving problems arising from the revolution, or were they rather part of a predesigned plan?

Notes

1. The materials for this chapter are taken from internal files of the Iranian Ministry of Foreign Affairs. The author has been a member of the Commission for the Implementation of Boundary Demarcation since early 1950s [ed.].
2. For the text of the declaration and other related texts see Tareq Y. Ismael, *Iraq and Iran: Roots of Conflict* (Syracuse: Syracuse University Press, 1982).

3

Analyses of the Risks of War: Iran-Iraq Discord, 1979–1980

KEITH MCLACHLAN

The history of the drift into the Iran-Iraq war, following the Islamic revolution, has become overshadowed by the changing fortunes in the war since its outbreak in September 1980. Yet the geopolitical, political, and sectional motivations that were at work in the prelude to the conflict retain importance of considerable magnitude. Any peace settlement will require an allocation of responsibility for the war under the political and juridical terms laid down by the Islamic Republic as a precondition for negotiations. The choice of 1979–80 as the core period in any chronology for determining how and through whose errors the conflict arose is a deliberate selection by the author. Sustaining this premise will be critical in the final resolution of the matter.

I will argue that there was an underlying movement into conditions where an Iran-Iraq war was feasible, perhaps even inevitable, in 1979–80. I examine two strands of evidence. First, I look at observers' writings, proclamations, and published opinions that were committed to print before the outbreak of the war to see what indications of incipient conflict there were and what they pointed to at that time. Second, I discuss the findings of the principal studies concerned with the war and published after its beginning. This contemporary review of the literature from sources other than the belligerents is designed as a first step in helping others make their own judgments about the situation.

The risks of a war with Iraq clouded the future of the nascent Islamic Republic from its early days. A large number of informed observers took the view, in 1979, that there was a possibility of a severe military conflict between Iran and Iraq. This conclusion has also been supported by the Iran–United States of America Claims Tribunal at the Hague, where the partial award in Case No. 56 (Amoco International Finance Corporation and the Government of the Islamic Republic of Iran, National Iranian Oil Company) was that "while it was impossible to forecast the war with Iraq as it actually developed, no one acquainted with the history of relations between the two countries could, in the circumstances prevailing at the time, discard entirely the risk of military actions, which would directly concern Kharg Island" (para 246).

The inexorable growth in diplomatic difficulties and military confrontations between the sides was neither sudden nor unexpected. As an academic authority on the Iran-Iraq dispute put it, "The Iranian revolution's success in early 1979 in toppling the monarchy was to effect a considerable destabilization in relations between Tehran and Baghdad. Saddam Hussein's accession as president of Iraq in July of the same year further accelerated such destabilization. It was by now clear that Iraq's Ba'ath rulers had signed the Algiers Accord as the only viable alternative to their imminent collapse and that, when the power equation was perceived to have altered across the Shatt Al-Arab, action would be taken to restore the river to its 'rightful owner.'"[1]

My own belief, after close analysis of the course of Iran-Iraq relations before and after the revolution, was that "during mid-1979 it seemed that the Ba'ath regime had given up its attempt to find a modus vivendi with the new Iranian government."[2] All the important evidence available indicated that there was awareness of the problem of Iranian-Iraqi conflicts from an early date after the revolution. On April 2, 1979, the Iranians complained of violations of Iranian air space by Iraq, and on April 7 they complained of Iraqi artillery attacks on the border town of Qasr-e-Shirin. There was a destabilization of relations between Iran and Iraq in 1979, exacerbated by the accession to the presidency of Iraq of Saddam Hussein in July.[3]

In May 1979, after Iraqi artillery and air strikes against the town of Mehran and Iranian retaliations there and elsewhere along the common frontier, the *Economist* Intelligence Unit warned that "the destabilization of Iran will adversely affect security in Iraq . . . [and] . . . might drag Iraq into further conflict with the Iranian central government."[4] On August 3, 1979, it reported that "the Iraqi-Iranian conflict will worsen," while characterizing the relations as "bitterness and anger."[5] Most important, the Iranian government suggested that it would seek full and absolute control of the Shatt Al-Arab on September 14, 1979.[6] On October 31, 1979, Iraqi officials threatened to abrogate the Algiers Accord of 1975 that governed relations between the two sides of the Shatt Al-Arab, the traditional area of friction. It had always been the first to be brought up in previous confrontations and now again was in violent contention. So less than nine months after the Iranian revolution, the political climate was poor and deteriorating.

The danger of war between Iran and Iraq was fully appreciated and documented by scholars, commentators, and risk analysts in 1979. Sepehr Zabih noted that relations between Iran and Iraq deteriorated almost immediately after the Islamic regime seized power in Tehran.[7] The key issue in the Iran-Iraq crisis during 1979 was therefore the extent to which the conflict would intensify. Some commentators were of the opinion that "talk of an imminent Iraqi-Iranian military confrontation and of continued border clashes is unlikely."[8] Nonetheless, they considered that warfare was feasible. In the United States, Anthony Cordesman, a respected authority on the Middle East, suggested that antagonism affected relations between the two states from the beginning of the Iranian revolution.[9] Other professional geopoliticians, G. Blake (Durham University, U.K.) and A. Drysdale (University of New Hampshire) made similar judgments: "Following the 1979 revolution, relations between the two states deteriorated. The boundary became a symbol of their hostility. Border incidents occurred with increasing frequency, more than 560 being reported by Iraq in 1979 and 1980."[10]

Perhaps the most indicative piece of evidence available to observers was the changing nature of Iraqi foreign policy under Saddam Hussein. The alteration in Iraqi orientation began in 1974 and was particularly noticeable after 1975. The culmination of the change came in the late 1970s as Iraqi policy consolidated toward challenging Iran on control of the Shatt Al-Arab, seeking hegemony in the key waterway of the

Persian Gulf and curbing the influence of Iran in the gulf area as a whole.[11] James Bill is unambiguous on the matter: "The real cause of the war was a political struggle for hegemony of the Persian Gulf. In the process, Iraq hoped to suffocate and destroy the Iranian revolution."[12]

The key plank in Iraqi policy was confrontation with Iran, and the locale was set firmly in the Persian Gulf arena—with all the implications it had for Iranian oil-exporting facilities, refineries, and petrochemical enterprises situated in Kharg Island at the heart of the Iranian presence in the gulf. The possibility of a military struggle between Iran and Iraq in the gulf, which would have inexorably included Kharg Island, as the Iran–USA Claims Tribunal stated (partial award, para. 246), could not be put aside lightly and undoubtedly put the southern Iranian oil fields and the export hub at Kharg at risk of disruption at that time.

In February 1980, the danger of war worsened perceptibly, to the extent that the official organs of the U.S. government were reported by Gary Sick (a member of the National Security Council staff until 1981) to be "quite aware that there were difficulties on that border and that there was a threat and that became more obvious as time went on."[13] In the early months of 1980, the consensus among responsible and informed commentators, as expressed in the media, journals, and analyses at the time, was that some form of conflict was brewing. January 1980 saw the arrangement of an extended arms supply agreement between France and Iraq. In February 1980 the *Economist* reported that "Iraq remains most violently antipathetic to Ayatollah Khomeini and his partners. A virulent propaganda campaign is in progress from Baghdad in support of the Arab guerrillas operating in Khuzestan. It is believed in Tehran that Iraq is actively training and equipping Arab, Kurd and Baluchi opposition groups. Iraq has, meanwhile, embarked on a policy of naval expansion designed to make the Iraqi navy the equal of Iran's and is determined to challenge Iran as the future power in the Gulf area in the near future. A number of clashes on the Iraq-Iran border took place in January, though not between regular troops. Iraqi diplomatic premises in Iran had been occupied, later closed, and some staff held hostage. Iraq responded by expelling Iranian nationals on a large scale."[14]

At the same time, there was fear in Baghdad that the new Iranian regime would use subversion against the Ba'ath as part of its ideological competition for the hearts and minds of the people of the Middle East and of the gulf area in particular.[15] There was also fear that Shi'ite revolutionary groups inside Iraq would gain Iranian support to undermine the government. Whether reliable evidence for subversion exists or not, the Iraqi regime apparently believed that Iran would use Iraqi proxies to promote its geopolitical aims.[16] Cordesman argued that the growth of covert conflict through paramilitary involvement by the two states in each other's affairs was a major cause of the outbreak of war.[17] The Iraqi demand in the first quarter of 1980 that Iran return the Persian Gulf islands of Abu Musa and the Tunbs and make concessions to Arab autonomists in Khuzestan added to the tensions.

It seems that feeling was also generated in Iraq that the time had come to regain the lands and self-esteem lost at the 1975 Algiers Accord on the Shatt Al-Arab. Phebe Marr (University of Tennessee) argued that Iraqi paranoia over the threat posed to it by the Iranian revolution was also stimulated by fears of new trouble in Iraqi Kurdestan as well as fear of growing hostility of the Iraqi Shi'a toward the regime in Baghdad. The leaders of the Kurdish Democratic party, Idris and Massoud Barazani, returned from Iran to Iraq in July 1979, thus posing a threat of a new Kurdish rebellion that would rekindle the Kurdish war. Opportunism in Baghdad was evident at this stage: "Events played into their [the Iraqi regime's] hands. . . . Rather than a strong Iran facing a weak and isolated Iraq, a strong Iraq appeared to face a weak and divided Iran. Saddam Hussein reasoned that Iraq would never have a more favorable opportunity to reverse the 1975 decision on the Shatt."[18]

The tendency for Iraq to press its credentials as the leader of the Arabs in the gulf area and its more ambitious belief in its destiny to lead the Arab world as a whole was brought to the attention of the world, albeit in slightly coded form, in the extremely important policy statement promulgated as the "National Charter" on February 8, 1980. In this document there were two closely related policies implicit in the Iraqi Ba'ath position. First, there should be Arab political and economic integration in general but specifically in the Persian Gulf area.

Second, Arab regional unity would mean joint confrontation against Iran. As G. Nonneman, a specialist on Iraqi political affairs, put it, "The principle of the Arab character of the Gulf meant opposition to Iranian (non-Arab) influence."[19]

Iraq systematically built up its alliances against Iran in 1980. An agreement was signed with Saudi Arabia in February 1979, reportedly including arrangements on mutual security.[20] Certainly, Iraq and Saudi Arabia moved closer together on a number of key policy issues, the most important of which was a joint security interest in the wake of the Iranian revolution.[21] The Iraqi authorities assiduously cultivated the Kuwaitis, and Crown Prince Shaikh Sa'ad Al-Abdullah made a five-day official visit to Iraq in May 1980. Saddam Hussein paid an unscheduled visit to the Saudi royal family on August 5, 1980, after which a joint statement emphasized the closeness of ties between the two states. It is in dispute whether talks between the Iraqis and other Arab leaders dealt in any specific way with the possibility of an Iraqi attack on Iran.[22] Even so, the pattern of Iraqi contacts with Saudi Arabia, Kuwait, Oman, and Ras Al-Khaimah pursuant to the issue of the "National Charter" was indicative of a regime establishing new pro-Iraqi "axes, to include all anti-Iranian forces."[23] This aggressive stance by Iraq and its quite demonstrable anti-Iranian objective was a further straw-in-the-wind warning of the hardening of confrontation between Iraq and Iran in the first half of 1980.

Throughout 1980 the situation deteriorated rapidly as each country acted against the other's interests, as Iraq acted more openly in support of Arab autonomist claims in Khuzestan and as the Shi'a opposition to Saddam Hussein in Iraq became more active. The expulsion of Iranian citizens from Iraq increased in tempo in April after accusations that Iranian interests were behind an attempt on the life of Tariq Aziz, a close political ally of the Iraqi president. There were also reports of constant armed clashes along the frontier during the first half of 1980. In some ways, the war was already in progress: "By April 1980, a low-level border war was clearly underway."[24] A declaration in Iraq in May 1980 that the Iraqi government took the position that the Iranian revolutionary regime should be replaced suggested strongly that armed conflict was inevitable. Iraq concentrated its troops along the border in

August 1980, and the artillery and other skirmishes along the border intensified significantly. Following Iraq's formal abrogation of the Algiers Accord on September 17, 1980, it immediately invaded Iranian territory, the principal military thrust of which was into the Iranian oil province of Khuzestan.

It is clear that the origins of the war are to be found in the complex history of Iran-Iraq relations. Insecurity and lack of confidence were inevitable legacies of the constantly shifting policies on the Shatt Al-Arab pursued by the two countries in the period before 1979. Iraq, however, had been a willing signatory of the Algiers Accord that had sought to settle outstanding issues between the two sides, and Iraq had failed to make any protest against its terms from 1975 to 1979. In the wake of the Iranian revolution, Iraqi authorities appeared to believe that Iranian internal weaknesses offered an opportunity for Iraq to change the balance of power in the Persian Gulf and possibly solve their problems in Kurdestan and the Shi'a domain of the south with one military stroke. By any fair measure, Iraq began the war against Iran in 1980 and must be considered the aggressor. This fact is recognized. In Bill's words, "It is also true that Iraq invaded Iran and was by any standard of international law the aggressor."[25] Iraqi artillery attacked Iranian targets. Iraqi troops invaded Iranian territory. Iran was not overwhelmed by these attacks, but it was caught by surprise. Altogether unready for a war that it had not expected, it took nearly one and a half years before Iran could push the bulk of Iraqi forces from Iranian land. In the words of the Iranians, the events of September 1980 must be accepted as an "imposed war."

Notes

1. R.N. Schofield, *The Evolution of the Shatt al-Arab Boundary Dispute* (London: Menas Publishers, 1986), 64.
2. K. McLachlan, "The Gulf War," *Economist* (1984): 32.
3. Schofield, *Shatt al-Arab*, 64.
4. *Economist* Intelligence Unit, "Iraq" (May 2, 1979): 8.
5. Ibid., 3.
6. A.H. Cordesman, *The Gulf and the Search for Strategic Stability* (Boulder, Col.: Westview Press, 1984), 665.

7. S. Zabih, *Iran since the Revolution* (London: Croom Helm, 1982), 176.
8. E. Ghareeb, "Iraq: Emergent Gulf Power," in *The Security of the Persian Gulf*, ed. H. Amirsageghi (London: Croom Helm, 1981), 216.
9. Cordesman, *The Gulf*, 665.
10. A. Drysdale and G. Blake, *The Middle East and North Africa* (London: Oxford University Press, 1985), 86.
11. G. Nonneman, *Iraq, the Gulf States and the War* (London: n.p., 1986), 14.
12. J. Bill, *The Eagle and the Lion: The Tragedy of American-Iranian Relations* (New Haven: Yale University Press, 1988), 304.
13. See G. Sick, "The Iranian Revolution and the Islamic Republic," conference proceedings, edited by N. Keddie and E. Hooglund (Washington, D.C.: Middle East Institute and Woodrow Wilson International Center for Scholars, 1982), 159.
14. *Economist* Intelligence Unit, "Iraq" (November 1980): 10–11.
15. I.E. Peterson, *Defending Arabia* (London: Croom Helm, 1986), 128–29.
16. M.S. Azhary, *The Iraq-Iran War* (London: Croom Helm, 1984), 1.
17. Cordesman, *The Gulf*, 397.
18. P. Marr, *The Modern History of Iraq* (Boulder, Col.: Westview Press, 1985), 292.
19. Nonneman, *Iraq*, 13.
20. Ibid., 14.
21. Ghareeb, "Iraq," 208.
22. G.H. Jansen, "The Attitudes of Arab Governments," in Azhary, *The Iraq-Iran War*, 81–82.
23. Nonneman, *Iraq*, 14.
24. Cordesman, *The Gulf*, 665.
25. Bill, *The Eagle and the Lion*, 304.

4

The War of the Cities

S. TAHERI SHEMIRANI

In its eight-year war of aggression against the Islamic Republic of Iran, the Iraqi regime was at fault not only for launching the war but in its conduct of the war. Two areas in which its behavior breached international law as well as humanitarian principles were the treatment of civilians and the use of forbidden and illegal means and weapons. The first was manifested in the way in which they bombed and shelled civilian targets, the so-called war of the cities. The second breach was Iraq's massive use of chemical weapons against both military and civilian populations. In this chapter I attempt an analytical report of these two areas.[1]

First, let us consider chemical weapons, the history of which is as old as the story of war itself. Prokipus reports that in the wars between the Sassanids and Rome, both sides used some form of chemical weapons, a practice used repeatedly by others later. In modern times the most extensive use was by Germany during World War I. By the end of the war, official statistics showed that more than one million people were exposed to chemical elements, about 100,000 of whom were poisoned to death.[2] During World War II all parties restrained themselves from using chemical elements, although the combatants had manufactured them (when the Soviet and American forces reached German soil, they encountered factories that produced chemical weapons). Since then, there has been less restraint, and chemical weapons have been used in wars in Vietnam, Yemen, Cambodia, and Afghanistan.

The widest use of chemical weapons, however, has been that of the Iraqi government during the past two decades. It first used them against the Kurds in its offensive in 1974.[3] Later, at the outbreak of the war with Iran, there were reports from the border region (in late September and October 1980) that Iraq was using chemical weapons. In response to the Iranian protest, Iraqi official radio denied the claim.[4] Wider usage came later. Iraqi planes dropped Iraqi-made chemical bombs in December 1983 during the Ramadan Operation. Subsequently, the Iraqi regime regularly used chemical weapons, particularly during any Iranian offensive. In the early days of the war, Iran suffered great casualties. For instance, in the Khaybar Operation of February 1984, Iraqi forces heavily pounded Iranian defense lines with chemical bombs and shells, using planes and artillery. Lack of sufficient experience, the enclave nature of the operation zone, and massive and multiple deployment of chemical gases compounded the effects on the regions as well as on the people, whether civilians or combatants.

During the next major event of the war, the Badr Operation in March and April 1985, the Iraqis diversified their usage of the various elements. Besides nerve gas and blister gas, the Iraqis deployed cyanide and blood-affecting gases. They were not successful in using chemical weapons in the Valfajr-8 Operation because Iranian forces hit Iraqi chemical arms depots in the Fao region. This, in turn, warned the Iraqis of the danger chemicals might pose to their own forces: It is reported that many Iraqi troops got their first exposure to chemical elements as a result of the explosion in these depots.

By the time of the Karbala-5 Operation, Iranian forces had learned to cope with chemicals. Despite that, the Iranians still suffered because during the operation, in the spring of 1987, the Iraqis used chemical weapons as freely as others use conventional ones. Moreover, the Iraqis, who did not succeed in achieving their expected goals, used chemicals against civilians, particularly in the cities of Basra, Khorramsharh, and Sardasht. In addition, a number of Kurdish villages were under heavy air attacks that discharged chemical weapons. The most venomous use of chemical weapons came in March 1988 when Iranian forces marched into the Kurdish city of Halabjah. Iraqi planes carried out twenty bombing missions, dropping one of the most lethal toxic gases, hydrogen cyanide, on civilians. It left about 5,000 dead and more than 7,000 seriously injured. Only then did the international community believe that the Iraqi government and armed forces had violated international principles in conducting war. The tables that follow display the attacks and damage done by Iraqi chemical weapons during the war. Tables 4.1–4.3 break down the chemical attacks on Iranian army and civilians. In total, more than 5,000 people lost their lives to chemical attacks and almost 45,000 were injured.

The use of chemical weapons had been forbidden since the Hague Conferences of 1899,[5] as part of a general effort to regulate wars and the way in which they should be conducted. In the Treaty of Versailles, in response to the massive use of chemical weapons during World War

Table 4.1. Chemical Rocket Attacks

Year	No. rockets	No. dead	No. injured
1981	2	1	—
1982	2	—	—
1983	8	—	1
1985	1	—	5
1986	6	—	5
1987	1	—	—
Total	20	1	11

Source: Statistics Department, Center for Documents of the Imposed War [formerly War Information Headquarters], Tehran, Iran. (The calendar used in the department is that of the Iranian year, which begins on March 21.)

Table 4.2. Chemical Air Attack

Year	No. attacks	No. dead	No. injured
1983	20	19	2,515
1984	47	34	2,343
1985	90	51	10,546
1986	47	11	6,573
1987	33	5,390	16,670
1988	47	260	4,284
Total	284	5,765	42,931

Source: Statistics Department, Center for Documents of the Imposed War, Tehran, Iran. (The calendar used in the department is that of the Iranian year, which begins on March 21.)

Table 4.3. Artillery Attacks

Year	No. attacks	No. dead	No. injured
1980	1	10	—
1981	2	—	—
1982	8	13	16
1983	18	3	277
1984	7	—	—
1985	14	—	320
1986	21	1	298
1987	2	—	120
1988	1	—	—
Total	74	27	1,031

Source: Statistics Department, Center for Documents of the Imposed War, Tehran, Iran. (The calendar used in the department is that of the Iranian year, which begins on March 21.)

I, the issue was treated carefully and the Hague principles were reiterated.[6] Later, the newly formed League of Nations mandated a conference to address this issue. The result—the 1925 Geneva Protocol—prohibited asphyxiating, poisonous, or other gases and bacteriological methods of warfare.[7] This document provided an effective mechanism for regulating and controlling chemical warfare.[8] Iraq signed the protocol in 1931. The principles of the 1925 convention have been reaffirmed many times by states as well as international organizations. These organizations have acknowledged that Iraqi use of chemical weapons against Iran throughout the Iran-Iraq war violated the aforementioned convention. The report of UN experts (SC 16433/March 26, 1984) explicitly showed that the Iraqis used chemical elements against Iran. Since then, in most resolutions passed by the UN, there are references to chemical weapons and their negative and destructive effects on people and the environment, but the UN did not put pressure on Iraq to refrain from such usage. Nor did it do much about the so-called war of the cities.

Iraq resorted to attacking civilians from the early days of the war. For instance, on the third day of the war, Ahwaz, the center of Khuzistan province and its largest city, was air bombed. The most serious attacks on civilians began with Iraq missile drops on Dezful, another major city in the province, less than three weeks after the war began. As a result of these attacks, at least 70 people died, 300 were injured, and a number of houses and stores in the city were ruined. After that, Iraq regularly attacked civilian areas. In June 1984 attacks on civilians took a new turn. Iran had to retaliate but only after suffering great losses.

During the festivities of the anniversary of the Islamic revolution in 1983, Iraq officially declared that it would attack the cities of Dezful, Andimeshk, Ahwaz, Kermanshah, Abadan, and Susa.[9] A few days later, the Iranian president, Seyyid Ali Khamene'i, declared that if Iraq resorted to such measures, Iran would retaliate by attacking Basra, Mandali, and Khaneqain. The president's statement was meant simply as a deterrent, and Iran refrained from any attack until June 1984. By that time, Iraq's continual attacks forced Iran to retaliate. On June 22, 1984, the secretary-general of the UN mediated an agreement between the two countries to put an end to the war of the cities. While Iran observed the principles of the agreement, the Iraqi regime continued its attacks under various pretexts. In September 1984, for instance, Iraq claimed that Abu-Moghaira, an Iraqi village near Basra, had been attacked by Iran, although the report of the UN experts showed that there were no signs of any attacks on this village.[10] The Iraqis continued attacking the cities and projected missiles at Dezful. Iran retaliated by hurling missiles at the oil field in Kerkuk, thus adding a new phase to the war of the cities. Until then, nobody believed that Iran had the capacity and the will to use missiles against Iraq. The UN secretary-general again tried to establish an agreement between the two countries, but Iraq sent missiles into Tehran just minutes before the agreement went into effect. The war of the cities temporarily came to a halt.

In December 1986, as Iran began the Karbala-5 Operation in the eastern part of Basra, the Iraqis launched a new phase of the war of the cities that lasted forty-two days and left 3,035 dead and 11,150 injured. During these attacks, missiles hit indiscriminate targets such as schools, hospitals, nurseries, and even a maternity hospital. The most destructive and disastrous attacks came in the beginning of 1988. This new phase began with Iraqi planes bombing and projecting missiles at Tehran on February 29 and lasted until May 1. The most important development in this phase was Iraqi deployment of long-range missiles. During the new phase, 133 missiles were dropped on Tehran alone. During the war of the cities, Iraq always started attacks on civilians and throughout the war (1980–88) attacked civilian areas 4,695 times, including 308 missile attacks, 2,695 air raids, and 1,693 artillery bombardments. These left 12,420 people dead and 53,118 injured, including the elderly, infants and older children, and noncombatant men and women. Tables 4.4–4.6 detail the number and kinds of attacks each year.

None of these attacks conformed in any way with the principles of public international law as it has developed over the centuries. The most explicit banning of attacks against civilians or use of projectile weapons that cause unnecessary damage came from the Hague Conferences of 1899 and the four agreements of 1907. The latter, entitled "1907 Convention Respecting the Law and Customs of War on Land," specifically delineated the limitations that each belligerent had to observe. Article 22 of the annex clearly stated that "the right of belligerents to adopt means of injuring the enemy is not unlimited."[11] It went on to enumer-

Table 4.4. Missile Attacks on Iranian Cities

Year	No. missiles	No. dead	No. injured
1980	16	289	838
1981	30	58	220
1982	6	105	499
1983	14	135	896
1984	16	351	1,900
1985	23	373	1,596
1986	21	204	804
1987	96	359	1,612
1988	86	352	2,340
Total	308	2,226	10,705

Source: Statistics Department, Center for Documents of the Imposed War, Tehran, Iran. (The calendar used in the department is that of the Iranian year, which begins on March 21.)

Table 4.5. Air Attacks

Year	No. attacks	No. dead	No. injured
1980	148	511	906
1981	95	286	1,088
1982	71	313	2,000
1983	80	381	2,157
1984	215	1,059	3,063
1985	206	858	2,535
1986	996	3,953	15,151
1987	537	702	3,735
1988	347	785	8,248
Total	2,695	8,848	38,883

Source: Statistics Department, Center for Documents of the Imposed War, Tehran, Iran. (The calendar used in the department is that of the Iranian year, which begins on March 21.)

Table 4.6. Artillery Used

Year	No. attacks	No. dead	No. injured
1980	206	646	192
1981	398	281	1,112
1982	386	200	1,579
1983	185	29	104
1984	375	87	241
1985	44	34	82
1986	56	39	61
1987	27	11	102
1988	16	19	57
Total	1,693	1,346	3,530

Source: Statistics Department, Center for Documents of the Imposed War, Tehran, Iran. (The calendar used in the department is that of the Iranian year, which begins on March 21.)

ate various prohibitions on deploying means that "cause unnecessary suffering" to the armed and uniformed men, let alone unarmed civilians, thus making an important distinction between military and civilian targets.

Explicit definitions of military objectives and targets have been presented in international forums. "Military objective means, so far as objects are concerned, any object which by its nature, location, purpose or use makes an effective contribution to military action and whose total or partial destruction, capture or neutralization, in the circumstances ruling at the time, offers a definite military advantage."[12]

In this passage, one should note the concepts "effective contribution" and "definite military advantage." The Iraqi forces, in their attacks on Iranian cities, indiscriminately dropped bombs and missiles only for political gain and possibly to undermine the solidarity of the Iranian people in their support for the war. In fact, it was reported that Iraqi leaders repeatedly acknowledged that they would take the war to any extreme to ignite the Iranian people against their leaders and the Islamic Republic. Thus, none of the destruction and killing of civilians by the Iraqis could have been considered a "definite military advantage." Instead, Iraqi objectives may have constituted interference in the internal affairs of another sovereign state. This objective in itself was in violation of international legal norms and practices.

Notes

1. In writing this chapter, I have used papers on chemical warfare and attacks on civilians from the War Information Headquarters of the Ministry of Defense. I acknowledge and express gratitude to the staff of the Statistics Division of the organization.
2. United Nations, *The Dangers of Chemical and Bacteriological Weapons* (New York: UN, 1969), 3.
3. *The Sunday Times*, April 28, 1974.
4. *The Sout-al-Jamahir* (December 8, 1981).
5. The 1899 Hague Declaration Concerning Asphyxiating Gases states that "the contracting Powers agree to abstain from the use of projectiles, the sole object of which is the diffusion of asphyxiating or deleterious gases." For the entire text, see Adam Roberts and Richard Guelff, eds., *Documents on the Laws of War* (Oxford: Clarendon Press, 1982), 35–39.
6. See Articles 171–91.
7. For the text, see Roberts and Guelff, *Laws of War*, 137–46.
8. Since 1966, the UN has been calling on its related organs to work for a new convention on banning chemical weapons.
9. The Iraqi News Agency (February 2, 1983).

10. See GA-Resolution 16750.
11. Roberts and Guelff, *Laws of War*, 52.
12. The 1981 United Nations convention restricted or prohibited the use of certain conventional weapons that may be deemed to be excessively injurious so as to have indiscriminate effects. For the text, see ibid., 467–82.

5

Cultural Identity in Danger

MEHDI HOJJAT

My concern here is with the cultural heritage of a people whose works, both intellectual and material, are grand and priceless. They are an invitation to meditation and deliberation. The founders of Iranian civilization and culture, its protectors and promoters, throughout history and at present, created awe-inspiring works that cause any beholder to bow in respect and charge not only Iranians but the people of the world to preserve their value. The identity of a nation is made up of its cultural heritage. Without appreciation of the heritage and recognition of its main components, no cultural planning will be fruitful.

The Islamic revolution has its roots in history, the understanding of which is necessary for further solidifying its foundations. Historical documents are often inaccurate because of their authors' intentional distortions or prejudices or because of their distance in time. Relics of the past could serve as a criterion to test the truth of historical events.

Archaeology is a tool for delving into the life of the ancient past; anthropology is the study of the present. Together with traditional crafts that represent the generations, they pave the way for understanding the past. To achieve this understanding, after the victory of the Islamic revolution the Organization for the Preservation of Cultural Heritage was founded. The foundation of this organization in the early stages of the Islamic revolution and the allocation of facilities, equipment, immediate funds, and an annual budget of approximately 5,000 million rials (about $60 million), even in the midst of war, indicates the value of cultural heritage for the Islamic Republic.

The members of the newly founded organization felt a great responsibility to preserve monuments, a necessary precondition for any kind of study and research. We assumed the task of preserving more than 8,000 monuments and historical sites. Approximately 1,100 monuments and 800 sites have been registered as national treasures. Three of the monuments are of extreme importance: Imam Square in Isfahan, Choghazanbil Temple, and Persepolis are registered as part of the world's cultural heritage. The oldest and vastest monuments of our country are located in the western and southwestern regions, that is, in Azarbayejan, Kurdistan, Kermanshah, Ilam, and Khuzistan. They include monuments dating from the fourth and fifth millennia B.C.

The value of the civilizations of the Khuzistan Plain and the vast historical site of Susa and the like are self-evident. The magnificent Temple of Choghazanbil is located on the Khuzistan Plain close to the border. The city of Dezful, considered a masterpiece of architecture in the Islamic period, and many other monuments are in the western and southwestern regions that came under enemy raids at the early stages of the Iraqi offensives. In the western regions of the country, some monuments of the Median, Elamite, Achaemenid, Parthian, Seljuk, Atabakan, and Safavid eras came under direct or indirect attacks. The reliefs known as Sheikh Khan, belonging to the third millennium, numerous Median monuments in Sare-Pole-Zahab, the Sassanid Palace, the Square Dome, and more have been occupied by the enemy for years, and most are already ruined. The raids of the enemy's forces were so widespread that no preventive or rescue operation was feasible. For more than several hundred kilometers, the offensives of several Iraqi divisions, together with air and ground weapons and rocket fire, destroyed mounds, monuments, cities, museums, and mosques. The people in the occupied region were slaughtered so savagely that no one could pay attention to preservation at that time

Abadan was besieged with artillery, and its museum containing fine relics was ruined. The city of Dezful received hundreds of missiles, and they destroyed more than 50 percent of its old quarter that, in addition to Sassanid monuments, contains buildings belonging to the Seljuk, Safavid, and Qajar eras. With the strong determination and extraordinary endeavors of the local officials in the district, we were able to transfer, under artillery fire, the relics of the Susa Museum. (We carried them by train, under constant attack, to Tehran and into the National Museum of Iran [Iran Bastan Museum].) Qasr-e-Shirin was occupied and the Sassanid Square Dome leveled. The remnant of the Sassanid Palace was attacked, and carvings and reliefs about 2,000 years old were destroyed as a result of the enemy's direct fire. The historic and religious sites of Susa, the tomb of the Prophet Daniel, and the Susa Museum were hit directly by artillery, and the historic mound of Susa and the existing archaeological center containing thousands of relics were damaged. The early air and missile attacks of the enemy badly damaged the business center (Bazaar) in Bakhtaran; the Mo'aven-ol-Molk passion plays theatre containing the finest paintings of religious rites on tiles and of the highest cultural value; the Biglar-Bagy passion plays theatre; the Hegmatane Mound in Hamadan; and the Bazaar in Urmia. The onset of air attacks on the residential areas of cities far from the frontier and on cities located in central Iran was an introduction to wider damages to cultural properties.

The air attacks on Isfahan were carefully planned and executed, and the places hit clearly indicate that the enemy's target was the old quarter of this area and the central district of the city. Part of the old section of the city and more than twenty old residential houses, the Sheik-ol-Islam passion play theatre, the Aqa Noor Mosque, the Haj Mohammad Jafar Mosque, the Seeid Mosque, the Khan Mosque and, most important of all, the Jame (congregational) Mosque (which can be considered the embodiment of an encyclopedia of the Islamic architecture and one of the finest monuments of art and architectural history) were hit by rockets. One of the rockets landed near the main dome and the other close to the northern dome. The mosque was hit at the time of the noon prayer, further evidence of the enemy's intentions. The attack on the sacred city of Qom, which injured people near the shrine and the bazaar, and the attack on the historic city of Burujerd close to its congregational mosque dating from the fourth century A.H./tenth century A.D. and on the girls' school, which caused the deaths of a large group of the city's youth, were other consequences of the attack on the cities.

The air and missile attacks on Tehran seriously threatened the relics concentrated in a large number of museums there. The Golestan Museum-Palace of the Qajar era, of tremendous value for its architecture and with thousands of precious objects, was badly threatened several times and suffered minor damage because it is located downtown and close to the bazaar. The missiles that landed less than 100 meters from the Decorative Arts Museum and others that landed near the National Art Museum caused minor damage. Fortunately, just at the start of the missile attacks on Tehran, the artifacts in the latter had been wrapped and transferred to a safer place and thus sustained no damage. It should be noted, however, that transferring items from more than ten museums all over Tehran, irrespective of administrative problems, inflicts damage to the artifacts; for museums, moving to a new place twice causes the same damage as one fire.

Iraq's aggression has had some side effects in addition to the direct damage to the cultural heritage. In a country like Iran, with thousands of historical sites, one effective method for preventing unauthorized excavations is controlling the borders to check for the presence of antiquities. If there were no possibility for smuggling the artifacts, there would be less incentive for unauthorized excavations. Of course, it was difficult to control more than 1,000 kilometers of border after the outbreak of war. For opportunists, profiteering would be a powerful incentive for smuggling antiquities and unique artistic and cultural products. Another harmful effect of the war is felt in fund allocation policies. As cultural affairs do not enjoy a high priority, particularly while a war is being waged, cultural trends suffer unforeseen and unwanted setbacks.

But, in my opinion, the most damage was what our president has termed "the raid on revolutions." Obviously, after the victory of a revolution or at least an Islamic one, the revolutionary enthusiasm of the people did not die. The war was imposed on Iran to diminish and wipe out the strong will of its people, and it was sustained for this purpose for more than eight years. In response, our strategy has been to restore and remove the damaged material even during the actual course of the war. After any destruction, a team of restorers rushed to the scene to begin restoration. For example, reconstruction of the destroyed sections of the congregational mosque of Isfahan was carried out on the basis of photogrammetric pictures, and in less than one year the mosque was restored to its original form.

After forcing the enemy out of the occupied territories, restoration was begun on the monuments of the Abadan Museum, the Susa Museum, the tomb of the Prophet Daniel, the House of Valy, the Bazaar of Urmia, the Biglar-Bagy passion plays theatre, and other damaged monuments, and they reopened after completion. Of course, the old quarters of the cities, ruined mounds, lost reliefs, and destroyed relics can never be revived, and the question is how these kinds of violations could be checked on an international scale. The 1954 Hague Convention immediately comes to mind. In view of the date of this convention, developments in war techniques, and the weapons invented during the past thirty years, the deficiency of the convention is abundantly clear. Delving into the articles of the convention shows that it was drawn up in a realistic way to protect cultural property at that time. Unfortunately, at present this convention is no more than moral advice and could not possibly be considered adequate.

Article 6 says that, "according the provisions of Article 16, cultural properties should be marked with special signs to be recognized presently." When a regime makes use of whatever is in its power to terrorize people and compel them to abandon their hometowns, marking cultural treasures could only be a step toward their destruction. The UNESCO mission, which was a response to Iran's request, was dispatched to survey the evidence of the damages in the war-afflicted provinces. After the survey, mission members admitted that it was necessary to conduct a more earnest discussion on implementing the feasibility of the convention.

Article 8 says that immovable property of considerable importance could be put under special protection under the conditions that (1) they are located a reasonable distance from industrial centers or any important military target considered to be a sensitive place, such as an airport, radio station, installations working for national defense, ports, and important railway stations and highways, and (2) they are not being used for military purposes. The congregational mosque, with its large dome, is one of the most prominent buildings in Isfahan and is easily recognizable. None of the above-mentioned conditions pertains to it, and the mosque was hit twice by rockets launched from an airplane in the daytime. One is forced to wonder about the utility of a convention if after eight years it has not had the smallest effect.

Based on Iran's request to execute the convention, UNESCO proposed that a general commissar for cultural property be appointed. A qualified person was selected from a list of individuals from different countries. Iraq rejected this person and did not suggest another, so nothing could be done to enforce the convention. In the latest general conference of UNESCO, the Islamic Republic of Iran proposed a resolution that was approved. In this resolution Iran asked for more attention to the convention and its enforcement. A letter sent by the general director to the Iranian Mission said that the Executive Council of UNESCO had, according to Resolution 8/10, asked UNESCO's Secretariat to accelerate the execution of resolution 11/2 approved by the 24th Session of the General Conference concerning a deeper survey into the methods of executing the Hague Convention. This points up the leniency of the execution and the problems in the text of the convention.

We hope that the laws' shortcomings and the ineptitude of the authorities will be ameliorated by further attention, careful discussion, and adoption of new methods. The Organization for the Preservation of Cultural Heritage, which has protected cultural property during the war, is well prepared to contribute to any national or international measure to study this topic and to perform its share of activities in the future.

Editor's note: Mehdi Hojjat, head of the Organization for the Preservation of Iranian Cultural Heritage since the revolution in 1979, is an architect by training. The information shared here is based on internal reports of the organization.

6

The War's Impact on Iraq

LAITH KUBBA

In order to carry out objective research on the impact on Iraq of an eight-year war, it is necessary to have access to both the people and the institutions inside Iraq. Such access has not been possible for several reasons, and the only data available are those of the Iraqi government, the opposition, and Western media. The information from both the government and the opposition is subjective, thus it was used with caution and a critical approach was necessary in quoting it. It has value because it reflects the attitudes of political groups in Iraq. Western media have also reported impressions of journalists who visited Iraq under strict supervision and had access to official data, which formed the basis for their reports. No accurate figures or statistics have been made public by the Iraqi government on the impact of the war on its economy, army, society, and so on.

I discuss the impact of the war in qualitative rather than quantitative terms, and my aim is to highlight how the war affected various institutions and groups in Iraq. This is an objective and realistic assessment of the effects of the war on Iraq, and it does not necessarily coincide fully with any particular model, ideology, or school of thought.

The Economy

Prewar Iraq had reserves in excess of $35 billion, a massive investment program to develop the infrastructure of industry, a growing skilled labor force, and increasing numbers of professionals. It had an oil-based economy and its main industries were its oil terminals, oil refineries, and petrochemicals. The war changed Iraq's economy in many ways.

(1) The main oil terminals (Al Bakr and Khour Al Ammya) and the Basra Oil Refinery were destroyed. However, Iraq opened a new pipeline via Turkey and is negotiating another via the Red Sea.
(2) Iraq's men were drawn to the battlefields (an estimated one million of regular and reserve troops). Iraqi women filled 30 percent of the vacancies; the rest were filled mainly by Arabs and Asians.
(3) Iraq was left heavily in debt (an estimated $100 billion), and its reconstruction program required an estimated $100 billion spread over ten years.
(4) The main cities that were destroyed were in southern Iraq and along its eastern borders with Iran, but little damage occurred in its western and northern cities. The damage included both residential and industrial installations. In Basra Province two fertilizers plants, a refinery, a steel plant, and a petrochemical plant were destroyed.
(5) The economy of Iraq adjusted to the war circumstances with efficient operators, partially contracted to foreign companies that supplied labor and management, and the economy became more liberalized, with a larger role going to the private sector.
(6) Industry was shifted from the south to the north, and Tikrit in particular became significantly important to Iraq's economy.

Effects on the Population

Iraq's population was polarized at the birth of the state of Iraq in 1920. The war strengthened such polarization and will affect further developments in postwar Iraq. In examining Iraqi institutions, politics, and attitudes, it is important to look at the ethnic-sectarian groups of the Iraqi population. Clear ethnic-sectarian trends marked Iraqi governments, the composition of the army, the distribution of national wealth, the growth of political movements, and other important aspects of the state and society. Therefore, it is necessary to examine the background of the various groups, their share of power, and overall trends.

Iraq's population can be divided into three major groups, Arab Shi'as, Arab Sunnis, and Kurds. Other small groups and minorities exist, but their small percentages do not make them relevant to the main political and social issues that face Iraq. It is more appropriate at this stage to focus on the impact of the war on the major groups of the population and its effects on issues that existed before the war.

Arab Shi'as

The Arab Shi'as are mainly tribes in the south with substantial presence in main cities all over Iraq. Now forming 55 percent of the population, they were a minority under Ottoman rule and traditionally were isolated from the administration of the country. Despite their majority presence in Iraq after 1920, the "deprived minority state of mind" has characterized Shi'a personalities, temperaments, and institutions. Their deprivation continued, and they were denied any say in the affairs of Iraq. Their sense of Shi'ism was secondary to their sense of tribal Arabism and of being Iraqi. No single political movement in Iraq has been based on their aspirations as a Shi'a group, and their struggle to achieve a better life in Iraq and some share in power was carried out through broad political and social movements (Islamic, socialist, nationalist, democratic, and so on). The Communist party has had some noticeable followers in mainly Shi'a areas, but its influence decreased in the past two decades. Later it was replaced by Islamic organizations and the religious influence of the Ulama.

The war against Iran divided the Shi'as, put them in a more difficult position, and exposed them to further sufferings. The main rank and file of the Ba'ath party are Shi'as, as are more than 90 percent of the soldiers and low-ranking officers. Although they have no say in decision making in the army, party, or government, they have to carry out the decisions and face the consequences. Iraq's human losses were mainly Shi'as, and they suffered more losses than any other group inside Iraq. Despite this, they were looked at as a "fifth column" by the Arab Sunnis, and their loyalty to Iraq was doubted because they share the same religious affiliation as the Iranians. The Shi'as were persecuted systematically at all levels in society, especially their religious centers and organizations. The state was careful not to lose Shi'a support, but at the same time it prevented their movements and crippled their organizations, crushing any potential for power. These policies have led to further suffering and created a deeper sense of resentment toward the ruling tribes. Historically, Shi'a political awareness is far less developed compared to the rest of the population's, mainly because of their lack of experience, their deprivation, and their restricted political activity. The war certainly increased their political awareness of the importance of the state and the processes of decision making. It brought to light Islamic organizations and politicized them. Thousands of Shi'a members are trained, armed, and fighting the regular armies of the central government. Urban terrorism did not spark an uprising, but it reflected the potential for confrontation.

Arab Sunnis

We must focus on the Arab Sunnis who rule Iraq to examine where the real power lies. The Arab Sunnis were the only group in Iraq who were not persecuted (ethnically or religiously) by the Turks and British, and they were used to administrate the country by both foreign powers. Later, the Sunnis played an important and positive role in the development of the state of Iraq. They can be divided into two main categories: tribal and urban.

The tribal Sunnis of the rural areas are mainly in northwest areas, villages and cities along two rivers, and they form less than 15 percent of the population. Their power developed quickly in the state of Iraq, especially after 1958, as a result of their presence in the army and their strong tribal bonds and loyalty. The increasing role of the army in Iraq's politics after 1936 simply meant the increasing importance of the tribal Sunnis, and, accordingly, they became influential in politics. In the last two decades they have become a ruling minority with strict controls over the majority of the population.

The urban Sunnis are in the main cities of Iraq (Baghdad, Mosul, and Basra), and they form less than 5 percent of the population. They were the elite, governing Iraq during Ottoman rule, and they did not lose that position during the British Mandate and the years of monocracy up until 1958. The urban Sunnis do not pose a threat to the ruling tribal Sunnis, and the former prefer the latter to Shi'as and Kurdish rulers.

The war had three important effects on the Arab Sunnis. (1) Their fear of losing power united both urban and rural Sunnis and concentrated the power in the hands of the tribal Sunnis from northwest Iraq. (2) The war brought support from the rest of the Arab Sunni world, namely the Persian Gulf and Middle East. (3) The war also developed their sense of religious sectarianism in the face of the Islamic sentiment of the revolution in Iran.

The Kurds

The Kurds are concentrated in northern Iraq and form more than 20 percent of the population. They are bound together by a sense of Kurdish identity, by language, and by close tribal ties. A minority of Kurds who lived in main cities have assimilated with the Arab Iraqis, but the tribal Kurds in urban and rural areas in northern Iraq remained culturally different from the Iraqi Arabs. Their national aspirations have been developing in Iraq since 1920, and their demands for fair representation and self-rule are well known. However, their political activities lack sufficient cohesion and coordination and collide with regional political realities. The war has revived their forty-year-old resistance against the government and has inspired their movements. They played an active role in military terms, but this role will likely end now that the war is over. The Kurds were exposed to extensive suffering and were considered potential enemies of the state. As such, they were exempted from national military service on the war fronts and were forced into relocation programs. These policies have intensified their national aspirations and demands for self-rule and further developed their political struggle and organizations. The Kurdish problem has become more complicated and cuts more deeply than expected into the future politics of Iraq.

There are other minorities in Iraq, including Christians (mainly Caledans, Assyrians, and Armenians), Turkomans (mainly Sunnis), Faiylis (Shi'a Kurds), Persian Shi'as, and Jews. The Faiylis and the Persian Shi'as suffered the most repression and have aligned themselves with the Islamic Republic in its war with Iraq. The Assyrians also aligned themselves with Iran, but the Caledans have entered into an alliance with Sunni tribes and benefited from being in power. Although these minorities do not exceed 5 percent of the population, it is likely that they would be polarized in postwar Iraq.

The Political Movement

Opposition groups survived government attempts to exterminate them, but they were displaced and isolated from the masses and their limited presence became only symbolic inside Iraqi cities. However, the war polarized the Iraqi people on new grounds that go beyond the political and ideological issues that used to dominate political life in the cities. The contradictions and differences in the interests of different socioeconomic ethnic groups are brought to light and are likely to leave a lasting impact on Iraq's political life. The slogans and compositions of political parties are likely to change accordingly, and new programs, slogans, and even new parties will probably develop. The struggle of the Iraqi opposition will probably concentrate on terminating the repressive institutions of future governments, demanding free elections, and ending the rule of Saddam Hussein.

There are no signs that the opposition will be able to topple the institutions ruling Iraq simply by mass mobilization, instigations, and provocations. However, it is possible to change the regime by relying on some of its own institutions such as the army, the party, and the intelligence service. This possibility can occur if and when there is international unity against the government of Saddam Hussein.

The Ruling Tribe

The war gave the ruling party an excuse to abolish the remains of civil rights under the pretext of "defending the nation." The powers of the army and the ruling tribes have been concentrated even beyond the norms of recent dictatorship ruling Iraq since 1958. It is extremely unlikely that the ruling group would agree to step down from its exclusive monopoly of power in Iraq, especially in light of the fact that the war institutionalized repression and gave extra powers to the government and its institutions. The government can try to buy out the resentment and dissatisfaction of the people, but it will not compromise on the issue of power and accountability. Disregarding the future of Saddam Hussein's government, the real issues in postwar Iraq go beyond the personality of Saddam Hussein. Traditional Iraqi opposition groups (Islamic, Kurdish, nationalist, and leftist) are unlikely to alter their programs immediately because of postwar political realities, and they will not challenge the monopoly of power by the minority in Iraq. However, it is likely that in the near future the issue will force itself on both existing and new political parties. The rule of the minority is unlikely to be concealed long in postwar Iraq.

The Army

The Iraqi army has been the key power behind Ba'ath rule in Iraq. Hence, despite its suffering and humiliation in the war, it seems unlikely that the army will alter its loyalty. It has developed its strength, growing to fifty brigades and mobilizing 800,000 regulars and 200,000 reserves (nearly all the working population of Iraq). It has also developed and modified its armed industry and is the largest producer and stockpiler of chemical weapons in the Middle East. The leadership of the army remains in the hands of the ruling tribe. The war has strengthened the army, thus it has strengthened the control of Iraq's ruling group. However, the army might hold Saddam and his officers responsible for the misconduct and miscalculation in the war, and it may survive future developments in the postwar era. Another serious possibility is that the army might not survive the pressures and strains within Iraqi society and would give way to a restructuring process that would produce an army more representative of the people of Iraq and their interests.

Foreign Policy

The government of Saddam Hussein bases its foreign policy on its central political objective that has not altered in the last twenty years: to stay in power. Therefore, its previous internal and foreign policy has been consistent. The ruling party in Iraq started the war to protect its self-interest in holding power, which coincided with the interests of other countries in the region that were threatened by the tide of Islamic fundamentalism and its main practitioner. Iraq's image did not suffer from the Arabic and foreign press after its aggression, and Iraq was seen as a country protecting regional stability and the interests of friendly nations.

The war did not alter Iraq's fundamental policy despite the fact that it changed its public stands on various central issues and changed its alliances. Iraq moved publicly against all its previous policies: it supported Egypt, defended the reactionary gulf states, formed liaisons with King Hussein, supported Islamic opposition in Syria against the Ba'ath, and reestablished a close, if temporary, relationship with the United States. However, the war meant that Iraq's leaders had become indebted to foreign countries to maintain their powers inside Iraq. Thus, the present (and future) government became dependent on foreign countries, and its foreign policies will be defined accordingly.

The Constitution of Iraq

Institutions in Iraq are unlikely to undergo radical changes, but Iraq itself as an institution will face the threat of civil wars, further polarization, and possible disintegration. There are many factors that could influence the results of such changes, and the Iran-Iraq war has made such changes possible in the foreseeable future. This does not necessarily mean that it is going to happen. The interests of both regional and international powers concerned with Iraq's future are against further instability in Iraq. The Kurds may receive sympathetic statements from Western countries and organizations, but it is unlikely that they will receive support for their desire for a separate state. Some form of self-rule within the state of Iraq may be encouraged, and the potential of further Kurdish unrest could accompany Iraq's future.

The war has had a strong impact in terms of human and economic costs, but these do not seem to be its most significant effect. The weaknesses of Iraq as a state and society and of the Iraqis as a people are the most important effects. The potential for a civil war, similar to Lebanon's, could develop into a reality if and when regional and international circumstances permit it and support it.

7

War Responsibility: Governments or Individuals?

ABDOLRAHMAN ALEM

In the beginning of the ninth decade of the twentieth century, the world once again witnessed open aggression of one state against another. Iraqi armed forces invaded the territory of the Islamic Republic of Iran and threatened its sovereignty, territorial integrity, and political independence. The consequences of such flagrant aggression, in accordance with the 1974 United Nations Resolution on Definition of Aggression, entail international responsibility for the aggressor state. I discuss here the responsibility of the Iraqi government vis-à-vis the government of Iran. I examine state responsibility from legal and penal standpoints, then I study questions relating to the responsibility of the Iraqi government and leaders.

The state is the supreme legal institution of a country. Absence of legal responsibility in internal matters relates exclusively to the nationals of the state. At the same time, states are members of an international system while demanding their own sovereignty and legal equality. In order to safeguard this sovereignty, rights and obligations that protect the existing order should be established. In international law, the violation of sovereignty rights by one state creates responsibility for the delinquent state, which has a duty to recognize the consequences of such a responsibility.[1]

Until the twentieth century, state responsibility had purely a customary status, and the delinquent state could have remedied the consequences of its actions by paying compensation or making reparations. For the first time, in Article 3 of the Fourth Hague Convention of

1907, rules and customs of land warfare found a legal structure. The article provides that "a belligerent party which violates the provisions of the said Regulations shall, if the case demands, be liable to pay compensation. It shall be responsible for all acts committed by persons forming part of its armed forces."[2] Thus, state responsibility becomes a supplementary part of customary international law and is binding.

Article 3, in addition to being a legal source for state responsibility, also determines the responsibility of a violator state for actions by its nationals, particularly those committed by its armed forces against the rights of another state. As will be discussed, individuals themselves are liable for their illegal actions, which are not necessarily similar to the responsibility of their government, but their governments are liable to compensate for their actions. This responsibility will be examined, and, in accordance with the relevant case, the responsibility of the government and leaders of Iraq will be determined.

According to customary international rules and regulations, the delinquent state, in addition to being liable to the injured state, is also responsible for its actions in the international system. Oppenheim asserts that "any break of a duty under international law is an international offense, and the injured state may by way of reprisal, or even war, force the delinquent state to fulfill its international obligations."[3] With the development of international law, this principle was accepted: all states have interests in observing the rules of international law, and, therefore, they should take collective action against the delinquent state and regain the violated rights of the injured state. Today, the principle of the responsibility of states toward the injured state and the international system is generally accepted.

The violation of the rights of one state no longer is considered to be relevant only to the injured or delinquent state. The international community also reacts to the commission of an international offense because the violation of the rights of one state endangers legal systems and international peace and security. Therefore, if a state violates customary rules or provisions of a convention, although it may concern the injured state initially, the international community supports the injured state and makes efforts to restore international order. International organizations, in conformity with the powers entrusted to them by the member states, may take direct actions against the delinquent state if a customary rule or regulation of international law is violated. For example, the United Nations, in which member states have entrusted the responsibility for the maintenance of peace and international security, may take collective action to remove threats to peace and suppress acts of aggression. In performance of such duties, the UN acts as the representative of the international community and reacts to violations of the delinquent state.

As a consequence, in international law an act of aggression changes not only legal relations between the aggressor and the victim of aggression but also the legal relations between the aggressor state and the international organization and all other states. General Assembly Resolution 3314 of December 14, 1974, on the "Definition of Aggression" (paragraph 5) considers a war of aggression a crime, creating international responsibility for the delinquent state. Paragraph 2 of Article 5 in the resolution stipulates, "A war of aggression is a crime against international peace. Aggression creates international responsibility." This paragraph clearly provides responsibility for states for their aggression or acts of aggression. In Article 2 of the same resolution, the responsibility of determining the occurrence of aggression has been entrusted to the UN Security Council.

The responsibility of states entails another consequence, namely, penal liability. This concept first found some proponents in the beginning of this century, particularly after World War II. The proponents were divided into two groups. One believed that penal responsibility of states emanates from international law and that penal responsibility of individuals results from municipal or civil law. The other tried to apply regulations governing the violations of obligations and duties, customary principles, and international law to individuals as well. Therefore, states are liable as legal persons, just as individuals are liable for their wrong actions in municipal law.

The first attempt to punish those responsible for committing war crimes was made after World War I, but most legal discussions on the responsibility of individuals took place after World War II. The Allies issued a number of joint and individual declarations on the punishment of war criminals: the first Allied Declaration in 1942 in London, the

Moscow Declaration of 1943, and the Nuremberg Charter. In addition, the charter of the International Military Tribunal (the Nuremberg Charter), adopted in August 8, 1945, by the governments of the United States, the United Kingdom, the USSR, and France, enumerated criminal acts against peace in Article 6.[4] Furthermore, the Nuremberg Charter was adopted by the General Assembly in accordance with Resolution 95 of December 11, 1946, as a document of international law that has given legal character to the penal liability of individuals. Declaration of the principles of international law concerning friendly relations and cooperation among states in accordance with the UN Charter (General Assembly Resolution 2625 of November 1970) provides, "A war of aggression is a crime against peace for which, in accordance with international law, there exists responsibility."[5]

Taking these points into consideration, the responsibility of the government of Iraq can be divided into three categories: international responsibility of the government of Iraq, the responsibility of the political leaders of Iraq, and the responsibility of the government of Iraq toward the injured state, namely, the Islamic Republic of Iran. These divisions are made to facilitate my discussion, because these three categories of responsibility are inseparable.

The International Responsibility of the Government of Iraq

The international responsibility of the government of Iraq falls into two categories: its breaches of international law and its aggression against Iran. The first stems from the violation of the following international treaties.

The First Hague Convention of 1907

Article 1 of the Convention of 1907 stipulated that international conflicts may not be waged without advance warning, declaration, or ultimatum. Iraq initiated an extensive undeclared attack on September 22, 1980, against airports, cities, rural settlements, civilian populations, commercial and economic centers, hospitals, and places of worship.

The Geneva Protocol on Chemical Warfare of 1925

The Geneva Protocol of 1925 prohibited the use of asphyxiating, poisonous, or other gases and bacteriological methods of warfare. It states that "whereas the use in war of asphyxiating, poisonous or other gases . . . has been justly condemned by the general opinion of the civilized world . . . the High Contracting Parties to Treaties prohibiting such use, accept this prohibition."[6] The government of Iraq signed this protocol on September 8, 1931, but by repeated use of asphyxiating, cyanide, mustard, and other gases, breached its international obligations according to this treaty. The extensive use of different kinds of gases in the city of Halabjah by Iraq, which caused the death of more than 5,000 Kurds, was a clear example of genocide. Before that, a large number of Iranian troops had been killed as a result of their exposure to various lethal gases used by Iraq.

The United Nations Convention on Prevention and Punishment of the Crime of Genocide

Under terms of the UN Convention on Genocide, "The contracting states confirm that genocide is a crime under international law that they undertake to prevent and punish." Other provisions of the convention enumerate the punishment of the violators.[7] The government of Iraq was one of the formulators of this convention and signed it on January 20, 1959. By mass extermination of Iraqi Kurds, Iraq breached its obligation and violated the legal principle of the inviolability of treaties.

The Four Geneva Conventions of 1949

On August 12, 1949, the participating states in Geneva ratified the four Geneva conventions that, more than any other document on the law of war, have been accepted by states. The main subject of all four conventions is the protection of war victims. The provisions of Articles 49, 53, 55, and 56 of the Fourth Convention are related to the protection of civilian persons in time of war.

Article 49 prohibits individuals or groups protected by the convention from being deported from occupied territory to the territory of the occupier state or any other territory, whether occupied or not, regardless of motive.[8] The government of Iraq displaced more than a million people and transferred large numbers of civilians from occupied Iranian territory to its own territory. The government of Iraq must be held accountable in accordance with this article.

Article 53 stipulates that "destruction of immovable and personal property belonging to individuals, associations, or private persons or governments or other public organizations, or social and cooperative associations by the occupier state is prohibited, unless such destruction is for absolutely necessary military operations."[9] Important economic centers of the Islamic Republic of Iran such as refineries, petrochemical complexes, power plants and bridges, residential areas, public and private institutions, customhouses, port facilities, transportation equipment, and the like were destroyed by Iraqi occupation forces. Furthermore, movable properties in the occupied territories were plundered, and some of the occupied cities were razed to the ground.

Articles 55 and 56 of the Fourth Geneva Convention relate to the duty of the occupier state to provide food and medicine and to maintain medical centers and hospitals in the occupied territories. The government of Iraq not only brutally maltreated civilian persons; it also refused to provide basic requirements and medical and health services. As a result, many of the maltreated prisoners of war and civilian persons in the occupied territories died. The government of Iraq ratified the four Geneva Conventions in February 1956.

The Charter of the United Nations

The government of Iraq is a member of the United Nations. In accordance with the provisions of its charter, which is a multilateral treaty, the government of Iraq has agreed to comply with the principles of the UN in its international relations and to fulfill its obligations with good faith. It has also agreed to resolve its disputes by peaceful means and to refrain from threat or use of force against the territorial integrity and political independence of other states.

By launching an attack against Iran, by refusing to resolve its disputes with Iran by peaceful means, and by threatening Iran's territorial integrity and political independence, the government of Iraq breached its obligations under the UN charter, proved its lack of good intention, and violated rules of international law.

The Treaty Concerning the State Frontier and Neighborly Relations between Iran and Iraq

In 1975, in order to settle their disputes, the governments of Iran and Iraq undertook, under the terms of the said treaty, to demarcate their land and river borders, establish security along their common borders, consider their obligations permanent, and resolve the disputes arising from the interpretation or implementation of the treaty by peaceful means. Iraq, however, annulled the 1975 treaty on September 17, 1980. Thus, by unilateral annulment of the 1975 treaty, Iraq violated the principle of inviolability of treaties and breached provisions of Article 62 of the Vienna Convention on the law of treaties concerning the permanency and inalterability of border treaties.[10]

The second category of Iraq's international responsibility, its aggression against Iran, is related to border encroachments. From early April 1979 to August 1980, Iraq repeatedly trespassed on the border areas of Iran. During this period, 135 aerial attacks took place; cities in Khuzestan and Ilam were bombed 152 times; border posts were invaded 119 times; rural settlements of Iran were attacked 63 times; and oil installations of Iran, including the Abadan Oil Refinery, were attacked seven times.

Iraq intensified its attacks on border regions a few days before its all-out invasion against the territory of Iran. Before September 22, 1980, Iraqi troops crossed the boundary lines of Iran on numerous occasions, including sixteen times in the border cities of Qasr-e-Shirin, Khorramshahr, Naft Shahr, Ilam, Mehran, and Dehloran. They attacked border posts 132 times, economic installations seven times, and rural settlements 39 times. On September 6, 1980, as a result of shelling by Iraqi artillery, five civilians were killed and six injured. On September 7, following clashes perpetrated by the Iraqi army, thirty-four civilians were killed in the cities of Mehran and Dehloran. On September 8, Qasr-e-Shirin was shelled by mortar and cannon fire, and a number of places in the city were razed to the ground, injuring eight persons and inflicting heavy material losses. These encroachments on the territory and border regions of Iran continued for some time, causing damage and casualties.[11]

The responsibility for such wanton and provocative acts lies with the government of Iraq. It must be held accountable to the international community for its aggression on the borders of Iran, violations of the existing border treaty, the endangerment of peace and international security, and actions contrary to its treaty obligations.

Further Iraqi aggression occurred in violation of Iranian sovereignty. On September 22, 1980, Iraq launched an extensive invasion against Iran along 550 kilometers of common border, using twelve armored mechanized infantry divisions, and simultaneously bombed airports and military and economic installations in Iran's major cities. Iraq also initiated a war at sea, thus waging a full-fledged war.[12]

There were a number of illegal elements in Iraq's actions. The first relates to its ill intentions in attacking Iran and violating its political independence. This ill intent is an important criterion for determining the responsibility of the aggressor state in the commission of crimes against international peace. The government of Iraq manifested its aggressive intention by instigating provocative acts in the province of Khuzestan and by its support of groups such as the "Arabistan Liberation Front," whose purpose was to subvert the government of the Islamic Republic of Iran. By exploding oil pipelines and bridges and planting bombs in urban centers and public transportation vehicles, the "Front" carried out terrorist acts supported, encouraged, and armed by Iraq. These actions not only contravened the generally accepted principles of international law but also demonstrated the Iraqi government's ill intention.[13]

The second element relates to anticipation in the commission of crimes. By carrying out an extensive and undeclared invasion against Iran, Iraq occupied large areas of Iranian soil and inflicted heavy material and human losses. Premeditation in the commission of crime, which is the prima facie evidence for an act of aggression, constitutes a criterion for aggression. Iraq's aggression against Iran was carried out in accordance with a calculated plan, therefore the government of Iraq is directly responsible for initiating a war of aggression.

The third element involves the gravity and consequences of the crime. As indicated, twelve divisions of Iraq's armed forces crossed Iranian borders and brought large areas of Iran under occupation. These forces entered Iran from the northern, central, and southern fronts. They occupied Khorramshahr, Susangerd, Bustan, Mehran,

Dehloran, Qasr-e-Shirin, Howeizeh, Naft Shahr, Sumar, Musian, and hundreds of square kilometers of Iranian territory. Iraq's aggression against Iran was of such gravity and consequence that it can be considered a full-fledged international tort involving responsibility of the government of Iraq.[14]

The Responsibility of the Political Leaders of Iraq

The UN General Assembly ratified the judgment of the Nuremberg Court by Resolution 95 of 1940 and made the principles in the said judgment part of the principles of international law. The first principle stipulates that any individual committing an act that is considered a crime in accordance with international law will be held responsible for the offense. Iraqi political leaders, by attacking Iran, committed an act that constitutes a war crime in accordance with international law. Thus, on the basis of the principle, Iraq is responsible and should be punished.

Political leaders and military commanders are responsible for acts committed by persons under their command. These acts include genocide and brutal treatment of prisoners of war. Existing documents and eyewitnesses recount massacres, maltreatment, displacement of civilian persons, plunder of public and private property in the occupied lands, and senseless destruction of cities, towns, and rural settlements by Iraq's armed forces. Iraq's political leaders, namely, Saddam Hussein and high-level officials, are responsible for war crimes committed by their subordinates.[15] Article 19 in the draft of the International Law Commission, which has also examined the responsibility of states and individuals for many years, states that the mere fact that an individual in his capacity as head of state or as another high-ranking official has not committed an international crime does not free him of international responsibility. Consequently, the nationals of a country, whether the head of state or an ordinary functionary, are responsible for the commission of war crimes. The fact that a defendant acted in pursuance to orders from his superior would not free him of responsibility, though it may be used as mitigation of his punishment.

The Responsibility of the Government of Iraq toward the Injured State

As mentioned, aggression creates responsibility. Iraq's acts of hostility against Iran make the Iraqi government responsible for reparations, in conformity with international customs and laws. According to these customs and laws, the delinquent state must make proper amends for damage and loss to the other state. The issue of reparation found its way into legal literature for the first time in the Paris Peace Conference. This conference appointed fifty-two specialized commissions, one charged with determining responsibility for initiators of war. The commission for the responsibility of the war concluded that the Central Powers of World War I (Germany, Austria-Hungary, Bulgaria, and Turkey) waged an aggressive war and were accountable for its consequences. Article 231 of the Versailles Peace Treaty dealt with this issue, according to which Germany was held responsible for reparation of loss, damage, and injury arising from its own and its allies' aggression.

Taking these points into account, the losses arising from Iraq's aggression can be categorized as financial damage, nonfinancial damage, and nonmaterial damage.

Financial damage and losses mean the amount that is needed to restore conditions to the state or position that existed before the damage or reduction of national production, decline in exploitation of natural resources, damage to agricultural output, fall in export earning, loss of markets for Iranian carpets, and profits lost.

Nonfinancial damage includes physical injuries such as death, injury, maiming, and damage caused by curtailing individual freedoms by imprisonment, detention, expulsion or banishment, and other acts of a similar nature for which the calculation of indemnification is difficult.

The nonmaterial losses arising from Iraq's aggression are countless. In addition to the destruction of precious historic relics, in violation of the Hague Convention of 1954, the psychological traumas arising from the war, the sufferings of the injured and their families, and the losses caused by missile and aerial bombardments have inflicted pain on Iran and the Iranian people. It should be determined which of the nonmaterial losses can be indemnified, and the government of Iraq should be held accountable for their compensation.[16]

Thus, the responsibility of the government of Iraq vis-à-vis the injured state, the Islamic Republic of Iran, involves compensation for its aggression against Iran, and the Iraqi government is obliged to make reparations in accordance with the legal liabilities arising from aggression. The modus operandi for determining the compensation is not difficult and can be calculated.

Notes

1. For the definition of state responsibility, see Reza Fioozi, *Mas'iliate Binolmelali and Hemayate Siyasi*, 2d ed. (Tehran: Center for International Studies, 1356/1977).
2. For the text of this convention and its annexes, see Adam Roberts and Richard Guelff, eds., *Documents on the Laws of War* (Oxford: University Press, 1982), 43–59.
3. L. Oppenheim, *International Law: A Treatise*, 2 vols. (London: Longman, 8th impression, 1967), 337.
4. Roberts and Guelff, *Laws of War*, 11.
5. *UN Treaty Series*, vol. 82 (1951), 285–88.
6. Roberts and Guelff, *Laws of War*, 140.
7. Ibid., 158–59.
8. Ibid., 288.
9. Ibid., 290.
10. See Nasrin Mosafa et al., *Iraq's Aggression against Iran and the UN's Position* (Tehran: Center for International Studies, 1366/1987), 10–12.
11. Ibid., 50–51.
12. Ibid., 74.
13. Ibid., 59–72; see also Ibrahim Tehrani's essay in this book.
14. *An Analysis of the Imposed War* (Tehran: Ministry of Foreign Affairs, 1361/1982), 132.
15. Ibid., 33.
16. Fioozi, *Mas'iliate Binolmelali*, 142–83.

Part II

Superpowers, International Law, and Politics

8

The USSR and the Iran-Iraq War: From Brezhnev to Gorbachev

MOHIADDIN MESBAHI

The Soviet Union and Iran: Paradigms and Objectives

Soviet policy toward the war is best understood within the general framework of its policy in the Middle East–Persian Gulf region and as a function of Moscow's perception of opportunities and risks in the region as a whole.[1]

What were traditional Soviet objectives in the region? Were there any modifications or changes in these objectives in the Gorbachev era? The answer given by Western Sovietologists to these questions, especially to the first, has generally been split along orthodox and revisionist interpretations of the cold war era and the intentions and objectives ascribed to Soviet global policy.

The orthodox view, while varying in degree of emphasis and rhetoric, sees Soviet traditional objectives as decidedly offensive and expansionist, motivated by a historical Russian *idée fixe* of the drive toward warm-water ports and the messianic impulses of Soviet communist ideology. Proponents of this school of thought have assembled evidence from the Russian and Soviet past and present. This evidence ranges from Peter the Great's mythical "will" and the Molotov-Ribbentrop Pact to Soviet intervention in Afghanistan, indicating a consistent forward-looking thrust in Soviet policy in the Persian Gulf region in the pre-Gorbachev era. Iran's geopolitical position as the only real physical barrier between the Soviet Union and the Persian Gulf has thus been the focus of the orthodox school and has informed to a large extent the West's Persian Gulf policy before and after World War II. More specifically, Iran became the cornerstone of U.S. containment strategy in the region. Although different postwar U.S. administrations had left the imprint of their own doctrinal idiosyncrasies, the overall thrust of the U.S. strategy of containment and its key actor in the region remained unchanged.

The revisionist or "the reactive" school viewed Soviet Gulf policy as an extension of the generally beleaguered Soviet state that reactively responded to the aggressive U.S. encirclement policy in the postwar era. Proponents of this school downgraded the role of ideology as having a significant place in actual Soviet policy but referred to the historical continuity of the West's militarization of Soviet southern border states, either through Western-sponsored alliance systems (CEATO or CENTO) or bilateral politico-military support and arrangements.

A third, more flexible and dynamic perspective has tried to accommodate both the offensive and the defensive thrusts of Soviet policy. A postrevisionist school of thought has argued that the two seemingly distinct features of Soviet foreign policy were in fact two sides of the same coin, reconciled by Soviet "legitimate" security interests and the fluctuating, though conceptually understandable, ambitions of a superpower.

Although the philosophical world view of the orthodox school is predominantly influenced by the primacy of Western idealism and the good-vs.-evil dichotomy, the reactive/revisionist school has benefited from more liberal and leftist (Western Marxist) perspectives, allowing a more critical view of U.S. foreign dynamics and objectives. The postrevisionist interpretation has been in large part committed to a less ideological intellectual tradition and adheres mainly to "power realism" as its intellectual roots and world view. It sees the Soviet Union as a typical big power, bent on protecting its security and interest by both accommodation and expansion. Ideology, the proponents of this view would argue, is generally irrelevant or at least only instrumental in ex post facto justification of Soviet policy objectives.

The latter model has the advantage of a "holistic approach," permitting a more sober, realistic assessment of diverse Soviet objectives and policies toward Iran and the Persian Gulf, but its contemptuous view of the role of ideology in Soviet foreign policy has been a noticeable handicap in analyzing that policy in the region. This model of assessing the international behavior of states, although practical and intellectually elegant, cannot adequately address the dynamics of crucial decisions Soviet leaders made about the region during the 1980s. Soviet attitudes regarding the Iranian revolution, the Iran-Iraq war, and the crisis in Afghanistan will be better understood if the complicated functions of Soviet Marxism-Leninism in informing their policy were to be taken into account or, better, if the Soviet foreign policy prism were allowed to speak for itself, rather than being forcibly adjusted to fit the requirements of a prevailing Western model.[2]

It is my thesis that Soviet ideological understanding of the "Islamic factor" was the key element in its policy toward Iran. Islam, either as a reactionary sociopolitical force and barrier or as a competitive ideology claiming a superior model of political development and mobilization, occupied a central place in Soviet policy perception and actions. From the early and formative years of Bolshevik policy toward Mirza Kuchek Khan to the more recent and complicated interaction with Ayatollah Khomeini, the Soviet perspective, in spite of its undeniable maturity and sophistication,[3] had been consistently distrustful of an Islamic alternative developing on its southern border.

This ideological factor was so prevalent that even the traditionally operative term of Soviet foreign policy, anti-imperialism, was subordinated to accommodate the more immediate concept of the containment of the perceived Islamic threat.[4] While one might argue that the potentials of the "Islamic threat" have been overblown and exaggerated, this argument remains largely irrelevant to the realities of Soviet policies that rightly or wrongly were greatly influenced by taking the "imagined" threat very seriously.[5] The Bolsheviks, after initial hesitation, refused to support Mirza Kuchek Khan's Islamically oriented movement and chose instead to work with Reza Khan's "national bourgeoisie." So, too, did Brezhnev and his successors overcome the initial temptation of strategic flirtation with the Islamic Republic, and, nostalgic of their peaceful coexistence with monarchical Iran,[6] chose a policy of containment.

What made the centrality of ideological conflict so critical in Soviet-

Iranian relations and, by association, in Soviet attitudes toward the region in general was the fact that neither Moscow nor Tehran harbored any fundamental confusion regarding the assessment of the other's ideological commitment or the parameters of its flexibilities and constraints. This relative clarity of perception was mutually reinforcing and thus left little room for a strategic rapprochement between Tehran and Moscow. Ideological compatibility in Soviet and Iranian anti-imperialist rhetoric, their occasional economic agreements, and tactical diplomatic support and maneuvers could not but reflect elements of "damage limitation" in a fundamentally irreconcilable relationship. Iran's "neither West nor East" foreign policy was not the typical nonaligned Third World policy familiar to the Kremlin leaders.[7] Not only did the policy reflect an unfamiliar and simultaneous symbiosis of anti-Americanism and anti-Sovietism, it also demonstrated Iran's frustrating disrespect for geopolitical realities and its apparent insensitivity toward the traditional calculations of its large neighbor's concerns and interests. Occasional flares of pragmatism toward Soviet interests could not at any time during the 1980s be sufficient to overcome the basic differences.

The Iran-Iraq War was the central development that encapsulated the ideological and political gap between Moscow and Tehran. Therefore, the study of Soviet policy regarding the war is in fact the study of Soviet-Iranian relations in the 1980s. The war was the central issue around which the dynamics of the Iranian revolutionary process matured and evolved. Domestically, it provided the subjective and objective basis of a conducive sociopolitical and psychological atmosphere, a situation of "national emergency," that directed the thrust of revolutionary processes toward the consolidation of clerical rule and the weakening or elimination of its opposition. In other words, the making of the ultimate ideological and political characteristic of the Iranian revolution and the regime became heavily embedded in and indebted to the war and its ideological and messianic impulse, an issue especially critical to Soviet policy toward Iran.

Internationally, the war symbolized the dialectics of the revolution's domestic ideological thrust and its external hopes and ramifications. The "imposed war" represented not only the heroic defense of a victimized revolution, but, as the major driving force of Iranian foreign policy, it was the mechanism through which an unorthodox state, irrespective of the extremity of its geopolitical environment, attempted to export its revolution. Iran's geographical location, bordering both the Persian Gulf and the Soviet Union, made the ideologized "imposed war" the most critical issue that shaped both Iranian foreign policy toward the outside world and the world's policy, including the Soviet Union's, toward Iran. Thus, in analyzing Soviet policy toward the Iran-Iraq war, the issue of ideological sensitivity in Soviet-Iranian relations has to be given adequate attention and should be added to the traditional mix of defensive and offensive thrusts in Soviet policy toward the region.

Soviet Policy toward the Iran-Iraq War

Several sets of interrelated concerns and perceptions helped influence and shape Moscow's policy toward the war. First, in Moscow's view, the war significantly enhanced the U.S. position in the region by providing the necessary justification for the United States to project its military power. The United States capitalized on the "Iranian threat," thereby convincing the otherwise reluctant states of the region to participate in a pro-American politico-military coalition. Second, the war further diminished the Soviet position by overshadowing the significance of the Arab-Israeli conflict, splitting the Arab world, and diminishing the Soviets' ability to utilize their traditional vehicle of influence in the critical post–Camp David period in the Middle East. Third, the war forced the Soviets to face the dilemma of maintaining good relations with the belligerents. They had to protect their position as a possible mediator without abdicating the flexibility of having major input into the final outcome of the conflict. Fourth, the future shape of the new revolutionary regime in Tehran was of utmost importance to Moscow's overall strategy in Iran. The war complicated domestic political dynamics and from Moscow's perspective was a leading factor in enhancing the political position of the conservative clergy and the concommitant rightward shift in the character of the Iranian regime. Finally, perhaps the most important Soviet concern was that the war magnified the threat of the Islamic factor. A military victory by Iran could have fundamentally altered the balance of power in the Persian Gulf and could conceivably have led to the emergence of an Iran-centric Islamic order. This would have had disastrous policy implications for the Soviet position in Afghanistan and the security of the Muslim republics of Soviet Central Asia. It is within the framework of the integrated and evolving dynamics of these perceptions and concerns that Soviet policy regarding the Iran-Iraq war should be addressed.

This policy went through three roughly overlapping yet distinctive periods. The first, between 1980 and 1982, was when Moscow pursued a policy of "strict neutrality." The second, a policy of "active neutrality," witnessed a gradual but definite shift toward Iraq between 1982 and early 1986. And the third stage of Soviet policy, coinciding with the ascendancy of Mikhail Gorbachev to power, saw a dramatic shift in Soviet policy of support for Iraq and "active containment" of Iran. This period started in mid-1986 and lasted until the acceptance of the August 1988 cease-fire by Iran.

Moscow's "Strict Neutrality": 1980–1982

When the war erupted in September 1980, the Soviets had little choice but to remain neutral. This neutrality, however, was not without its complications as both Iraq and Iran presented the Soviets with considerable potential and opportunities that Moscow could hardly ignore.

Iraq, a long-time Soviet ally with a longstanding Treaty of Friendship and Cooperation, was the emerging Soviet partner in the Persian Gulf and the Arab world. Iraq's political and strategic value had only increased as a result of the Camp David Accord and the finalization of the Egyptian decision to join the United States' Middle Eastern scheme. In addition, Iraq was a major recipient of Soviet arms and a reliable exporter of oil to the Soviet Union and its East European allies. Finally, the Soviets must have pondered the negative repercussions that a lack of support for Iraq might have had on Soviet-alliance credibility as the perennial supporter of the Arab states in the postwar era.

Iran, on the other hand, presented the Soviet leadership with a unique and unprecedented opportunity. The Iranian revolution of 1979 had, with remarkable speed, removed one of the staunchest allies of the United States in the region. As a result, the cornerstone of U.S. containment of the Soviet Union in the region had been removed; instead, a promising though fluid target of opportunity had presented itself to Moscow. The fluidity of Iranian domestic dynamics and the uncertainties surrounding the ultimate shape and orientation of the Iranian regime was one, if not the key, factor in the initial Soviet decision not to support Iraq's war effort against Iran. Soviet policy, also reflected in the Tudeh party's strategy toward the Islamic Republic, showed that during the first two years of the conflict Moscow clearly hoped that it could influence the dynamics of Iran's internal politics. The Soviets wanted, first, to prevent at all cost the reemergence of a pro-Western regime in Tehran and, second, to leave their options flexible and relevant so as to influence the optimal features of the Iranian polity.

Further, the Soviets had to consider possible Western reaction to Soviet support for either Iran or Iraq.[8] Soviet support, especially for Iraq, not only might have prompted a U.S. response, but, in view of the uncertainties of Iranian politics, might have pushed Iran into a policy of reconciliation with the West, strengthening the hands of the "bourgeois trend" in Iran.[9] This, presumably, might have paved the way for the return of a pro-Western regime in Iran, a scenario totally unacceptable to Moscow.

The interplay of opportunities and constraints that emerged from Soviet evaluation led to its adoption of a position of neutrality at the start of the war and to the suspension of arms sales to Iraq. Soviet declaratory policy, in fact, indicated a mild criticism of Iraq and sympathy for Iran.[10] Although the Soviets were clearly unhappy about Iraq's ill-conceived decision to invade Iran, Moscow eschewed from publicly condemning Baghdad and labeling Iraq as the aggressor. Moscow supported a political settlement through negotiations. The final document of the CPSU 26th Congress, in its assessment of the war, called for an immediate end to the war that directly contradicted the interests of the countries involved by "weakening their anti-imperialist potential."[11] General Secretary Leonid Brezhnev, in a statement carried by *Pravda*, announced that "we do not intend to intervene in the Iran-Iraq conflict. We support a political solution to this conflict as soon as possible."[12]

The official position of "nonintervention" was repeatedly emphasized by many Soviet commentators during the first stage of the war, from September 1980 to the early fall of 1982.[13] Numerous Western media reports suggesting Soviet arms sales to both Iran and Iraq were repeatedly rejected by Soviet officials and observers. Henry Trofimenko, deputy director of the U.S.A. and Canada Institute in Moscow, in an interview with *Al Waten*, reflected on the cautious Soviet policy and stated that "we do not want to contribute to its prolongation by offering military aid to this or that party. That would only deepen the conflict. We want a speedy and negotiated settlement."[14] In October 1981, the Iranian prime minister, Mohammed Ali Rajaee, dropped an unpleasant bombshell when he announced that the Soviets, through their ambassador in Tehran, Vladimir Vinogiadov, had offered Iran a substantial arms package that he had rejected. Moscow angrily denounced the suggestion as a "gross lie" and strongly reiterated its observed neutrality.[15]

As argued, Soviet concern over the internal political dynamics of Iran was a major factor behind Soviet neutrality. The intense political struggle in the Iranian domestic scene waged among different groups within the broad spectrum of the postrevolutionary leadership, and the emerging armed struggle initiated by the underground "left" against the government, all in the midst of a deteriorating economic situation, made Iran, from the Soviet perspective, vulnerable and thus a target of opportunity. The Soviet theoretical interpretation of the political trend in Iran suggested a desire to support the "petty-bourgeois Islamic forces" against both "the bourgeois trend" and the armed "left." Moscow hoped that the "radical" forces within the "petty bourgeois Islamic trend" would be able to consolidate their hold on power, thereby enabling the Soviet Union to consolidate its influence in Iran by forging an alliance between the Tudeh and the radical petty bourgeois. Yevgeni Primakov, director of the Institute of the World Economy and International Relations of the USSR Academy of Science and one of the future architects of Soviet "new thinking," in an authoritative article published in the mid-1980s, encapsulated Soviet ideological assessment of the Iranian political development. After dividing the predominant trends within the Islamic forces into "radical" and "conservative" "petty bourgeois," Primakov argued that in the first few years of revolution "the petty bourgeois Islamic forces, both conservative and radical, united against the Iranian bourgeois and the individual who represented its interests in the Islamic movement."[16]

Primakov's authoritative analysis reflects a clear early Soviet hope that in the confrontation between the competing political trends in Tehran, the "Iranian bourgeois," led by "Iran's Liberation Movement" and other associated groups and individuals collectively branded as "Liberals," would be defeated. The Soviets clearly saw in the Liberals' broad platform the danger of a political comeback by the United States and the reversal of the revolution's anti-imperialist potentials and gains. It was not a coincidence that the main thrust of the Tudeh party's propaganda campaign in the first two years of revolution was directed against the Liberals. In fact, one can argue that the label itself to a certain extent was coined and popularized by the Tudeh party, a label that soon became one of the most enduring and widely utilized political terms of postrevolutionary Iran.[17] "It was precisely this period," Primakov has argued, "that witnessed the most radical slogans and measures of Iran's Islamic leadership: anti-monopoly appeals, the imposition of restrictions on the activity of big capital, the sequestration of the property of the capitalist . . . the promotion of agrarian reforms, etc."[18]

It is clear that the Soviets, confined in the neatly organized Soviet Marxology, had overlooked the complexity of the interdependence among the different trends within the Islamic forces. Moreover, the Soviets underestimated the power and political resilience of the so-called conservative petty bourgeois, namely the clergy, and the unique role of Imam Khomeini in bringing together and personifying both the "radical" and "conservative" trends. What the Soviets clearly hoped, and theorized about, was the anticipation that the clerical rule of the "conservative petty bourgeois" would soon be replaced by, or consumed into, a more secular Islamic radicalism of the Algerian variety, one that would have allowed continued Soviet influence and presence in Iran. In a nonfundamentalist and secular, though Islamic, Iran, Soviet geopolitical proximity and reach, combined with a penetrative and skilled pro-

Soviet Communist party (the Tudeh party), could have created a sustainable base for Moscow's long-term influence in Iran and the Persian Gulf region. Such a scenario would have eased Soviet problems in Afghanistan and Central Asia and strengthened the hands of the Soviet leadership to bring the Iran-Iraq war to a desirable and speedy end.

Thus, the Soviet policy of "strict neutrality" during the period 1980–82 was a deliberately cautious one, reflecting Moscow's understanding of the complexity of the conflict, its aspiration for influencing a desirable political development in Iran, and its determination to remain unentangled in a potentially dangerous yet localized and stalemated conflict.

Moscow's "Active Neutrality": 1982–1986

The war of stalemate of 1981 came to an end when Iranian military momentum, through several successive offensive operations, broke the siege of Abadan, retook Bustan, and liberated Khorramshahr in May 1982. This military turning point was followed by the most critical decision of the Iranian leadership in the short history of the new republic: to adopt a maximalist war objective and carry the war into Iraq in July 1982.[19] Tehran's demand for the punishment of the aggressor and consequent shift in its military strategy to an all-out offensive led to a shift in Moscow's position on the war. In this new phase of the war, from the summer of 1982 to February 1986, Soviet policy retained its formal posture of neutrality as Moscow continued to promote a diplomatic solution and maintained relations with both sides. However, it began gradually but *actively* to tilt toward Iraq in order to prevent the collapse of the Saddam Hussein regime. Moscow therefore resumed open military and economic aid to Iraq.

The shift in Soviet policy in favor of Iraq was the result of Moscow's reassessment of the implications of an Iranian victory in the war and the interplay of opportunities and risks that such a development might entail. Although Iran remained the key strategic prize, the prospect of a dramatic change in the balance of power in the region in favor of Tehran did not present the Soviet government with any reliable prospect of influence and advantage. There was no reason for Moscow to believe that a victorious Iran would be willing to forge a cordial alliance, let alone a strategic one, with the Soviet Union. More than the mere change in the military positions of the belligerents, it was the political decision behind the Iranian military effort that was most disturbing. Iran's "puritan" war objectives of removing the aggressor (Saddam Hussein) and liberating Qods (Jerusalem)[20] through the liberation of Karbala,[21] meant an outward expansion of Islamic revolution through the conduct of a revolutionary war against Iraq. Victory over Iraq seemed, from the Soviet perspective, the first step in Iran's conduct of the "permanent revolution."[22]

The continuation of the war also meant that Iranian domestic politics would be influenced, to a large extent, by the dynamics of the war itself, a situation of "national emergency" that did not allow for a more predictable political evolution in which Soviet interests and political input could play a more meaningful role in shaping Iran's political future. It was primarily Moscow's concern over the twin issues of the revolution's external expansion and its internal consolidation that forced the Tudeh party to commit itself to a policy of opposing the regime's new war objectives. Given the depth of the Iranian leadership's commitment to the prosecution of the war and the tense internal atmosphere of domestic politics, this policy seemed then, and proved later, to be suicidal.[23] The similarity of editorials in *Nameh Mardom* (Tudeh's main organ), *Pravda*, and *Izvestiya* in opposing continuation of the war was unmistakable. While *Nameh Mardom*'s editorials questioned the soundness of Iran's war objective and its "negative consequences on the socio-economic progress" of the country[24] and on its "anti-imperialist potentials,"[25] *Pravda* and *Izvestiya*, in less circumspect language, blasted Iran's war objective as "without precedence in international practice"[26] and one that "drives the conflict between Iraq and Iran into an impasse."[27]

Moscow's tilt toward Iraq did have some additional justifications. Soviet credibility in not allowing a signatory of a Treaty of Friendship to be toppled was also tested. Furthermore, in the larger Middle East picture, the new shift in the Iran-Iraq war coincided with the Israeli invasion of Lebanon and the defeat of Syria and its mainly Soviet-equipped army. "Both the failure of Soviet arms in Lebanon," as Chubin has observed, "and the diminishing number of entry points for Soviet influence in the Middle East, argued for an emphasis on and commitment to the Iraqi connection."[28]

In view of a now consolidated hostility between Iran and the United States, the new Soviet tilt toward Iraq reduced the prospects for serious escalation and superpower confrontation in the Persian Gulf. Moscow was more doubtful than before that the United States would support Iran. Iranian insistence that the "imposed war" was in fact a U.S.-sponsored war waged by "the Zionist puppet in Baghdad" was more than simple rhetoric; it was indeed a widely held conviction among key decision-making circles in Tehran. In fact, the perceived "American hands" behind Iraq's aggression was one of the key factors in intensifying and deepening U.S.-Iranian hostility. The depth and degree of the U.S.-Iranian alienation provided Moscow with a necessary geopolitical cushion to bypass the fear of U.S.-Iranian rapprochement, providing Moscow with more regional maneuverability than it had had.

Soviet support for Iraq also opened new windows of opportunity in the Middle East and the Arab world. The restoration of political relations with Egypt in 1984 marked the culmination of Soviet efforts since their expulsion from that country to "re-establish some influence in Egypt and to expand Soviet leverage in a broader Middle Eastern context."[29] Egypt had been one of Iraq's arms suppliers during the war,[30] and Iraq had acted as a conduit for Egypt's reentry to the Arab world and the end of its isolation resulting from its peace treaty with Israel. The Soviet pro-Iraqi stand also facilitated the diplomatic offensive in the Persian Gulf region. After years of hesitation and contemplation, the Soviets finally succeeded in establishing full diplomatic relations with Oman and the United Arab Emirates and improved the atmosphere of their relations with Saudi Arabia through indirect contacts. Moscow's relations with Kuwait also improved, and new agreements for the delivery of Soviet arms, including air defense components such as SAM-8, were signed.[31]

This new opening for the Soviets in the region was more a function of the political consensus reached among the key regional actors as to the necessity of Iran's containment than a result of any new regional policy initiative originated in Moscow. Moscow, in fact, was reaping the benefits of the "trickle-down effects" resulting from the regional Arab coalition against Iran and the coalition's support for Iraq as the cornerstone of the containment of "Iranian expansion" and its brand of "Islamic fundamentalism." Soviet diplomatic opportunism and flexibility in making some inroads into the Persian Gulf was not enough, however, to become a real factor in tempering the U.S. drive for a monopoly of influence in the area. Soviet gains were modest, and the essential Soviet concern remained—that, on balance, Washington had gained more, and the prolongation of the conflict had become an effective instrument of U.S. influence building in the region.

Despite the fact that the Soviet tilt led to the improvement of Soviet-Iraqi relations, Baghdad finalized its gradual opening to the United States with full-fledged diplomatic relations in 1984 and the development of closer cooperation with Washington throughout the conflict with Iran. In fact, by the mid-1980s, the United States "became Iraq's silent ally."[32] But the resumption of Soviet arms supplies to Iraq and its support for Iraq's call to end the hostility reflected Moscow's determination to remain influential and competitive in Iraq. The U.S.-Iraqi courtship could not have gone unchallenged, as Moscow was determined to prevent a repetition of its previous setback in Egypt and the "Sadatization" of Saddam Hussein and "Egyptianization" of Iraq.[33]

Soviet-Iraqi rapprochement predictably led to a worsening of Soviet relations with Iran. A marked increase in criticism in Iran of the Soviet presence in Afghanistan was followed by more emphasis on an unambiguous "neither West nor East" policy, and, more importantly, by the crackdown on the Tudeh party and the expulsion of groups of Soviet diplomats on the charge of espionage.[34]

The arrest of the Tudeh party's leaders and a number of its members was a turning point in Soviet-Iranian relations. It was rather remarkable, as argued above, that the Soviet leaders could have ignored or downplayed the degree of the Tudeh party's vulnerability and, perhaps, overestimated Iran's sensitivity to Moscow's reaction over a possible crackdown. Moscow's overconfidence, it appears, was a function of its perception of Iran's isolation and its expectation of Tehran's natural tendency not to aggravate its large neighbor unnecessarily. This unwarranted confidence was a key factor in emboldening the Tudeh leadership to continue criticizing Iran's prosecution of the war with Iraq and, further, to perform an important intelligence function for Moscow through expansive penetration of Iran's governmental institutions and the military.[35] The Tudeh party's aggressive opposition toward the continuation of the war also reflected fundamental Soviet concerns over the negative and disruptive impact of the war on a desirable political make-up of the Iranian regime.

Throughout the second phase of the war, Soviet policy on the issue of military balance between Iran and Iraq derived fundamentally from the assumption that the level of military support given to Iraq was sufficient for it to withstand the continuous but inconclusive Iranian offensives. Iraq's strategy of "mobile defense," designed to absorb, envelop, and then destroy Iranian "human wave" assaults, seemed to have proved effective.[36]

Thus, by the end of 1985 and the beginning of 1986, the Soviets, and for that matter the rest of the outside actors involved in the conflict, had concluded that in spite of occasional eruptions, the Iran-Iraq war had reached a state of strategic stalemate that would continue until the ultimate erosion of Iran's economic and human resources would force it to accept a diplomatic settlement. This complex regional conflict appeared to have acquired a life of its own, to be a "forgotten war," as though it were a permanent, though nondefinitive, component of regional politics. This seemingly manageable situation, however, ended in 1986, and Soviet policy went through another marked shift.

Gorbachev and the Policy of "Active Containment": 1986–1988

The Soviet policy shift in 1986–87 was a function of both the reinforcement of Moscow's original perception of threat and several new dynamics. Collectively and simultaneously, these factors prompted a new level of involvement and activism in the conflict in favor of Iraq. The impressive Iranian military victories (especially the conquest of the Faw Peninsula), combined with the Soviet decision to withdraw from Afghanistan, the growing Soviet "Islamic problem" in Central Asia, and, finally, Gorbachev's *perestroika* at home and "new thinking" abroad, were the new elements that influenced Soviet policy toward the conflict and its protagonists.

The Iranian conquest of the Faw Peninsula was a stunning victory that, unlike the previous human wave assaults, was a sophisticated, carefully planned amphibious operation. It not only provided a significant foothold inside Iraq's territory but also sent a psychological shock wave throughout the region. Iran's follow-up operation toward Umm-al-Qasr, designed to cut off Iraq completely from the Persian Gulf, was contained only with considerable cost to Iraq's Republican Guard, the core of Iraq's best fighting units.[37] "Iranian troops reached the Khor Abdullah waterway opposite Kuwait, and there were even reports that Iranian forces had surrounded the Iraqi naval base at Umm-al-Qasr. . . . Iran also captured Iraq's main air control and warning center covering the Gulf, which was located north of Faw. This resulted in near panic in Kuwait and Saudi Arabia."[38]

Iran's military achievements were not followed by immediate victory in the war. Yet, while the fear of a decisive Iranian victory was unwarranted, the psychological impact of the new offensive reinforced the nightmarish apocalyptic projection of an eventual Iraqi collapse. Iraq's unsuccessful counterattack to retake the Faw only added to the atmosphere of near panic in the region's capitals. In a highly publicized operation, Iraq occupied Mehran, a small Iranian border town, only to be pushed back, leaving behind considerable military hardware, casualties, and POWs.[39]

The new military developments again rekindled old Soviet anxieties over the real probability of Iraq's military collapse and thus reinforced Moscow's threat perceptions. A noticeable increase in Soviet diplomatic and political activities and media coverage in February and March 1986 indicated the significance for Soviet policy of Iran's military breakthrough in the Faw Peninsula. Several meetings, apparently hurriedly arranged, between top Soviet officials (including soviet Foreign Minister Edward Shevernadze and Deputy Foreign Minister Yuli Vorontsov), and Iraqi Foreign Minister Tariq Aziz (also representing the Arab League) reflected the immediacy of the perceived threat. Criticism of Iran's intransigence in continuing "a war which can only benefit the imperialists," and open expressions of support for "Iraq's open call for an immediate cease-fire and a peaceful settlement," were repeatedly expressed by the Soviet media covering the meetings.[40]

With the "prospect" of an Iranian victory now intensified, the Arab states of the Persian Gulf looked toward Washington for more protection and closer involvement. Moscow's fundamental concern over the growing U.S. manipulation of the Iranian "bogeyman," as the mechanism for influence building and military projection, was further reinforced. So far, the conservative Arab states of the Persian Gulf had been content with an "over-the-horizon" U.S. presence as the main deterrent against Iranian expansion, while they simultaneously cultivated Soviet friendship as a way to isolate Iran further and enhance their own political leverage. In view of the new developments on the war front, and the subsequent intensification of the "tanker war" by Iraq, the United States had a clearer and more "justifiable" pretext for converting its over-the-horizon presence into a real military presence, thus seizing the role of Arab protector. Later developments in 1987 indicated that Soviet anxiety was not unwarranted. From the Soviet view, the "reflagging operation" and the unprecedented level of the U.S naval presence and access marked the culmination of an eventual outcome of the continuous war between Iran and Iraq, that is, the consolidation of a qualitatively new level of U.S. influence and presence in the Persian Gulf.[41]

The intensification and internationalization of the war and the prospect of an Iranian victory had now also given an added significance to the Soviet position in Afghanistan. Although they were concerned during the two initial phases of the war, the Soviets felt that the impact of the Iran-Iraq war on the Soviet-Afghan entanglement was manageable because Moscow's strategy in Afghanistan was based on a long and irreversible political and military commitment. With Gorbachev's decision early in 1987 to withdraw from Afghanistan and the danger of a "fundamentalist" takeover in Kabul, the implication of a victorious fundamentalist Iran seemed more significant. An emboldened and victorious Iran could only have added to Soviet problems in Afghanistan.

Moscow's concern over Afghanistan was linked directly to the core of the Kremlin's ideological anxiety over its own growing Islamic problem. Here again, an old issue that seemed a prospective and manageable problem was rapidly becoming an immediate and serious one. Though still in its initial phase (1986–87), Soviet *glasnost* allowed for a more sober and realistic assessment of Soviet problems in the Muslim republics of Central Asia. Soviet analysts and officials now discussed openly the seriousness of the revival of pan-Islamic ideas among the Muslim population of the Soviet Union and harshly questioned previous official optimism regarding the political attitudes and ethnic challenges of Soviet Islam.

It is worth noting that most Soviet alarmist discussions of the war focused primarily on Islam in its ideological aspect rather than on the more recent balanced Soviet treatment that reflects an appreciation of the ethnic dimension of Islamic revival in the Soviet Union. Earlier commentaries reflected Moscow's concern over the external and security aspects of its Islamic problems and the significance of the impact that the regional revival of Islam in Southwest Asia might have on the Soviet Muslim population. In an article in the January 1987 issue of *Pravda Vostoka*, R. Usmankhojaev, first secretary of the Central Committee of the Uzbekistan Communist party, expressed serious concern over the role of religion in undermining Soviet domestic security and foreign policy interests. Commenting on the role of Islam in encouraging nationalism and chauvinism, he observed that the "long-obsolete ideas of pan-Islamism are being revived and nationalistic passions are being inflamed."[42] Igor Beliaev, a long-term Soviet observer of the Iran-Iraq war, in his article, "Islam i Politiki" ("Islam and Politics") published in *Literaturnaya Gazeta*, warned the Soviets about the painful reality of an existing "Islamic substructure" in Soviet Central Asia.[43]

A full discussion of the recent dynamics of Soviet Islam is beyond the scope of this study. What is significant here is that an alarmist view of Islam, especially the role of outside influences (i.e., the Islamic revolution in Iran and the war in Afghanistan) on the dynamics of Soviet Islam since 1986–87, dominated Soviet thinking. Soviet sensitivity was also expressed over the impact of foreign broadcasts targeted at a Soviet Muslim audience. "On the Soviet-Iranian border alone," Beliaev complained, "there are thirty-eight broadcasting stations talking about Islam and [the] Islamic Revolution. Clearly the aims of these broadcasts are subversive, although officially they are talking only about religion and pretend that exporting the 'Islamic Revolution' is not hostile propaganda."[44] Pointing to the flourishing underground religious publications, and in an obvious reference to the propaganda techniques used in the Iranian revolution, Beliaev argued that "Islamizdat is functioning, religious publications are largely typed and Xeroxed, cassettes with sacred Muslim texts and talks by Muslim authorities are recorded. I would not be surprised to discover that some of these cassettes reaching Tadzhikistan and Uzbekistan, and other areas of the USSR, are made and fabricated abroad."[45]

Similar Soviet commentaries reflected Moscow's acute sensitivity toward the vulnerability of Soviet Central Asia's Muslim population to external religious dynamics and the exploitation of this sensitivity by outside powers.[46] "From Afghanistan and Iran," Alexandre Bennigsen argued, "Soviet Muslims receive the message that Soviet power is not invisible, that mighty empires can be brought to bay."[47] It is within the context of the triangular dynamics of Soviet Islamic problems in Central Asia, Afghanistan, and Iran that Soviet policy toward the new military developments in the Iran-Iraq war must be analyzed. In a nutshell, from 1986 onward, the "Islamic factor" performed a much more significant and immediate role in shaping the parameters of Soviet threat perceptions. The renewed prospect of an Iraqi collapse (so prevalent after the conquest of the Faw in 1986), and the emergence of an Iran-centric Islamic order in the Soviet Union's southern republics that might align with fundamentalist Afghanistan, became not only a worry for Washington but a nightmare for Moscow.

The interdependence of Soviet domestic and regional security, and the dynamics of the Iran-Iraq war, was further complicated by the changes in Soviet domestic and foreign policy, specifically, perestroika and "new political thinking." The reduction of international tensions, arms control, and the resolution of Third World conflicts were prerequisites for the successful implementation of the Soviet restructuring program and the new images of Soviet global policy. The resolution of regional conflicts through negotiations and political accommodation had in fact become one of the most visible components of Soviet new thinking, particularly of the new world order that Gorbachev and other Soviet officials repeatedly outlined and promoted.[48]

Although the conflict between Iran and Iraq fit into the overall Soviet concept of regional conflicts, it differed from other military conflicts in the Third World both in its geopolitical makeup and in the requirements for its resolution. First, the hotbed of the conflict was in the most sensitive geopolitical real estate of the Third World, the Persian Gulf, a region both contiguous to the Soviet border and close to the heart of areas of vital interest to the United States. Second, contrary to many other conflicts, such as those in Nicaragua, Angola, and Afghanistan, where Soviet political influence and involvement was a key asset in the imposition of a political settlement, Moscow lacked similar capability in this conflict. Iran had refused to allow Soviet penetration, and Moscow's diplomatic gestures and maneuvers had repeatedly failed to pressure Tehran to comply with Soviet political objectives. Soviet credibility had been further compromised by its initial neutrality in the 1980–82 phase of the conflict, where the bluntness of Iraq's aggression required a more just Soviet position—a direct and unequivocal condemnation of Iraq as the aggressor. The contrast between the Soviet refusal to condemn openly Iraq's invasion of Iran in 1980 and its openly expressed concerns and condemnation of Iran after Iran moved the war into Iraq's territory signaled Moscow's fundamental bias in favor of Iraq and its lack of credibility as an honest mediator in the eyes of Iran. Third, this conflict, as discussed, was interdependent with Soviet security interests in Afghanistan and political stability in Soviet Central Asia. Thus, Gorbachev's familiar approach in the resolution of other Third World regional disputes was a nonstarter in the one between Iran and Iraq.

In a letter to the fifth conference of the Organization of Islamic Countries, the USSR Supreme Soviet Presidium expressed Moscow's profound "concern for the preservation of the seats of military tension and regional conflicts." Referring to the significance of this new political thinking and the "Delhi Declaration,"[49] the letter addressed "the fratricidal war between Iran and Iraq" and emphasized Moscow's determination "to end this tragic conflict and settle it by peaceful political means."[50] A speedy end to the war would have served Moscow's interest, but by mid-1986 prospects of a diplomatic solution seemed as remote as ever. Iran's main condition for ending the war—the punishment of the aggressor—was unacceptable to Moscow.[51]

The Soviet policy of "active neutrality" (tilting toward Iraq and maintaining its defensive capability), a policy implemented between 1982 and 1986, no longer seemed sufficient. The credibility of Iraq's "mobile defense" strategy had lost its apparent invincibility and assurance as a result of the "close call" in the Faw. Furthermore, the new regional and international dynamics relating to the war urged a more aggressive military approach than the existing war of attrition, which was the philosophy behind a mobile defense strategy adopted by Iraq after 1982. The Soviet fear, shared by many in the West, was that although the conquest of the Faw and subsequent operations did not lead to an immediate collapse of Iraq's military, Iraq's ability to contain similar and successive offensives by Iran was in doubt. A speedy end to the war by political means seemed impossible and achievable only by a shift in the military balance between the belligerents. Iraq's inability to recapture the Faw and its unsuccessful offensives against Mehran, both in 1986, indicated that its attack structure was clearly insufficient for implementing an offensive strategy. Some Iraqi senior officers also shared the Soviet analysis of the military balance and had privately assessed Iraq's inadequate strength, both in organized manpower (fresh mechanized infantry divisions) and equipment, as a major impediment to undertaking an offensive strategy.[52] Thus, Moscow's policy during the third and most critical phase of the war, 1986–88, reflected a determination by the new Soviet leadership to end the war by providing Saddam Hussein with a massive military package that would force Iran to accept a political settlement.

The decision to give Iraq the military edge over Iran was universal. Not only the Soviet Union but the entire Western alliance system, largely financed by conservative Arab states, engaged in the most comprehensive and massive arms transfer in history to a Third World state involved in conflict. France alone, in less than two years, supplied Iraq with arms valued at about $5.6 billion. China, Great Britain, West Germany, Brazil, Egypt, Colombia, Spain, the United States, and many other countries also provided Iraq with an enormous amount of high-tech conventional and chemical weapons. The "Western package" for Iraq, however, paled in comparison with the Soviet's. Between 1986 and 1988, the Soviets delivered to Iraq arms valued at roughly $8.8 to $9.2 billion, comprising more than 2,000 tanks (including 800 T-72s), 300 fighter aircraft, almost 300 surface-to-surface missiles (mostly Scud Bs), and thousands of pieces of heavy artillery and armored personnel vehicles.[53] Most of these weapons reached Iraq via the Jordanian port of Aqaba, thereby giving Jordan a significant logistical role in the Iraqi military buildup.[54]

As a result of this massive arms sale by the Soviets and others,[55] Iraqi armed forces increased their major weapons systems by more than 40 percent in less than two years. On the eve of recapturing the Faw Peninsula in April 1988, a military victory that proved to be the decisive point of the war, the Iraqi army had roughly 5,000 tanks, 4,500 armored fighting vehicles (AFV), 5,500 artillery pieces, 420 helicopters, and 720 operational combat aircraft.[56] This impressive accumulation of weapons systems was complemented by at least 300 Scud surface-to-surface missiles[57] and a large quantity of chemical munitions.[58]

Iraq's absorption of these massive quantities of arms almost enabled Baghdad to double its ground forces, from twenty-six divisions in 1986 to fifty divisions in 1988. This buildup reflected real growth in both force structure and operational capabilities and was a significant step in changing the overall strategic balance in the Persian Gulf. The increase in trained Iraqi military manpower also clearly demonstrated the Soviet contribution in providing the training backup that enabled the Iraqi army to absorb the massive injection of Soviet arms and complete its reorganization.[59]

The decisive Soviet policy shift in support of Iraq only increased the distance between Moscow and Tehran. The Soviets, of course, maintained their familiar diplomatic flexibility toward Iran through diplomatic maneuvers that now had the Gorbachev touch of Soviet "new thinking" and "openness." Soviet flexibility and activism were multifaceted and included tactical diplomatic support and expansion of economic ties with Iran. For example, after the adoption of UN Security Council Resolution 598 in June 1987, that called for, among other provisions, an immediate cease-fire, the Soviets opposed the second UN resolution that was designed to punish Iran for its noncompliance by imposing an arms embargo and economic sanctions.

Soviet diplomatic activism, "shuttle diplomacy" between Baghdad and Tehran,[60] and several diplomatic exchanges in Moscow between Andre Gromyko and both Iranian and Iraqi officials[61] reflected Moscow's determination to maintain the posture of neutrality and to search for a political solution. First Deputy Foreign Minister Yuli Vorontsov's shuttle diplomacy indicated a rather ambitious and tempting Soviet desire to perform the role of mediator between Iran and Iraq—a role reminiscent of the Soviet-sponsored Tashkent peace talks, which had put an end to the Indo-Pakistani War more than two decades earlier. In large part, Iran decided not to reject the UN resolution flatly but to leave open a window of opportunity for badly needed breathing space in Iranian war diplomacy. The Soviets were encouraged by this opening and were determined to maintain communication with Tehran, hoping that a process of approximation between the views of Tehran and Baghdad through Soviet mediation could lead to a political settlement and a real diplomatic coup for Moscow.[62]

The Soviet mediation effort was accompanied by an increase of economic ties between the two countries. A series of discussions on the resumption of natural gas shipments to the Soviet Union were held in both Moscow and Tehran. A new pipeline agreement on the transfer of oil from Iran to the Black Sea, transit of Iranian goods over Soviet territory, and the arrival of Soviet technical experts in Tehran figured prominently in the new economic agreement.

Soviet diplomatic gestures toward Tehran also included opposition to the U.S. reflagging operation in the Persian Gulf. The Soviet position on this issue was not surprising, for it reflected the traditional Soviet concern over a U.S. military presence and Moscow's desire for its elimination through demilitarization of the Persian Gulf and Indian Ocean theaters. Moscow's diplomatic activism, its gestures toward Tehran in opposing the second UN resolution and the U.S. reflagging operation, and the new economic agreements led to Arab and Western speculation and concern over a Soviet tilt toward Iran in 1987. The gulf media quoted Taha Yasin Ramadan's statement that "the presence of

U.S. naval ships in the Gulf waters is linked with ending the war." The Iraqi deputy prime minister further reminded Moscow that "those who call for separating the security of navigation in the Gulf, from the Iran-Iraq War, harbor no good intentions toward Iraq."[63] The *New York Times* reported "a mini crisis" in Iraqi-Soviet relations.[64] Commenting on Soviet opposition to the U.S. reflagging of Kuwaiti shipping, Carol Saivetz observed that "it cannot be emphasized strongly enough that Iran remains the strategic prize in the region. An Iran with strong economic links to Moscow is less likely to reestablish close ties to Washington." According to this view, the intense cultivation of Tehran by Moscow was "a reaction to the increasing American role in the Gulf War" and, in light of traditional Soviet objectives in the Third World in opposing the U.S. presence, an understandable utilization of Iranian anti-Westernism.[65]

The Soviet tilt was, however, devoid of any real political substance. The strategic gap between Tehran and Moscow was just too wide. The tilt was no more than a new version of the old "damage limitation" tactic, motivated by the longstanding Soviet diplomatic tradition of maximizing its investment in multiple arenas. Publicized economic ties were bogged down in protocol and never materialized into real and meaningful economic relations commensurate to the generated expectations. The political and public relations aspects of Soviet-Iranian economic ties in the 1980s should not be ignored, however. It is only in the 1990s that one might give that aspect of the relationship its proper and substantive place.

Contrary to conventional wisdom, Soviet manipulation of Iranian anti-Westernism had lost most of its value and effectiveness, for Iran did not believe Soviet anti-American rhetoric—including the opposition to the reflagging operation—nor did Moscow see anti-Americanism as the essential instrument and objective of its diplomacy with Iran. Iranian anti-Americanism had failed to deliver a desirable political result in Iran: that is, a secular, radical, Third World political system susceptible to Soviet ideological penetration and political influence. Instead, the "conservative petty-bourgeois" regime, to use Primakov's label, had consolidated its power and was pursuing a foreign policy that was detrimental to Moscow's interest. Concerning the utility of Iran's anti-

Westernism, Primakov reminded his colleagues at the Oriental Institute that "anti-imperialist appeals are still being made, but now, as a rule, they are accompanied by anti-communist and anti-Soviet slogans and actions. According to the ideologists of the 'Islamic revolution,' there is no basic difference between the imperialist states and the socialist community, and they emphasize that the 'Islamic revolution' is directed primarily against the 'superpowers.'"[66] Other Soviet observers and scholars complained that although the struggle waged by an Islamic revolution against oppression to achieve social justice "makes it anti-imperialist, it's being inseparable from the Islamization of society has in many respects predetermined and continues to predetermine its anti-Communist features."[67]

From the Soviet perspective, the war had a negative impact on Iran's sociopolitical dynamics and was directly responsible for the consolidation of the role of the clergy and the suppression of the left, including the Tudeh party. Reflecting on the position of the CPSU's twenty-sixth Congress on the impact of the war in "strengthening the position of local reactionaries," Primakov argued that "the protracted Iranian-Iraqi War has been clearly instrumental in bringing about the general shift to the right in Iran."[68]

What most of the analysts in the West ignored or refused to see was the shallowness of Gorbachev's opposition to the U.S. naval presence in the area in the 1987–88 period and the emergence of an implicit superpower consensus to contain Iran. The cold war ended in Iran much earlier than in Europe. Iran's "Russia-American 'card' " was, in reality, a myth. It took both Washington and Moscow some time to realize the seriousness of the most important result of the Iranian revolution: a genuine and strategic desire in Iran to have an independent foreign policy. Ironically, superpower recognition of this fact led to relaxation of the traditional fear of an Iranian "tilt" toward the East or West and crippled Iran's policy in the war.

Briefly, despite the Soviets' traditional nervousness, the U.S. naval presence was not directed primarily against Soviet interests but rather against Iran. The U.S. presence played an important function in its containment strategy, the fundamentals of which Moscow understood and shared. In a strategic sense, the reflagging operation was essential to the Iraqi war of the sea. It provided Baghdad with a strategic umbrella with which to cripple the Iranian economy by attacking its oil shipments. Iran could not retaliate against the oil shipments of Iraq's regional allies, Saudi Arabia and Kuwait, because it would have meant a military encounter with the United States.[69]

On land, however, the Soviet effort had been essential. By early 1988, reorganization of Iraq's military machine was complete, and the stage was set for an Iraqi shift from a "mobile defense" to an offensive strategy. The missile attacks against key Iranian urban centers, especially Tehran, and the effective use of chemical weapons and the realistic prospect of their use against civilian targets had already shaken Iranian determination to continue the war. (The indirect message of Iraq's use of chemical weapons against its own Kurdish population in Halabjah was not lost in Tehran.)

Iraq's well-coordinated blitzkrieg in April 1988 led to the recapture of the Faw Peninsula and the reoccupation of more than 2,000 square kilometers of Iranian territory. The Faw's recapture, as was the case in its 1986 capture by Iran, marked the turning point of the last phase of the Iran-Iraq conflict. The strategic significance of its recapture did not escape Soviet observers. In an article written immediately after the Iraqis recaptured the Faw, and published in the June 1988 issue of *Mezhdunarodnye Zhizn*, Igor Beliaev, a long-time observer of the war and persistent critic of Iran, reflected on the significance of the changed military balance and, as it turned out, correctly anticipated that "in analyzing the development in the Persian Gulf, one should proceed from the fact *that conditions for establishing peace there may soon appear*. . . . I think that the practical terms of, first, an armistice and then a comprehensive peace treaty between Iran and Iraq can be formulated and discussed in the summer or autumn of this year" (emphasis added). The momentum of the Iraqi blitzkrieg forced Iran's acceptance of a cease-fire in July 1988, leading to the official ending of the conflict on August 20, 1988. The Soviet policy of "active containment" had succeeded.[70]

Author's note: This discussion deals primarily with the Soviet policy toward the Iran-Iraq war from September 1980 to August 1988 and does not address the diplomatic and political activities in the post–cease-fire period.

Notes

1. In spite of a considerable number of publications on the Iran-Iraq war in the West, few have dealt with Soviet policy toward the conflict. For a comprehensive bibliography on the Persian Gulf war, see Anthony J. Gardner, *The Iran-Iraq War: A Bibliography* (London: Mansell Publishing Limited, 1988), and Shahram Chubin and Charles Tripp, *Iran and Iraq at War* (London: I.B. Tavris and Co. Ltd. Publishers, 1988). For studies on Soviet policy about the war, see Karen Dawisha, "Moscow and the Gulf War," *The World Today* (January 1981); Dennis Ross, "Soviet Views toward the Gulf War," *Orbis* (Fall 1984); Fred Holliday, "Moscow Makes Up to Baghdad," *Nation* (August 8, 1981); Robert O. Freedman, "Soviet Policy toward the Persian Gulf from the Outbreak of the Iran-Iraq War to the Death of Konstantin Chernenko," in *U.S. Strategic Interests in the Gulf Region*, ed. William J. Olson (Boulder, Col.: Westview Press, 1987) and "Gorbachev, Iran, and the Iran-Iraq War," in *Neither East nor West: Iran, the Soviet Union and the United States*, ed. N. Keddie and M. Gasiorowski (New Haven: Yale University Press, 1990); Mohiaddin Mesbahi, *Moscow and Iran: From the Islamic Revolution to the Collapse of Communism* (forthcoming); Herbert Sawyer, *Soviet Perceptions of the Oil Factor in U.S. Foreign Policy: The Middle East–Gulf Region* (Boulder, Col.: Westview Press, 1983); Aryeh Y. Yodfat, "The USSR's Attitude to the Gulf War," *Asian Affairs* (October 1982), and *The Soviet Union and the Arabian Peninsula: Soviet Policy Towards the Persian Gulf* (London, Croom Helm; New York: St. Martin's Press, 1983); Chubin, *The Role of the Outside Powers; Security in the Persian Gulf* (Totowa, N.J.: International Institute for Strategic Studies, 1982); Ahmad Shekhzadeh, "Thorny Soviet Dilemmas of the Gulf War," unpublished paper, Columbia University, 1986; and Carol R. Saivetz, *The Soviet Union and the Gulf in the 1980s* (Boulder, Col.: Westview Press, 1989). For Soviet views of the war, see V. Viktorov, "The Persian Gulf: Washington's Imperial Ambitions," *International Affairs* (Moscow, July 1982), and Igor Beliaev, "Mideast Versions," *International Affairs* (Moscow, June 1988).

2. For different perspectives on the similarities and differences between Western "power realism" and Soviet views on "correlation of forces," especially the role of ideology as an important component of power, see Vernon Aspaturian, *Power and Process in Soviet Foreign Policy* (Boston: Little, Brown, 1971); Margot Light, *The Soviet Theory of International Relations* (New York: St. Martin's Press, 1988), 249–85; Alen Lynch, *The Soviet Study of International Relations* (Cambridge: Cambridge University Press, 1987), 89–104; V. Kubalkova and A. Cruickshank, *Marxism and International Relations* (Oxford: Oxford University Press, 1988) and *Thinking New about Soviet "New Thinking"* (Berkeley: University of California Press, 1989), 63–91, 109–16.

3. See, e.g., Muriel Atkin, *The Subtlest Battle: Islam in Soviet Tadjikistan* (Philadelphia: Foreign Policy Research Institute, 1989).

4. In fact, some Western Sovietologists have suggested that the fight against the threat of Islam's fundamentalism could be an area of cooperation between the Soviet Union and the West. For example, see Jerry Hough, "The End of Russia's Khomeini Era," *World Policy Journal* (Fall 1987), and Elizabeth K. Valkenier, "New Soviet Thinking about the Third World," *World Policy Journal* (Fall 1987): 63–65.

5. The potential impact on Soviet Central Asia of the Islamic revival in the Middle East, especially in Iran, has generated considerable debate among the Western observers of Soviet Islam. While scholars such as Bennigsen and Wimbush considered the Soviet problem as internally intractable and greatly susceptible to outside influence, others such as Olcott and Atkin have emphasized the indigenous roots of Soviet Islamic trends and its eventual manageability. See, for example, Alexandre Bennigsen and Marie Broxup, *The Islamic Threat to the Soviet Union* (London: Croom Helm, 1984); Alexandre Bennigsen and S. Enders Wimbush, *Mystics and Commissars: Sufism in the Soviet Union* (Berkeley and Los Angeles: University of California Press, 1986); Martha Brill Olcott, "Soviet Islam and World Revolution," *World Politics*, 34, no. 4 (July 1982); Olcott, "Moscow's Troublesome Muslim Minority," *Washington Quarterly* (Spring 1986), 73–84; Olcott, "Soviet Central Asia: Does Moscow Fear Iranian Influence?" in *The Iranian Revolution: Its Global Impact*, ed. John L. Esposito (Miami: Florida International University Press, 1990); Atkin, *The Subtlest Battle.*

6. A.Z. Arabdjan, director of the Iranian Department of the USSR Academy of Sciences Institute for Oriental Studies, a Soviet specialist on Iran, made a revealing remark: "The so-called 'Islamic revolution' . . . constitutes a step backward from the Shah's rule from the point of view of serving crucial historical and economic tasks," cited in David Segal, "The Iran-Iraq War: A Military Analysis," *Foreign Affairs* (Summer 1988): 962.

7. Perhaps the only country that might have presented similar foreign policy rhetoric was Albania, which theoretically placed both the United States and the Soviet Union in the same category as imperialist powers. But the geopolitical insignificance of Albania and its socialist nature did not qualify it as a "third force," as was the case with Islamic Iran.

8. For a good overview of the Soviet perception of the U.S. role in the war, see Viktorov, "The Persian Gulf"; Beliaev, "Iranian Gambit," *Literaturnaia Gazeta* (November 26, 1986); V. Gudev, "An Unnecessary and Dangerous Conflict," *New Times*, no. 47 (1982); L. Medvedko, "The Persian Gulf: A Revival of Gunboat Diplomacy," *International Affairs* (Moscow), no. 12 (1980); E. Primakov, "U.S.A.: Policy of Destabilization in the Middle East," *International Affairs* (Moscow, March 1984); and, especially, Beliaev, "Mideast Versions."

9. Yevgeni M. Primakov, "Dialectics of Social Development and Ideological Struggle: The Wave of Islamic Fundamentalism: Problems and Lessons," *Soviet Oriental Studies Annual 1986* (Moscow: Nauka Publishers, 1987), 14.

10. For a detailed account of Soviet declaratory policy in this period, see Yod-

fat, "The USSR's Attitude," 243–44; Yodfat, "Iraq-USSR: Between Friendship and Suspicion," *Soviet Analyst* (May 10, 1982): 1–2; Freedman, "Soviet Policy toward the Persian Gulf."

11. *Documents and Resolutions of the 26th Congress of the Communist Party of the Soviet Union* (Moscow, February 23, March 3, 1981), 18–79.

12. *Pravda*, January 17, 1981.

13. See, e.g., *Sovietskaya Rossiya* 11 (August 1982); *Pravda*, July 17, 1982; and Radio Moscow in Persian, August 24, 1982, cited in *FBIS-SOV*, August 26, 1982, p. 7.

14. *Al Waten*, cited in *FBIS-SOV*, November 4, 1982. In a conversation with the author in March 1983, Trofimenko indicated the extreme complexity of this conflict as unprecedented in the history of Third World conflicts.

15. *Tass*, October 23, 1981, cited in FBIS-SOV, October 23, 1981.

16. Primakov, "Dialectics of Social Development," 14–16.

17. Marxist-Leninist jargon played an important role in the overall development of political language in Iran after the revolution and directly contributed to the rhetorical atmosphere that made the term *liberal* one of the most stigmatized in contemporary Iran. For the best content analysis of the Tudeh party's journals, especially *Nameh Mardom*, in radicalizing the political language of the Iranian revolution, see Kazem Sajjadpour, "Iranian-Soviet Relations in a Security Perspective, 1979–1986" (Ph.D. diss., George Washington University, 1991).

18. Primakov, "Dialectics of Social Development," 14.

19. "Today, a treacherous Saddam has realized," observed Ayatollah Khomeini, "that he will not be able to escape the trap which has been placed in his path. He and his infidel Ba'athist Party of Iraq, will have no fate except downfall and death": *Tehran Domestic Service* (in Persian), *FBIS-SAS*, May 28, 1982, pp. 11–14. Hashemi Rafsanjani, speaker of the Parliament, echoed a similar theme: "The Saddam regime, after all the crimes it perpetrated against the nation of Islam, cannot survive. We will prosecute Saddam as a criminal of war, within the right given to us by international norms": *Tehran Domestic Service* (in Persian), *FBIS-SAS*, May 28, 1982, p. 15. President Ali Khamene'i called on the Iraqi army to "put an end to the last days of this corrupt mercenary of Israel and rest assured that Saddam is finished": *Tehran Domestic Service* (in Persian), *FBIS-SAS*, May 10, 1982, p. 19.

20. "Rah-e Karbala as Qods Migozarad" (The path to Jerusalem is paved through Karbala) became the motto of Iranian political objectives in the war. The slogan indicated continuous commitment to the Palestinian cause, the achievement of which was preconditioned to the removal of the "Zionist agent in Baghdad, Saddam Hussein."

21. Karbala is the second most sacred religious city of Shi'i Islam after Mecca and is the burial site of the third Shi'i Imam, Hussein ibn Ali, whose martyrdom has been the most enduring symbol of revolutionary sacrifice and zeal in pre- and postrevolutionary Iran.

22. "Export of revolution through war by Iran is similar to what some of our Bolsheviks including Trotskyites wanted to do in 1917. It was wrong then and it is wrong now": conversation with Trofimenko, Miami, 1983.

23. For a comprehensive look into the divergent functions of the Tudeh party and its value for Soviet policy, see Sajjadpour, "Iranian-Soviet Relations," esp. 82–113.

24. *Nameh Mardom* (in Persian), August 26, 1982, p. 2.

25. Ibid., September 16, 1982, p. 1.

26. *Pravda*, November 14, 1982, p. 2; see also *Pravda Vostoka* (12), November 1982.

27. *Izvestia*, November 24, 1982, p. 4.

28. Chubin, "Soviet Policy in the Middle East," in *Security in the Middle East*, ed. S. Wells and M. Bruzonsky (Boulder, Col.: Westview Press, 1987), 268. See also Freedman, "Soviet Policy toward the Persian Gulf," 59–60.

29. "Active Soviet Policy Pursued in the Near East," *Soviet World Outlook*, August 15, 1984, p. 6.

30. For a discussion of the Egyptian role in the war, see Philip H. Stoddard, "Egypt and the Iran-Iraq War," in *Gulf Security and the Iran-Iraq War*, ed. Thomas Naff (Washington: National Defense University Press, 1985), 40. The Egyptians also played an important role in cultivating U.S. support for Iraq; see, e.g., the insightful article by Paul A. Gigot, "A Great American Screw Up: The U.S. and Iraq, 1980–1990," *The National Interest* (Winter 1990/91).

31. For a background discussion of the opening of diplomatic relations among the Soviet Union, Oman, and the United Arab Emirates, see D. L. Price, "Soviet-Omani Relations on a New Level," *Soviet Analyst*, October 9, 1985. For the Soviet view, see D. Zegersky, "Establishing Relations," *New Times*, no. 41 (1985): 8–10 and "Oman's Open Door," *New Times*, no. 44 (1985).

32. For a short and interesting overview of U.S. policy toward Iraq, see Gigot, "Great American Screw-Up."

33. My interpretation of this aspect of the Soviet policy shift was supported by several Soviet commentators and Middle East observers who expressed similar views during my recent visit to the USSR Academy of Science, Oriental Institute in Moscow (June 9, 1990).

34. Chubin, "Soviet Policy," 268.

35. Among the key military figures arrested was Admiral Afzali, the commander of the Iranian navy. For an account of the Tudeh party's role in penetrating the Iranian military after the revolution, see Sajjadpour, "Iranian-Soviet Relations," 91–96.

36. Soviet commentary on the military situation reflected its overall assessment that Iraq's "more organized, better armed army" has proven its "defensive effectiveness" by managing "Iranian numerical superiority" and the "overzealous Kamikaze mentality" of its soldiers. For a sample of Soviet observations, see *Pravda* October 13, 1985, p. 6; *Sovetskaya Rossiay*, November 20, 1985, p. 8; and *Krasnay Zvezda*, March 13, 1984, p. 10 and December 16, 1985, p. 8.

37. For an assessment of the political and military significance of the Faw operation see Segal, "The Iran-Iraq War"; Milton Viorst, "Iraq at War," *Foreign Affairs* (Winter 1986–87): 352–53; Efraim Karsh, "The Iran-Iraq War: A Military Analysis," *Adelphi Papers*, no. 220 (Spring 1987); and, thus far the best military treatment of the war, Anthony H. Cordesman and Abraham R. Wagner, *The Les-*

sons of Modern War: The Iran-Iraq War (Boulder, Col.: Westview Press, 1990), 2:219–24.

38. Cordesman and Wagner, *Modern War*, 221.

39. For details of the operation in the Faw Peninsula, see ibid., 227–30.

40. See, e.g., *Pravda*, February 18, 1986; *Izvestiya*, February 18, 1986; *Tass*, February 20, 1986, cited in *FBIS-SOV*, February 21, 1986, p. H1; Radio Moscow Commentary (in Russian), "The Need to End the Iran-Iraq War," cited in *FBIS-SOV*, February 21, 1986, p. H1; "The Iranian Scene," *New Times* (February 1986); and "Foreign Ministry Spokesman on the Gulf War," *Tass*, February 14, 1986, cited in *FBIS-SOV*, February 15, 1986.

41. The U.S. role in the war was covered by the Soviet media almost redundantly. See Viktorov, "The Persian Gulf"; Beliaev, "Mideast Versions" and "Iranian Gambit"; Gudev, "An Unnecessary and Dangerous Conflict"; Medvedko, "The Persian Gulf"; and Primakov, "U.S.A.: Policy of Destabilization." For the general Soviet view, see two major editorials in *Izvestiya*, March 25, 1986, and *Pravda*, June 25, 1986. On the U.S. "reflagging operation," see "U.S. Moves in the Gulf," *Krasnaya Zvezda* (June 1987); "Mikhail Gorbachev's message to the U.S. on the Iran-Iraq War," *Tass*, cited in *FBIS-SOV*, July 21, 1987; and *Izvestiya*, May 31, 1988. The intensification of the war, especially the "tank war," had also brought China, another Soviet rival, into the equation. Reports of Chinese arms supplies to Iran, including Silk Worm missiles, could only add to Soviet anxiety. For Soviet commentary on China's military sales, see "Chinese Arms in the Gulf," *Tass*, April 12, 1988, cited in *FBIS-SOV*, April 13, 1988, pp. 7–8. For more details on Chinese arms sales in the area, see *The Military Balance, 1988–89* (London, IISS, 1989), 94.

42. *Pravda Vostoka*, January 31, 1987.

43. Beliaev, "Islami i Politika" (Islam and Politics), *Literaturnaya Gazeta*, May 13, 1987.

44. Ibid., May 20, 1987, the second in a two-part article that Beliaev wrote on the subject. See also the following articles in the official Soviet journal *Argumenty*, which specializes in dealing with propaganda from abroad: A. Akhmedov, "Pod flagom islama" (Moscow: Politizdat, 1981), 5–36, "Islamskii faktor' v planakh imperializma i reaktisii" (Moscow: Politizdat, 1982), 63–85; and "Fal' shivye tesizy" (Moscow: Politizdat, 1984), 40–60. Also by the same author, see *Islam v sovremennoi ideinopoliticheskoi bor'be* (Moscow: Politizdat, 1985).

45. Beliaev, "Islam i Politika." Interestingly, Beliaev, in a recent conversation with me in Moscow in June 1990, repeated a similar concern. Soviet security and sensitivity, he argued, has been ignored by the Iranian propaganda campaign to export Islam to the southern regions of the Soviet Union.

46. There has been considerable material published in the Soviet media on the issue of "Islam," "fundamentalism," etc., during the 1989–90 period, which basically continues to reflect a similar alarmist perspective. But since my discussion here reflects the Soviet mode of thinking on the issues during 1986–88, a period of renewed Soviet activism in the Iran-Iraq War, the following sources provide a comparative Soviet perspective: Vladimir Volinskiy, "Ties with the Islamic Revolution

in Iran," on Radio Moscow in Persian to Iran, cited in *FBIS-SOV*, October 5, 1982, p. H-10; Mosamir Gulakhomadov, "Atheist Education and the Requirement of Time," Dushanbeh Domestic Services, Tadzhik, cited in *FBIS-SOV*, March 19, 1986, P.R. 3; and R. Guseynov, "Beneath the Green Banner: Reflections on the Role of Islam in the Light of Contemporary Society," *Comsomolskaya Pravda*, September 27, 1988, pp. 3–6.

47. Alexandre Bennigsen, "Unrest in the World of Soviet Islam," *Third World Quarterly* (April 1988): 786. "Most serious Soviet scholars of Islam," Olcott observes, "particularly those from Central Asia, have been uncomfortable with the thesis that the rise of Islamic fundamentalism is largely a product of external machination": Olcott, "Soviet Central Asia," 220.

48. Mikhail Gorbachev, *Perestroika: New Thinking for Our Country and the World* (New York: Harper and Row, 1987), 171–88; text of Gorbachev's interview with the Algerian journal *Revolution Africaine*, cited in *Pravda*, April 3, 1986; Primakov, "USSR and the Regional Conflict," *International Affairs* (Moscow, June 1988); Edward Shevernadze, "USSR Military of Foreign Affairs Report," *International Affairs* (Moscow, June 1990); D. Volskiy, "We and the Third World: Through the Prism of Modern Thinking," *Izvestiya*, December 22, 1988; I.F. Usachev, "Universal and Class Foundations in World Politics," *Kommunist*, July 1988; E. Pozdniakov, "Nacionalnye, gosudarstvennye: Klasovye interesy v mezhdvnarodnyhk otnosheniakh" (National, state and class interests in international relations), *Mirovaia ekonomika i mezhdvnarodnye otnosheniia* (*MEMO*), May 1988; V.I. Maksimenko, "Socialist Orientation: A Restructuring of Ideas" (*MEMO*), February 1989; N.N. Spasov, "Old and New Elements in the Middle East Conflict" (*MEMO*), March 1990. For a Western interpretation of the new Soviet policy toward the Third World, see W. Raymond Duncan and Carolyn McGiffert-Ekedhal, *Moscow and the Third World under Gorbachev* (Boulder, Col.: Westview Press, 1990).

49. The "Delhi Declaration," a document that was signed between India and the Soviet Union during Gorbachev's visit to that country, set forth the "principles of peaceful coexistence." It was used repeatedly by the Soviets as the guiding document for the promotion of peace and the resolution of conflicts. See, e.g., Primakov, "A Big Step Forward: Thoughts Following M.S. Gorbachev's Visit to India," *Pravda*, January 5, 1987, p.6.

50. For the full text of the letter, see *Izvestiya*, January 26, 1987, p. 1.

51. Early in 1987, the Soviets once again, this time in language indicating their frustration with the Iranian position, issued an official statement strongly urging the parties to the conflict toward a negotiated settlement of the war. Soviet media coverage of Moscow's diplomatic exchanges with both Baghdad and Tehran indicated a further tilt toward Iraq and open displeasure with Iran. (The latter was reflected in the characterization of Soviet official meetings with their Iranian counterparts as being "frank" and "businesslike.") See "Government Issued Statement on the Iran-Iraq War," *Izvestiya*, January 8, 1987, and *Tass*, January 13, 1987, cited in *FBIS-SOV*, January 15, 1987. For a follow-up analysis of the government statement, see "The Senseless Gulf War," *Krasnaya Zvezda*, January 1987.

For a more explicit expression of Soviet support for Iraq, see the two interviews of Soviet Foreign Ministry officials by the official Kuwaiti newspaper, *Al-Anba*, January 30, March 13, 1987.

52. Many Western analysts also argued the need for an offensive strategy and especially the significance of retaking the Faw to restore the badly shaken military balance between Iran and Iraq. See Viorst, "Iraq at War," esp. pp. 352–53 and Karsh, "The Iran-Iraq War." For the best Western analysis of Iraq's military problems, see Cordesman, *The Iran-Iraq War and Western Security, 1984–87: Strategic Implications and Policy Options* (Janes, 1987), 92–104, and Cordesman and Wagner, *Modern War*.

53. The estimates of Iraq's arms imports varies according to different sources, but the fact that Baghdad has been the leading importer of arms in the Third World throughout the 1980s has not been disputed. For example, in the 1982–86 period alone, Iraq imported $31.7 billion worth of arms, of which $14.3 billion was provided by the Soviet Union and approximately another $1 billion by other East European countries. During the same period, France continued to occupy second place after the Soviet Union. For these figures, see *World Military Expenditures and Arms Transfers, 1987* (Washington: U.S. Arms Control and Disarmament Agency, 1987), and *SIPRI Year Book* (1986), 344–45. Cordesman's more detailed estimate indicates the Soviet and French leading position in earlier periods. According to him, the Soviets in 1979–83 alone provided $7.2 billion worth of arms to Iraq, and France and Great Britain followed by $.8 billion and $280 million, respectively. See Cordesman, *Iran-Iraq War*, 26–27.

54. For this and also a discussion of the details of the Iraqi buildup in 1986, see Karsh, "The Iran-Iraq War," 25–28.

55. According to *The Military Balance* (London: IISS, 1988–89), the total Iraqi military expenditure in 1987 soared to an all-time high of $13.996 billion, 60–62 percent of which had been traditionally allocated for importing arms, indicating the figure of $8.4 billion for the year. A more conservative U.S. estimate (Cordesman, *Iran-Iraq War*) has put the constant Soviet share of Iraq's arms market at 55 percent, or $4.6 billion for the year 1987. Cordesman's suggested percentage of the Soviet share is roughly similar to my estimate of $4.4–$4.6 billion *yearly* during the 1986–88 period.

56. For a slightly different estimate of Iraqi strength in mid-1988, see Cordesman, *Iran-Iraq War*, 42. It is important to note that although his figure does not include 1988 numbers, it does approximate, and, in certain categories, such as tanks and artillery, exceeds my estimate for the 1986–88 period. Cordesman's figure on combat aircraft does not include several new deliveries by the Soviets and the French in early 1988, especially the SU-25 Frogfoot, MIG-29 Fulcrum, and Mirage F.1.

57. Iraq apparently modified the Soviet Scud missile into two medium-range SSMs called Al-Abbas and Al-Hussein. Modifications were mostly on payload-range ratio, not on accuracy. Nevertheless, the psychological and political significance of missile attacks against Iran's civilian targets, as in the case of Iraq's attack against allied targets in the Gulf War crisis, largely compensated its purely military

utilities: "[T]he U.S.S.R. provided substantial technical advice and actual support during their use in combat" (Cordesman and Wagner, *Modern War*, 367). In addition, according to Segal, "The chemical munition used on Iraq's Soviet-made 122-, 132-, and 152-mm guns and its BM-21 multiple rocket launchers appears very similar to the standard Soviet chemical munitions for these weapons" ("Iran-Iraq War," 962).

58. The Soviet role in providing chemical bombs to Iraq is not clear. To a large extent, the crisis in the Persian Gulf and the U.S.-Iraqi confrontation have demystified the stories of Iraq's enormous chemical weapon capabilities. The West, especially West Germany, played a decisive role in selling chemical components and technological know-how to Iraq. Iraq's own indigenous expansion also played an important role. Earlier Iraqi attempts to use chemical weapons, especially in 1986 during the Faw operation, had proven ineffective (see Cordesman, *Iran-Iraq War*, 97). But the sophisticated and well-integrated application of chemical weapons, including hydrogen cyanide and nerve gas by Iraq against Iran in the 1980 campaigns, indicated technical and instructive support from outside, possibly from the Soviet Union. Both the Soviets and Americans had, of course, long been interested in combat experimentation and the opportunity of a massive application of these weapons. The interest, in fact, had been rekindled in the late 1960s by the superpowers' increasing emphasis on nonnuclear conflict options in Europe. For the role that Western companies played in Iraq's chemical buildup during the Iran-Iraq war, see a series of three informative articles by John J. Fialka, "Outlawed Weapons: A Scourge Returns," *Wall Street Journal*, September 15, 16, 19, 1988, and Cordesman and Wagner, *Modern War*, 506–12.

59. For a discussion of the significance of the "manpower struggle" between Iran and Iraq, see Cordesman, *Iran-Iraq War*, 40, 41 and Cordesman and Wagner, *Modern War*, 353–57.

60. Moscow World Service, June 18, 1987, in *FBIS-SOV*, June 19, 1987, p. CC2.

61. For Soviet coverage of meetings between Andre Gromyko and Mohammed Javad Larijani (Iran's deputy foreign minister), see *Izvestiya*, July 19, 1987, p. 6. Gromyko had earlier met Taha Yasin Ramadan (Iraq's deputy prime minister) on July 2, 1987; see *Izvestiya* July 6, 1987, p. 3.

62. For an expression of Soviet efforts to reconcile the views of Tehran and Baghdad on UN Resolution 598, see the interview with the chief of the "Arab Gulf Section" in the Soviet Ministry of Foreign affairs by *Al Anba*, August 20, 1987, p. 1. Soviet flirtation with the idea of mediation continued after the August 1988 ceasefire between Iran and Iraq. For the Iranian position on the Soviet mediation after the ceasefire, see Tehran *IRNA*, *FBIS-NES*, January 16, 1990, pp. 20–32.

63. *WAM* (Abu Dhabi), September 12, 1987; *FBIS-MEA*, September 14, 1987, pp. 12–13. *Al Anba*, August 20, 1987, p. 1, warned that the USSR, "which has concluded important agreements with Iran . . . is placing itself in the position of being almost a friend of that aggressive state." For a discussion of the Arab reaction toward the Soviet "tilt," see Saivetz, *Soviet Union and the Gulf*, 99–110.

64. Elaine Sciolino, "Soviet-Iraqi Ties Hit Snag on Iran," *New York Times*,

October 3, 1987, p. 3. See also Patrick A. Taylor, "Hussein Sees Summit More as a Message to Moscow," *Washington Post*, November 14, 1987.

65. Saivetz, *Soviet Union and the Gulf*, 101.

66. Primakov, "Social Development," 17. For a thorough assessment of the role played by revolutionary Islam, see Primakov, "Islam i protsessy obshchestvennogo razvitiia stran zarvbezhnogo vostoka," *Voprosy Filosofi*, no. 8 (1980): 31; L.R. Polonskaya, "The Ideology of Moslem Political Movement at the End of the 1970s—The beginning of the 1980s," *Soviet Oriental Studies Annual 1986* (Moscow: Nauka Publisher, 1987), 218–19; S. Aliev, "Antimonorkhicheskaia i anti-imperialisticheskaia revoliutsiia v Irane," *Narody Azii i Afriki*, no. 3 (1979); R.A. Ul'ianovskii, "Iranskaia revoliutsiia i ee osobennosti," *Kommunist*, no. 10 (1982); G.F. Kim, "The Urgent Tasks of Soviet Oriental Studies," in *Oriental Studies in the USSR Annual 1987* (Moscow: Nauka Publisher, 1987), 11–27.

67. Polonskaya, "Moslem Political Movement," 218–21.

68. Primakov, "Social Development," 14.

69. For Ramadan's comment on the direct and positive linkage between the U.S. naval presence and the Iraqi war effort, see *WAM*, September 12, 1987, in *FBIS-NEA*, September 14, 1987, pp. 12–13.

70. For an analysis of the dramatic changes in Soviet-Iranian relations since 1988, see Mohiaddin Mesbahi, "Moscow, Iran and Persian Gulf Security," in *Reconstruction and Regional Diplomacy in the Persian Gulf*, ed. N. Entessar and H. Amirahmadi (London/New York: Routledge, 1991), and *Moscow and Iran*.

9

Saudi Arabia and the United States: Partnership in the Persian Gulf

A. REZA SHEIKHOLESLAMI

The U.S. government has characterized the Islamic Republic of Iran as the major threat to the stability of the oil-producing countries in the Middle East. Warning the Arab countries of the Persian Gulf that revolutionary upheaval, fed by Islamic "fundamentalism," will sweep through their countries, it has managed to assuage their fears of the notoriety of public cooperation with the United States. The United States has provided a military shield, presumably ensuring the security of the states that have waged war on Iran by massive financial and logistic support for Iraq.

It is my thesis that the major threat to the Arab countries of the Persian Gulf is the internal contradictions that have decayed the bases of the present rulerships. The absence of political legitimacy, the regimes' inability to develop effective bureaucratic structures because of their patrimonial nature, pervasive corruption, and the emergence of a new social structure eventually would have brought down the Arab monarchies and sheikdoms. However, the rapid economic decline resulting from their support for U.S. oil policies and the failure of industrial and agricultural programs have intensified the conflict over economic exploitation between the patrimonial princes and their immediate cohorts, on the one hand, and the members of the bourgeoisie who were coopted during the boom years, on the other. Finally, the blatant association between the United States and the Arab regimes of the Persian Gulf and the effort by these regimes to put the Palestinian issue on the back burner and focus instead on Iraq's war against Iran will, more than any other issue, delegitimize the Persian Gulf Arab countries. The Arab people apparently realize they are paying for a war machine that serves U.S. interests in alliance with Israel, as exemplified by the AWACS program.

U.S. policy toward Iran is to wage war on it, in conjunction with the dependent regional states, in an effort to cripple the Islamic revolution and prevent its exportation. The revolution does not need to be exported because such revolutions are responses to internal conditions and external associations. The United States, unbeknown to itself, is fanning the flames that it wishes to extinguish.

THE UNITED STATES assembled in the Persian Gulf the largest naval armada since the Vietnam War. The apparent objectives of this task force were to guarantee freedom of navigation in the Persian Gulf; ensure free oil flow; and prevent Soviet penetration in the gulf region. U.S. claims and propaganda that attempted to galvanize the military and political support of other Western countries were patently spurious. "The shocking fact," Senator John Glenn observed on his return from a Middle East fact-finding mission, "is that [the Iran-Iraq] war has not even begun to seriously interfere with the flow of oil out of the Gulf. There has been less than one percent reduction in the flow of oil. . . . As to ship damage," the senator went on, "this is probably the most 'unlethal' war in all of history. . . . [I]n the past 5 1/2 years not a single ship has been sunk in the Persian Gulf."[1] The highest U.S. military authority, Admiral William Crowe, chairman of the Joint Chiefs of Staff, admitted during the same hearings that "commercial air traffic . . . has continued to all the littoral countries. As a matter of fact, the Persian Gulf is one of the busiest air spaces in the world." He went on to confirm that "air and sea traffic continues apace. Drilling rigs are operating normally." Moreover, the admiral pointed out that "the Gulf is not a no man's land. In fact, it is still a thriving and bustling commercial crossroads."[2] Michael Armacost, undersecretary of state for political affairs, said that "Iran's rhetoric [is] full of menace, but Tehran's conduct [is] marked by great prudence in the Gulf."[3]

U.S. officials were well aware that the Soviet government had learned a painful lesson in Afghanistan and did not have much interest in repeating the experience in Iran. The officials recognized that the only way in which the Russians could gain was if Iran, besieged by America, sought assistance from the Soviet Union. Erroneously or not, U.S. policy makers dismissed this possibility, citing the historical conflicts between the two countries. The cold war rhetoric, however, was necessary in order to mobilize U.S. public opinion in support of military actions.

The reasons stated by the United States for beating the war drums are clearly misrepresentations. Its true objectives lie elsewhere. The administration, in the tradition of all conservative governments in history, hoped to crush a revolutionary system or, at the least, to punish it so severely that the revolutionary ideas would lose their appeal to the surrounding peoples. The patterns of war imposed on the French and the Russians after their revolutions is now orchestrated by America in Cuba, Nicaragua, Angola, and Iran. In pursuing this policy, the United States found it necessary to participate in the Iran-Iraq war and effectively ally itself with Iraq. A report issued by the Committee on Foreign Relations of the U.S. Senate clarifies U.S. objectives in the area. The report makes it obvious that it was the fear of the fall of the Ba'athist minority regime in Iraq and a subsequent Iranian victory, not freedom of sea lanes, that prompted the United States to interfere in the war more directly.

> The principal danger to Western interests lies not in an oil cutoff through a conflict in the Gulf waterway, but in the geopolitical implications of an Iranian victory in the Iran-Iraq war. An Iraqi defeat, which must now be regarded as a realistic possibility, would immediately threaten the sparsely populated Arab Gulf monarchies.
>
> All along its 900-mile front with Iran, Iraq is under heavy military pressure, and its ability to stand Iran's assaults indefinitely is an open question. On the southern front, Iraq's loss of Basra looms as a distinct possibility with enormous consequences.
>
> . . . Meanwhile in the north, Iraq's position has deteriorated dramatically . . . and in the central sector, Iraq's superiority in armor could be challenged by Iran with the help of TOW anti-tank weapons. . . .
>
> Thus far, Saddam Hussein's minority Ba'athist government continues to control Iraq. But if the military situation dramatically worsens, resentment against Saddam Hussein and his cult of personality could boil over in both the civilian population and the military.[4]

When Iran was invaded by Iraq in 1980, Iran immediately took its case to the UN Security Council, where the Iranian complaint received an unsympathetic hearing from the United States. In fact, America supported a resolution for a cease-fire in place, which would have meant that the Iraqi troops could hold on to the territory they had occupied in their surprise attack. In 1982, when Iran ousted the invading force, U.S. policy changed perceptibly. In the words of a report by the Committee on Foreign Relations, "the tilt included: (1) "Operation Staunch," an active U.S. diplomatic effort to identify and halt arms shipments to Iran; (2) the provision of Commodity Credit Corporation credits to Iraq for . . . purchases in the United States; (3) vocal condemnation of Iran at the United Nations and other arenas; and, (4) the provision of military intelligence to Iraq."[5] Finally, in 1984, the United States, after seventeen years, opened diplomatic relationship with a country that the same report describes in the following terms: "Political dissent in Iraq is unknown. Ba'ath political control is maintained through a harsh penal code that imposes the death penalty for a wide range of crimes. These include economic sabotage, dissension, and publicly insulting the president. Torture often followed by execution, is a common means of dealing with dissent. An elaborate neighborhood spy system keeps the security apparatus informed."[6]

Somehow, to the foreign policy makers of a liberal democracy, the fall of this house of torture seemed to open a Pandora's box. Indeed, the fall of a totalitarian regime that was supported by a network of spies appeared detrimental to the true interests of a liberal democracy. It was viewed as a harbinger of greater changes to come. But the sanctimonious misstatements failed to convince even the congressional supporters of the administration's policy. The Gulf of Tonkin Resolution, by comparison, was a far more effective form of concealment. But the failure of the public and the media to question the policy is odd, though understandable, in the face of pervasive anti-Iranian propaganda.

U.S. support for Iraq and the untruthfulness of official claims were routinely acknowledged in Congress. Congressman Robert Dornan, a Republican from California, during a hearing on the Persian Gulf concerning Iraqi ties with the Western world, stated that the Iraqis "have naval and air superiority to the Iranians because they have conduits to the West and a lot of this weaponry comes in on Kuwaiti tankers," which are reflagged and escorted by the U.S. navy. He went on to say, "So Iraqi supports go through Kuwait. Now, Iraqis in 1985, used air power against Iranian ships in a ratio of 3:1, so Iran decided to fight back. So it is disingenuous to tell the world that the United States is there as a peacekeeper, like we tried in Lebanon. The reality is that not only we are tilting toward Iraq, but we are trying to help Iraq win the sea war by guarding Iraqi and Kuwaiti shipping."[7]

Senator Glenn was baffled as to why his government had taken a duplicitous course by taking refuge under the banner of the "freedom of the seas." He thought it was advisable "[t]o tell our people the truth: that a Persian Gulf in unfriendly hands affects their jobs, which could vanish if energy prices stayed too high, too long; it affects their pocketbooks, too. They should remember the impact on their pocketbooks of increased prices."[8] The senator bluntly, but apparently correctly, pointed out that the purpose of the military intervention was to maintain a web of regional rulerships that serve the global economic interests of the United States by maintaining low prices for commodity exports, unrelated to the inflated prices of their imports from the Western world. Admiral Crowe agreed that "our absence would lead to Iran realizing its goal of regional dominance." Moreover, he said, "there is little doubt in my mind that a U.S. departure would thrust our Arab relations into deep and perhaps irreparable disarray."[9]

The proposition that, above all, the purpose of U.S. military intervention was to suppress revolutionary Islam is supported by a report issued by the Senate Committee on Foreign Relations. "U.S. policy makers express near universal agreement," the report reads, "that incalculable harm would be done to Western interests in the event of an outright Iranian victory over Iraq. Such an outcome would inevitably renew the radical fervor of the Iranian revolution and almost surely place at risk the moderate governments in the smaller Gulf states."[10]

William Colby, a former director of the CIA, agrees that an Iranian victory would have endangered U.S. economic and political interests in the region. Thus, he concludes that "it is in the interest of the United States, the Western world and even the Soviet Union that Iraq successfully withstand the Iranian assault. . . . The United States better make direct efforts to strengthen Iraq against Iran."[11] Indeed, it seems that his advice was unnecessary, as this process had been ongoing for a long time. However, Iranian claims were dismissed by the Western media as propaganda and the U.S. propaganda was presented as facts!

Colby's statement highlights another fact: conflict in the world is increasingly between Third World revolutionary ideologies and the "haves" of the Northern Hemisphere. This conflict is in contrast to the harmony of the world vision developing between the capitalist camp and the Eastern bloc. A communist Iran, which would accept the present economic and political divisions and modes of international conduct, would be more acceptable to the United States than an Iran with a new vision and an indigenous ideology with appeal to the regional peoples.

In the charged atmosphere of Iran-bashing, not only were some recent legislative developments such as the War Powers Act sacrificed at the altar, but no reasonable question received a response. Senator Edward Kennedy, however, gave a satisfactory answer when he commented that "the administration's rationale on freedom of navigation is much weaker. It is Iraq that initiated this phase of the [tanker] war and that conducts the preponderance of the assaults. If we support freedom of navigation in the Gulf, and we should, we must seek to end all attacks, not just those by Iran. Any protection we offer to Kuwaiti ships should be linked to efforts to press Baghdad to end its own attacks against shipping in the Gulf." The senator defined U.S. interests in a manner that ran counter to the policy objectives of the Reagan administration. He advised, "Our interest is in ending the tanker war and the wider war, not entering it and escalating."[12] It is significant that Senator Kennedy's comments were completely ignored by his colleagues, and the debate centered on whether the United States should announce its policy objectives honestly or whether it should take cover behind a shroud of shaky excuses.

Undersecretary Armacost stated the true U.S. objective in the Persian Gulf: "standing by our friends in the Gulf whose stability and security are directly threatened not only by the war between Iran and Iraq, but by radicalism which is a part of the Iranian revolution."[13] Now the question becomes whether the stability of these regimes can be saved, and, if so, is America choosing the correct approach? I shall discuss the case of Saudi Arabia with which, in the lexicon of the present administration, there exists a "special relationship," and which, of course, is the most significant country on the southern shores of the Persian Gulf.

THE FOREIGN POLICY of the United States toward the Middle East is often hampered by inadequate information or gross misconceptions. For instance, as recently as 1957, a confidential State Department profile referred to the Saudi monarchy as "radical," "prone to follow the Soviet line," and "increasingly anti-American."[14] The study concluded that so long as the Saudi dynasty was in power, no improvement in Saudi-American relations was feasible. Although still misunderstood, Saudi Arabia has oddly become a cornerstone of American foreign policy in the Middle East. President Carter, seriously but naively, expected that Saudi Arabia would be willing and able to sell the Camp David Accords to "moderate" Arab governments like that of Jordan. President Reagan had similar hopes in regard to his plans for Palestinian autonomy in the West Bank in association with Jordan. On another occasion, Reagan categorically committed his country to the defense of the Saudi regime, stating that the United States would not permit the events that had led to the fall of the shah to be repeated in Saudi Arabia. The feared implications of the president's statement were noted in the Arabian peninsula and did not help the Saudi regime's credibility or legitimacy. Moreover, he committed America to a dangerous and possibly fruitless course. The Saudi kingdom is internally immobilized. The old institutions that supported the regime and permitted the flow of information and grievances to the rulers have decayed. New institutions have not replaced the old ones. The opulence has only hidden the internal weaknesses of the Saudi regime.

The Saudi kingdom seemingly has many of the markings of power and success. When the Camp David Accords were signed, the country provided 30 percent of total OPEC production. Two years later the value of its exports ranked only behind the United States and the Federal Republic of Germany, and Saudi Arabia was the tenth largest importer in the world. No less impressive was the tempo of change. As recently as 1968, the Saudi GNP per capita was only $311; in 1982, it was over $12,000. For 1,300 years after the advent of Islam, it is said, nothing new was introduced to Arabia except coffee and guns. Today, one-fifth of the Saudis travel abroad annually, and the number of foreign visitors to the country equals half of the native population. In 1955, there were only three high schools in the kingdom and no girls' schools existed until 1960. Today, about 1.3 million students are registered in schools and 300 girls' schools are in operation—major successes in a country in which the native population, in spite of official claims, is between 5 and 6 million.

The infusion of petro-dollars into Saudi Arabia has integrated the once fragmented Arabian society and economy. Differences among tribes and clans have been replaced by differences of income and access to central authority. The erosion of local and primordial bonds has increasingly led to the development of a nation with an embryonic modern class structure. Contemporary Saudi society is remarkably similar to that of Iran on the eve of its revolution. Social and economic improvements are rapidly restructuring the society and economy so that the regime is becoming anachronistic.

In spite of fundamental social changes, rulership has remained personal. The Saudi state is essentially a family matter that was once in harmony with the familial mores of the society. Bureaucratic and political positions are still considered as revenue pieces to be distributed among the ruling clan. The king is, therefore, the premier, and his brother, Abd Allah, is the deputy premier. Minister of Defense Prince Sultan is the king's full brother, as is Minister of the Interior Prince Naif. Their deputies are their nephews. Important governorships are also distributed among the important members of the royal household. The governor of the Western Province is Prince Abd al-Majid, King Fahd's brother. The king's most trusted brother, Salman, is entrusted with the important governorship of the capital city of Riyadh. Still another brother, Abd al-Muhsin, rules over Medina, the city of the Prophet. The Eastern Province, the home of the Shi'ites of Arabia, has been under the harsh rule of the Jiluwi branch of the royal family since the formation of the kingdom. In fact, almost all governorships are monopolized by the Saudis, indicating that this is not a state but a family endowment.

Some positions, in the Ministries of Oil and Planning and Religious Affairs, for instance, requiring specialized training, are filled by nonroyal individuals. Their fathers, however, had performed crucial services for Abd al-Aziz during the period of state formation. Indeed, the most important contractors in the kingdom are also in this category. The Juffali brothers, Ghaith Far'un, and Adnan Khashoggi are the sons of physicians and confidants of Abd al-Aziz. None of them, with the partial exception of the Shaikh family, have independent political bases. They are not politicians or enterprising capitalists. They are simply granted monopolies by the family. The Juffalis, for example, built the telegraph system for Jiddah, brought electricity to Mecca, and are sales agents for about 300 companies, among them IBM and Siemens.[15] The value of these business families is the access they enjoy, not the business skills they master.

The regime is faced with the dilemma of giving access to the growing number of educated middle-class Saudis and losing its cohesion, or of withholding power from the middle class and thus alienating them. The state has so far failed to build a bureaucracy worthy of the name. Areas of jurisdiction are intentionally confusing and overlapping. Many bureaucrats hold other full-time jobs. Absenteeism, according to some studies, reaches 50 percent. Cynicism is the norm. A rationalized bureaucracy, manifesting professionalism and esprit de corps, would militate against the personalistic norms of the state and is consequently avoided.

In the absence of bureaucratic institutions, the state has come to depend on the military in order to survive. Yet the military is feared. To forestall coups, the army is divided into the tribally recruited National Guard and the regular military. The state of rivalry and distrust between the two makes a successful coup improbable, but should the regime face a major crisis they will be unable to act in harmony. Both forces are internally immobilized, devoid of initiative, and unable to communicate with each other. All communications are vertically directed toward Riyadh. The 100,000-strong military makes Saudi Arabia the least defended country in the Middle East, in view of its vast expanse. But given the small population, the military cannot be expanded.

The Saudis' major claim to legitimacy has been their puritanism, but it has been challenged by persistent rumors of corruption among the members of the royal family, particularly Prince Mohammed, a partner in Arabia Bechtel Company and a son of King Fahd. He reportedly receives commissions of up to $100 million for a single agreement and has collected as much as $368,200 a day on the sale of oil to Japan. The construction of giant and questionable projects such as the Jiddah Airport, which on completion at the cost of $10 billion will be bigger than Kennedy, Newark, La Guardia, O'Hare, and Los Angeles airports combined, is considered by many Saudis to be the consequence of collusion between the regime and foreign entrepreneurs to defraud the nation.

Corruption has been always a pervasive aspect of the kingdom. St. John Philby, Abd al-Aziz's closest advisor for thirty years, estimates that of over $1.25 billion in revenue, only $90 million was spent on public projects between 1946 and 1953. The present scale of corruption is much higher and, given the emerging concept of citizenship, steals even more legitimacy. King Fahd's son, Prince Mohammad, ran Petromonde, a small office in London, in the early 1980s that showed a profit of about $11 million a month.[16] Corruption of this proportion necessarily affects both the efficacy and the legitimacy of the government. Clearly, the history and politics of Saudi Arabia are not marked by a traditional pattern of rulership, legitimized through Islam and the mechanism of tribal structure, as U.S. officials depict. Rather, the country has been marked by pervasive corruption that has generated a series of conflicts, including some within the family.

Of all of Abd al-Aziz's successors, only one, Khalid (1975–82), has been allowed to die peacefully, still a king. Ibn Saud (1953–64) fell in a military coup that divided the family, and Faisal (1964–75) was assassinated by a relative. The myth of smooth transfers of power is merely the wishful thinking of U.S. officials. Members of the family are not as united as it seems. During Nasser's presidency, some princes, known as al-Umara al-Ahrar, fled to Egypt where, on the "*Arab*

Voice," they asked the populace to rise up in rebellion against the monarchy. The clan of the Sudairi Seven is enviously regarded by descendants of Abd al-Aziz from other wives. Some members of the royal family are known to have been so outraged by the family's behavior and policies that they have publicly expressed their anger.

There were two coup attempts in 1969 alone. One stemmed from the dissatisfaction of military officers who were imbued with Nasserist ideology and sympathetic to the Aramco workers' antipathy to the Saudi regime and U.S. exploitation of oil resources. The other resulted from the dissatisfaction of the bourgeoisie.[17] There have been major strikes in the oil fields, especially in 1953 and 1956, and much political agitation during this period and after. Likely the memories of these events, as well as political activities of radical members of the Union of the People of Arabia, the Workers' Committee, and the National Liberation Front, will serve as watersheds for future rebellions. Even more likely is that the regime will fall to a radical Islamic movement.

The uprising of Juhaiman took place only in 1979, and, given the fact that it took the state two weeks to reoccupy the Ka'aba with casualties of 427 officers and troops, clearly involved many more than 200 guerrillas, which the government claims. Rumors that French troops were permitted inside the holy shrine in order to fight the guerrillas affected not only the religious legitimacy of the state but caused many to wonder about its efficacy as well. The government tried to depict the rebels as atavistic barbarians who simply objected to football and technology. The enthusiasm with which different political groups claimed the rebels indicated the failure of the government's smear tactics. A former Saudi ambassador, with a long history of service to his country, put Juhaiman's uprising in perspective. He found it long overdue. "There are," he said, "spreading feelings of unrest and impatience with the uneven justice, with the huge commission paid to the princes, with the double standard we have to live with." The Saudi ambassador drew attention to the political demands of the rebels: "The people in Mecca were asking for change in the ruling system. They were saying that the royalty is non-Islamic. Even if I do not agree with that I tell you this movement is much bigger than its leadership suggests."[18] Nor was this the only act of religious defiance. Many general disturbances occurred at the religious college of Medina in 1979 and turmoil at the religious college of Mahd al-Da'wah in Mecca. At the same time, there was a major Shi'ite uprising in the Eastern Province.

Now the Saudi economy has taken a turn for the worse. Gross domestic production has steadily decreased since 1985. In fact, the decline started in earnest when Saudi Arabia, in conjunction with U.S. policy, lowered the price of oil, its major product. This is the first time in recorded history that a government argued for lower prices for 90 percent of its exports. In 1983, the GDP growth was –20.9 percent. The decline continued into 1984, with –10.4 percent.[19] In 1985 the GDP dropped by 13 percent, and the next year by 12 percent.[20] The United States, it seems, in trying to exhaust Iran and prevent it from "exporting" revolution to Saudi Arabia, exported an economic recession to Arabia proportionally greater than what America suffered during the depression. If the Saudi subjects need a reason to rebel, their government's unctuous support for U.S. policies and their own resulting rapid economic decline are much more immediate than the appeal of the Iranian revolution. While the per capita income of the Saudis has fallen by $5,000, a 40 percent drop in the past five years, the Saudi and Kuwaiti governments, again in conjunction with the U.S. policy of engaging Iran in war, had extended as much as $70 billion in credit to Iraq by the end of 1985.[21]

Since 1984 government spending has dropped by more than 30 percent and government spending on salaries has gone up. The government, concerned about discontent, has attempted to co-opt every unemployed university graduate into its administration. The bureaucracy, an arm of the government, likely contains many possibly disgruntled individuals who can, at any time, close down the Saudi bureaucracy just as Iranian bureaucrats did in 1978.

From 1983 to 1984, annual budget deficits of over $10 billion and current account deficits of over $15 billion reduced Saudi official assets by more than $60 billion.[22] Finally, in 1983, the Saudi government, sitting on 200 billion barrels of proven oil reserves, more than a quarter of the world's proven reserves, was forced to borrow money.[23] By 1987, the $99 billion oil revenues of 1982, accounting for 90 percent of the kingdom's total revenues, was reduced to $16.8 billion.[24] The impact of this shrinkage is serious. The number of licenses issued for industrial ventures was almost halved between 1984 and 1986. Joint ventures dropped 32 percent in 1985 alone. Bank profits fell 48 percent in 1985 and 44 percent in 1986. Construction dropped 20 percent in 1986.[25] Any of these statistics would have been viewed with alarm as an indicator of economic collapse had they taken place in the United States. All sectors of the Saudi economy are in decline as a consequence of its oil policies, massive financial contributions to Iraq, and military buildup, all aimed at controlling the exportation of the Islamic revolution.

The economic decline, cushioned by reserves and unusual prosperity of the past, is straining relations among members of the ruling class. A case in point is the conflict between the powerful importers of cement and the equally powerful heads of domestic cement companies. Collapse of the construction sector and the sharp reduction of demand for cement have pitted the importers and the producers against each other in a quota war. In 1987 the demand for cement was 11 million tons, a drop from 17 million tons in 1985. The country's production capacity is 15 million tons. The Saudi Arabian Monetary Agency has calculated that until 1986 more than 24 percent of Saudi Industrial Development loans have gone to a mere eight cement companies. Now, it is not only public knowledge that this aspect of industrialization was a system of connections and corruption; it is also public knowledge that the producers need subsidies of 100 percent for every ton of cement they sell in order to show any profit.[26] It is not only the system's legitimacy that is questioned; its efficacy is equally questionable. To placate importers such as Ghaith Far'un's Redec Company, the country is producing only 50 percent of its capacity.

The country's proclaimed agricultural development is another case in which connections have led to monopolies and to inefficient programs that are handsomely rewarded by the state. Merchant families are, as usual, the junior partners to members of the royal family. The "self-sufficiency" program has actually made Saudi Arabia more dependent than previously. Agricultural imports, seeds, machinery, and services are costing the country $2 billion more than the food it used to import. Agricultural subsidies and monopoly rights have not only cost the country dearly (in the form of interest-free credit—purchasing price for

Saudi wheat is six times the world market); they have also helped to privatize public land. The subsidies help the rich. The average values of loans, for example, was over $1.1 million in 1985. The powerful agricultural lobby will not permit pursuance of a more reasonable agricultural policy. In Saudi Arabia today, the Americans and Europeans manage complex farms, Asians work them, the state foots the bill, and a few Saudis and Western companies become much richer at a cost of a nation in the grip of depression.[27]

The United States has used the debts accrued by Third World nations as a vehicle to force these nations to export as much of their natural resources as possible. Third World nations are pitted against each other, lowering price levels for their commodities.[28] Saudi Arabia does not have much debt, but it has enormous amounts of oil. Persistent political leverage is used to force Saudi Arabia to pump more than it needs, to bring down the prices, and to incur major expenditures that would necessitate unbridled oil exportation. Development of industrial cities, such as Jubail, that require gas and some petro-products, not only has wasted financial resources but has also necessitated high levels of oil production. The product of this inefficient industry requires a price support of about 100 percent to make it marketable. Consequently, the Saudis need to produce even more oil to pay for the products of their wasteful industrialization program.

The United States, however, enthusiastically supports the sale of Saudi Arabia's irreplaceable resources below the going rates. A State Department bulletin, arguing for the sale of military hardware to Saudi Arabia, commends the kingdom, for it has, on occasion, "maintained oil production at high levels to offset shortages and has priced Saudi crude well below OPEC levels to preserve price stability in the world oil market."[29] The State Department, moreover, finds Saudi Arabia "a force for moderation in the Arab and Islamic world." The linguistic hypocrisy of "price stability" and "moderation" for pauperization of the Third World and support for U.S. policies is at least replaced with openness when it comes to Israel. King Fahd, the bulletin reads, has brought about "a major breakthrough in moving Arab states away from confrontation with Israel."[30]

Even more honestly, the bulletin admits that the sophisticated weaponry is to be used to support U.S. interests in any case: "Saudi Arabia is now actively supporting U.S. naval operations in the Gulf." Saudi AWACS (Airborne Warning and Control System) aircraft, the report says, "provide critical air defense data to our forces; Saudi F-15s protect both Saudi and U.S. AWACS. . . . When we have asked for logistical and other support as well as emergency assistance, the Saudi Government has responded positively."[31] The report is clear on why Saudi Arabia has become a storage facility for sophisticated weapon systems. The kingdom reduces the need for direct American "military deployment to the area. If, however, U.S. forces are required in a crisis, they will find Saudi Arabia a cooperative partner equipped with comparable, U.S.-origin defense systems."[32]

On a single page of published hearings of the Executive Session for the Senate's Armed Services Committee, even with seven sensitive passages deleted, it is clear that there are several secret military agreements between the United States and the kingdom and that the kingdom is to provide support for U.S. forces. Undersecretary Armitage testified that "we have additional agreements from the Saudis. . . . The Saudis have made the Jubail Naval Base Hospital open to us, and their facilities open to us; as well, they are instructing their National Guard, their Civil Defense and their aviation SAR helicopters to work with us right now so they can be in a position, should a problem develop."[33]

From these sanitized pages of congressional hearings, it is clear that the kingdom has provided air bases to the United States. For instance, it says that "the Middle East Force has direct communication links with both the U.S. AWACS aircraft based in Riyadh . . . and with the Saudi AWACS. . . . The AWACS keep track of all air traffic in the region, and, in effect, assist U.S. naval operations in the Gulf."[34]

Sandra Charles, director of Near Eastern and South Asian Affairs, Department of Defense, simply but forcefully summed up the purpose of the kingdom's air force. "We have AWACS flying in the region, and if the AWACS encountered a problem, the Saudi F-15s are there for that purpose." Although she said much regarding refueling, port visits, and logistical support, when she was pressed by Congressman Mel

Levine as to what other military supports were given by the Saudis, she said that beyond what she had said already, she could not comment in open session.[35]

The manner in which Saudi Arabia has become an appendix to U.S. military designs in the Persian Gulf, while paying for the honor of serving, is manifest in Assistant Secretary of State Murphy's written statement to the House of Representatives. Supporting the sale of AWACS to Saudi Arabia, he pointed out that "the U.S. will save about $100 million annually in costs associated with keeping our AWACS in the Kingdom. Moreover, the Saudi AWACS and associated ground equipment could become the nucleus of support for U.S. forces." Although the Saudis only pay for the AWACS and provide ground support, Murphy still emphasized that "delivery of the AWACS will not adversely affect Israel's security."[36] Indeed, one may argue that since only the United States can operate the aircraft, gather intelligence, and interpret the data, the security of Israel is favorably affected by the sale.

Undersecretary Armitage assured Congress that a U.S. "security manager" will be in charge of security of the AWACS that are paid for by the Saudis and that "the president has assured the Congress that we will have continuous and complete access to the information which is gained by RSAF AWACS." In fact, it seems that the Philippine government placed more restrictions on Clark Air Base than the Saudis have over much of their military. Not only did the Philippine government not pay for U.S. planes; it received compensation in the form of rents.

In order to generate congressional support for the sale, State Department officials listed the Saudis' political services for the United States. Congressman Gilman said, "Mr. Murphy, I would like to ask if you would tell us some of the major areas in which Saudi Arabia has been helpful to us in the peace process." In the American lexicon, peace process means U.S.-imposed solutions. The list of Saudi political services on behalf of the United States is a long one. Assistant Secretary Murphy listed "the role they tried to play in the Iran and Iraq War," developing "their own defensive systems, [their] role in the Gulf Council in organizing the joint military efforts, on Lebanon . . . in 1982, on the Reagan initiative," and destroying the Arab "consensus that existed from 1967 onward—the Arab consensus were the three noes of Khartoum: no negotiation, no recognition, and no conciliation with Israel." Murphy also noted "on Libya," when the United States carried out an air raid, killing many civilians, "they have not given aid [to Libya], their links of communication with the Syrians on occasion have served our interests. . . . [T]he AWACS operations in Saudi Arabia are based on U.S. national security interests," and, finally, Saudi regime supported President Amin Jemayel's recognition of Israel worked out by Secretary George Shultz on May 17, 1983.[37]

To this long list, one may also add the efforts of Saudi Arabia at the Arab Summit in 1987 in Amman. The Saudis and their "moderate," i.e., pro-U.S. allies, succeeded in mobilizing against Iran and declared the occupation of Palestine only a secondary issue.[38] The Palestinian uprising, of course, demonstrated the fallacy of the "moderates."

There are also other curious coincidences. "In the week that Saudi Arabia announced its decision to sever links with Iran," *The Economist*'s Intelligence Report pointed out, "the USA carried out a most effective 'retaliatory' raid against Iranian naval interests and may have helped Iraq in its recapture of Faw. It announced that . . . it expected to step up arms sales to Saudi Arabia."[39] In fact, the day after the Saudis broke relations with Iran, the Reagan administration informed Congress that they planned to sell to the Saudis $850 million worth of arms. The administration had decided earlier to let the sale remain pending.[40] This was preceded by another coincidence after the massacre in Mecca. A usually pro-Saudi *New York Times* reporter observed that the Saudi officials were "obviously grateful that the Mecca confrontation coincided with the Reagan administration's decision to send United States naval vessels into the Persian Gulf."[41]

U.S. foreign policy in the Persian Gulf is a sad reminder that history indeed repeats itself for those who refuse to learn. For years the United States assumed that the only threat to the shah of Iran was an external one. For years they ignored the tension that ran through Iranian society. And for years, through military support for the shah, they compounded his economic and political problems and, through closer association, made his regime more odious to his people. Like the southerners who fought integration by claiming that problems were simply generated by northern liberals and like the Israelis who claim that the Palestinian uprising is the work of outside agitators and TV cameras, the U.S. government assumes that the threat to Saudi Arabia is simply of Iranian origin.

Under U.S. tutelage, Fahd has become an autocrat in contrast to his predecessors and much in opposition to the Arabian tradition of limited rule. Collective responsibility that characterized the regime has given way to emerging tyranny. The country's cautious behavior of the past, which gave it stability, has given way to adventurism in conjunction with U.S. policies in the Persian Gulf. The United States does not understand that the kingdom's fragile system is incapable of carrying such heavy loads. The political system is overburdened. The present euphoria of Fahd and his cohorts is even less justified than the shah's grandiose plans in the early 1970s. The political system requires thousands of Western specialists to run its economy and military. It is so frightened of a few Shi'ites in the Pakistani garrisons stationed in Saudi that it plans to replace them with 16,000 Turkish troops with the condition that the troops exclude Shi'ites.[42] The Saudi Kingdom is indeed a house built on sand. It is weaker, more backward, and more decayed than Rome just before it collapsed. The pomp and ceremony, overconsumption and luxury, and dependence on foreign legions can only accelerate the decline and fall.

Notes

1. Senate Committee on Armed Services, *U.S. Military Forces to Protect "Re-Flagged" Kuwaiti Oil Tankers*, 100th Cong., 1st sess., June 5, 11, 16, 1987, p. 11. Undersecretary of State for Political Affairs Michael Armacost summed up the situation. "The [U.S.] interest in the unimpeded flow of oil is not dramatically challenged at the moment. Less than one percent of the ships transitting the Gulf are being attacked. The price of oil is not going up appreciably. Insurance rates are not going up dramatically. Our friends and allies are securing a steady flow of oil. The Strait of Hormuz is open" (p. 35).
2. Ibid., 17.
3. Ibid., 29.
4. Senate Staff Report, Committee on Foreign Relations, *War in the Persian Gulf: The U.S. Takes Sides*, November 1987, pp. vii–viii.
5. Ibid., 21–22.

6. Ibid., 20.

7. House Committee on Foreign Affairs, *Overview of the Situation in the Persian Gulf*, Hearings and Markup before its Subcommittees on Arms Control, International Security and Science, and on Europe and the Middle East, 100th Cong., 1st sess., May 19, June 2, 9, 10, 11, 23, 1987, p. 95.

8. Senate Committee on Armed Services, *"Re-Flagged" Kuwaiti Tankers*, 13.

9. Ibid., 18.

10. Senate Committee on Foreign Relations, *War in the Persian Gulf*, 3.

11. William E. Colby, "Support Iraq Not Iran," *Washington Post*, November 24, 1986.

12. Senate Committee on Armed Forces, *"Re-Flagged" Kuwaiti Tankers*, 9.

13. Ibid., 27–28.

14. Cited in Department of State, Division of Research for Near East, South Asia, and Africa, "Saudi Arabia: A Disruptive Force in Western Arabia," *Intelligence Report* 7144 (January 16, 1957): 5.

15. A. Reza S. Islami and Rostam Kavoussi, *The Political Economy of Saudi Arabia* (Seattle: University of Washington Press, 1984), 11.

16. Ibid., 80. For the riot caused by a grandson of Abd al-Aziz, see Robert Lacy, *The Kingdom* (New York: Harcourt Brace Jovanovich, 1982), 368–71.

17. House Committee on Foreign Affairs, *Situation in the Persian Gulf*, 102; see also David Holden and Richard Johns, *A House of Saud* (London: Pan Books, 1981), 260–62.

18. Youssef Ibrahim, "New Data Link Mecca Takeover to Political Rift," *New York Times*, February 25, 1980. For the report that some of the rebels were members of the National Guard, see "Les Forces Saoudiennes auraient repris controle total de la grand mosquée de la mecque," *Le Monde*, November 24, 1979. For more information on the opposition, see James Buchan, "Secular and Religious Oppositions," in *State, Economy and Society in Saudi Arabia*, ed. Tim Niblock (New York: St. Martin's Press, 1982), esp. 112–13.

19. "Country Report: Saudi Arabia," *The Economist* Intelligence Unit 2 (1988): 2.

20. U.S. Department of Commerce, International Trade Administration, *Foreign Economic Trends and Their Implications for the United States: Saudi Arabia*, September 1987, p. 3.

21. George Joffe and Keith McLachlan, "Iran and Iraq: The Next Five Years," *The Economist* Intelligence Unit (February 1987), p. 20.

22. Department of Commerce, *Foreign Economic Trends*, 5.

23. *The Economist*, "Look Who's Having to Borrow," June 18, 1988, pp. 40–41.

24. Department of Commerce, *Foreign Economic Trends*, 5; *Saudi Arabia and the United States: The New Context in an Evolving "Special Relationship,"* report prepared for the Subcommittee on Europe and the Middle East of the Committee on the Foreign Affairs, p. ix.

25. Department of Commerce, *Foreign Economic Trends*, 5–7.

26. Dorian Hancock, "The Saudi Cement War," *The Middle East*, no. 155 (September 1987): 35–37.

27. The information on Saudi Arabian agricultural programs is drawn from Vahid Nowshirvani's excellent article "The Yellow Brick Road: Self-Sufficiency or Self-Enrichment in Saudi Agriculture?" *Middle East Report* (March–April 1987): 7–13.

28. Susan George, *A Fate Worse than Debt* (New York: Grove Press, 1988).

29. Bureau of Public Affairs, Department of State, "U.S. Arms Sales to Saudi Arabia," *Gist* (October 1987).

30. Ibid.

31. Ibid.

32. Senate Committee on Armed Forces, *"Re-Flagged" Kuwaiti Tankers*, 69. For other relevant passages regarding provision of air bases, see pp. 5, 37, 39, 41, 59, 62, 71. See also Senate Committee on Foreign Relations, *War in the Persian Gulf*, 33.

33. Senate Committee on Foreign Relations, *War in the Persian Gulf*, 41; House Committee on Foreign Affairs, *Situation in the Persian Gulf*, 56.

34. House Committee on Foreign Affairs, *Situation in the Persian Gulf*, 59.

35. House Committee on the Foreign Affairs, *Presidential Certification on the Delivery of AWACS to Saudi Arabia*, hearing before the Subcommittee on Europe and the Middle East, 99th Cong., 2d sess., July 15, 1986, 7.

36. Ibid., 15–17.

37. Ibid., 43–44, 58–59.

38. Ibrahim, "Arab Summit Talks Opening Today," *New York Times*, November 8, 1987.

39. "Country Report: Saudi Arabia," *The Economist* Intelligence Unit 2 (1988): 5.

40. Ibid., 7.

41. Francis X. Clines, "Saudis Pledge to Demolish Iran 'Monster,' " *New York Times*, August 29, 1987, 1–2.

42. "Saudi Arabia," *The Economist* Intelligence Unit, 9.

10

U.S. Reflagging of Kuwaiti Tankers

ELIZABETH GAMLEN AND PAUL ROGERS

In 1986–87 the Kuwaiti government approached members of the UN Security Council with requests for help in protecting its tankers from attacks in the Persian Gulf. This request led to a major expansion in the gulf of naval warships belonging to outside powers and substantially increased the level of hostilities between Iran and the United States. We provide an outline of the so-called Tanker War, including a consideration of its legal inference and its impact on exports from the Persian Gulf region. We study the reasons for Kuwait's request and the United States agreement to the request. We consider the consequences in terms of international reaction and escalation of conflict in the Persian Gulf. Finally, we propose some implications of this U.S. intervention.

After the outbreak of the war, Iran destroyed two oil terminals near Faw, instituted a naval blockade, and effectively closed off all Iraqi access to the sea. Consequently, Iraq had to rely on overland pipelines to export its oil and on friendly nations, notably Kuwait, to transship war materials.[1] After these moves by Iran, both Iranian and Iraqi maritime military action was limited almost entirely to attacks on merchant vessels and other nonbelligerent shipping. Until the first phase of the Tanker War was initiated in earnest in February 1984, such attacks were infrequent and were perpetrated solely by Iraq. After 1984, Iraq appeared to have twin goals: to tempt Iran into trying to close the Straits of Hormuz and thus interrupt the West's supply of oil and precipitate Western action to end the war, and to limit Iran's oil exports and its ability to finance its war effort.[2]

The first strategy was foiled when Iran made no attempt to close the straits and by a surprising degree of international indifference to attacks on neutral civilian shipping. Iran did not launch retaliatory attacks on any shipping until May 1984, and even then, as can be seen from table 10.1, retaliation was not on a one-for-one basis. However, it is worth noting that, in response to threats from Iran to close the Straits of Hormuz, Western powers did plan for military operations to ensure access if necessary.[3] The rationale behind the Iraqi strategy (and Western planning) is difficult to understand because almost all Iranian oil is exported through the Straits of Hormuz. Clearly, Iran would not make any attempt to close the straits unless their exporting capability had been so devastated that the closure would make little difference to them or unless they found an alternative means of exporting their oil. The geographical asymmetry of Iran and Iraq meant that if Iran wished to retaliate in kind for attacks on shipping, it could only attack vessels servicing gulf states, not Iraq itself. The legal basis of attacks by either side on civilian shipping is questionable.

Iraq's attacks on tankers did significantly affect Iran's ability to export its oil and thus weakened its economy. Iran was forced to adopt a "shuttle service" of small tankers to transship the oil to less vulnerable loading points farther down the gulf.[4] However, Iran's refusal to be provoked into extensive retaliation had its effect, and the Tanker War died down until Iraq came under severe pressure again in the land war when Iran captured Faw in February 1986. Although the exact numbers of attacks are unobtainable, it can clearly be seen from the following tables that until 1987 Iraq persistently attacked far more ships in the gulf than Iran did (a ratio of approximately 3:1 in 1984, 2.5:1 in 1985, 1.5:1 in 1986, and almost equal numbers in 1987). Iraq's responsibility can be further established by a detailed study of each phase of the Tanker War. Almost invariably, the first attack was carried out by Iraq.

Contrary to popular belief these tanker attacks only marginally affected oil supplies, in part because of the substantial increase during the 1980s in the use of pipelines that bypass the Straits of Hormuz,[5] and in part because at the time the United States made its decision to reflag

Table 10.1. Attacks on Ships by Belligerents, 1980–87

Attacker	1980	1981	1982	1983	1984	1985	1986	1987	Total
Iraq	0	5	22	16	53	33	66	88	283
Iran	5	0	0	0	18	14	45	91	173

Sources: O'Rourke, "The Tanker War," U.S. Naval Institute Proceedings in *Naval Review* (1988); *U.S. Center for Defense Information Press Release 129*, October 2, 1987. Both cite a number of sources.

Table 10.2. Attacks on Ships by Belligerents, by Months, 1987

Attacker	Jan.	Feb.	Mar.	Apr.	May	June	July	Aug.	Sept.	Oct.	Nov.	Dec.
Iraq	6	8	5	7	5	2	3	4	12	13	8	15
Iran	6	3	4	4	10	5	4	5	16	7	10	17

Source: O'Rourke, "The Tanker War," U.S. Naval Institute Proceedings in *Naval Review* (1988), 30, citing CDI sources.

Kuwait's tankers only about 1 percent of ships had been affected by the war.[6]

Although Iran's attacks were concentrated on the shipping trade of Kuwait and Saudi Arabia, the tables show that only eight Kuwaiti-flagged ships and eight Saudi Arabian–flagged ships had been attacked by December 1987.[7] These numbers were low because a large proportion of exports were transported on ships registered under so-called flags of convenience.

Kuwait requested help on the grounds that it needed assistance in protecting its exports. According to the United States, in September 1986 Iran began to single out for attack both Kuwaiti-flagged vessels and vessels bound to or from Kuwait.[8] This claim may have some justification if only the attacks that occurred in 1986 are considered, but, as can be seen from table 10.4, it is not an accurate picture of Iranian attacks since the start of the Tanker War.

Clearly, Iran concentrated on ships bound to or from Kuwait or Saudi Arabia from the start, so perhaps other factors precipitated the sudden Kuwaiti request for outside help. Kuwait's claim that its prime concern was the safety of its exports is further undermined by the fact that it relied heavily on non-Kuwaiti-flagged vessels for transporting its

Table 10.3. Attacks on Merchant Ships in the Gulf by Flag of Registry, June 1984–December 1987

Liberia	61	Singapore	6	Sri Lanka	2
Iran	46	U.K.	6	Pakistan	2
Panama	41	Japan	6	Italy	2
Cyrus	39	South Korea	5	Qatar	2
Greece	26	West Germany	5	Philippines	2
Malta	9	India	4	Soviet Union	2
Kuwait	8	France	3	U.S.	2
Saudi Arabia	8	Spain	3	Maldives	2
Turkey	7	Bahamas	3	Other/unknown	28
Norway	7	Denmark	3		

Source: O'Rourke, "The Tanker War," U.S. Naval Institute Proceedings in *Naval Review* (1988), 30, citing UN sources. (The figures in these tables were taken from a number of sources, as no single set of authoritative figures exists. Consequently there are some discrepancies.)

Table 10.4. Iranian Attacks on Vessels Bound to or from Mideast Countries.

Country	1984	1985	Jan.–July 1986	Aug.–Dec. 1986
Abu Dhabi	—	1	—	—
Bahrain	—	2	6	—
Dubai	—	1	—	—
Iran	—	1	—	—
Kuwait	6	4	—	5
Qatar	—	—	—	1
Saudi Arabia	6	6	15	6
U.A.E.	—	—	—	1
Unknown	2	—	1	4

Source: Information from a memo submitted by Lloyds of London Press, Ltd., to the U.K. House of Commons Defense Committee, and cited in the 3d Special Report of the Committee, Session 1986–87, "Protection of British Merchant Shipping in the Persian Gulf," May 1987. Figures include offshore oilfields.

exports. The eleven reflagged tankers account for only about 20 percent of Kuwait's daily export of crude and refined products.[9] If Kuwait's main concern was to protect its ability to export, an initiative to protect all neutral shipping would have been more effective than one directed only at Kuwaiti-flagged vessels. A more plausible explanation is provided by linking the Kuwaiti request with the state of the Iran-Iraq war. In February 1986, Iran captured and held a significant piece of

Iraqi territory—the Faw Peninsula. Thus Iranian troops were, for the first time in the war, entrenched close to the Kuwaiti border. Iran also made slow but steady gains elsewhere on the war front.[10] Iraq's response to these gains was a substantial increase in its attacks on Iran's oil exports. The assaults on Kharg Island had already forced Iran to use a shuttle service to Sirri and Larak oil-loading terminals. In August 1986, Iraqi planes succeeded in attacking Sirri Island for the first time. Kharg Island was temporarily closed in October, and in November Iraq extended its attacks to Larak.[11]

Iran adopted a number of diplomatic and military strategies to cope with this destruction of its oil industry. It launched missile and shell attacks against Iraq, pressed OPEC for changes in policy, increased its threats to retaliate against GCC states for their support of Iraq, and increased its naval inspections of vessels passing through the Straits of Hormuz. It also increased its tanker attacks and, in October 1986, began for the first time to attack them at night.[12] Although only a small proportion of tankers in the gulf were being attacked, the combination of these tactics, and Iran's successes in the land war, increased feelings of insecurity of the GCC states.

It seems reasonable, therefore, to suggest that Kuwait requested help largely to draw international attention to the war, because of fears for its safety, rather than because of any physical problem with its export shipments. According to officials of the government-owned Kuwaiti Oil Tanker Company (KOTC), "Kuwait simultaneously approached both the U.S. and USSR in September 1986 seeking the protection of their ships. The U.S. response was positive in principle but only if Kuwait could qualify under stringent U.S. codes and regulations . . . [and] did not . . . offer to provide naval protection for the reflagged ships."[13] By contrast, the Soviet response was an immediate offer of full cooperation, and in January 1987 KOTC delegates went to Moscow "to negotiate specific terms." The Soviets lacked the larger tankers Kuwait needed and agreed to a Kuwaiti suggestion that it reflag some Kuwaiti tankers. Only when these talks were made known to the United States did Secretary of Defense Caspar Weinberger declare U.S. willingness to reflag all eleven vessels and provide them with naval protection.[14] The United States learned of the Soviet agreement to reflag and protect five

Kuwaiti tankers in late February, and on March 2 KOTC asked for six vessels to be put under the U.S. flag.[15] On March 7 Kuwait was informed that the United States would protect all eleven vessels in question. There are a number of indications that the United States refused to help Kuwait if any of the tankers were reflagged by the Soviet Union.[16] The Kuwaitis then compromised by accepting U.S. reflagging of all eleven tankers and limited the Soviet role to chartering three vessels (retaining an option to increase the number).[17] The original approach to the Soviets was probably a deliberate tactical decision to force the hand of the United States, and if so it was extremely successful. Kuwait's subsequent insistence on not excluding the Soviets altogether was a reflection of the fact that its past policy toward the superpowers has been considerably more balanced than that of some of the other Arab states in the gulf.[18]

Kuwait subsequently requested similar help from all the permanent UN Security Council members. Their responses varied. There was little publicity about the request to the French. It was presumably refused as there appears to be no record of any Kuwaiti ships being reregistered in France. Kuwait announced on June 9, 1987, that it had asked China to reregister some Kuwaiti vessels under the Chinese flag.[19] The Chinese Foreign Ministry said that it was "considering" the request,[20] but no further action was reported. (China would not normally deploy its navy in the Persian Gulf. The request by Kuwait appears to have been merely a formality, as part of its policy to approach all the permanent UN Security Council members.) Britain was formally approached by Kuwait on July 15, 1987.[21] Kuwait was informed that registration of vessels in Britain or the Dependent Territories was a matter of "commercial and procedural arrangement," not one that required a governmental policy decision.[22] Subsequently, three KOTC vessels were reregistered in Britain. Because the Kuwaiti request appears to have been politically motivated, the British government's refusal to involve itself in the matter was disappointing for Kuwait, especially in view of the earlier response of Britain's close ally, the United States.

If the KOTC version of events is correct, and the basic outline has certainly been corroborated by other reports,[23] the United States was initially reluctant to reflag and protect the Kuwaiti tankers. The decision to do so appears to have been taken hastily and without adequate study of the military implications. For example, congressional notification of the decision, revealed in closed testimony in March 1987, was made with "scant notice of the protection aspect of the plan."[24] Although consideration had been given to the possibility of shipping lanes being mined, little was done to reduce the danger. Further, no formal interagency assessment of the risks involved was requested,[25] and U.S. allies were not consulted until well after the decision had been made.[26] The official rationale for the United States to agree to the reflagging was twofold: "First to help Kuwait counter immediate intimidation and thereby discourage Iran from similar attempts against the other moderate Gulf states; and second to limit, to the extent possible, an increase in Soviet military presence and influence in the Gulf."[27] (Two other factors that are widely thought to have played important parts in the U.S. decision, although rarely acknowledged officially, were the need to regain the confidence of Arab states in the wake of "Irangate"[28] and U.S. unwillingness to permit an Iraqi collapse.[29])

The first rationale was based on the belief that Kuwaiti exports had become the target of a sustained series of attacks by Iran to pressure Kuwait into reducing its support for Iraq and to discourage other gulf states from emulating Kuwait. There appears to be little basis for this belief because no major change had occurred in Kuwait's export situation.

The second rationale refers to the Kuwaiti invitation to the Soviet Union to assist in protecting Kuwaiti exports. It was a longstanding policy of the United States to deny that the Soviet Union had reason to be concerned about affairs in the Persian Gulf and (unlike the United States) that it had no right to send ships to the region. The grounds for this U.S. assertion was that the Soviet Union was not dependent on oil exports from the region.[30] This reasoning does not take into account the fact that the Persian Gulf is only some 700 miles from the Soviet's southern border and that Iran is contiguous to it. It may also be argued that it reflected a refusal on the part of the United States to recognize the reality of the situation. The Soviet Union had visited ports in the Persian Gulf since (and possibly before) 1968 and had a permanent presence in or near it (escorting Soviet merchant vessels through) since two Soviet freighters were temporarily seized by the Iranians in September 1986, on suspicion of carrying contraband bound for Iraq.[31]

Notwithstanding doubts about the justice of its desire to exclude the Soviet Union, the United States could have attempted to minimize the Soviet presence without resorting to the provocative action of reflagging. For example, it could have attempted to persuade the Soviets not to go ahead with their plans to reflag on the grounds that it was not in the interest of either superpower to inflame tensions in the gulf further. It could have persuaded Kuwait to withdraw its invitation (especially because other GCC states were doubtful about the wisdom of Kuwait's plan) and offered to use its influence at the UN to press for an end to the war. Finally, the United States could have recognized the inevitability of a Soviet naval presence in the region and defused its significance by accepting some kind of multinational force, perhaps under UN auspices. Several proposals for such a force were made, including one by the Soviet Union, which was welcomed by the GCC states[32] but rejected by the United States and the United Kingdom.[33] Despite serious practical problems with establishing a UN naval peacekeeping force, the Tanker War clearly demonstrated that if the UN is to fulfill its role of international adjudicator it must develop a credible ability to deal with conflicts at sea, as it has attempted to do with those on land.

The revelation that the United States had been secretly selling arms to Iran was a substantial shock to the GCC states. The United States has a continual problem in trying to maintain good relations with both Arab and Israeli regimes, and the entire framework of U.S.-Arab relations was undermined by the revelation that Arab interests could, under some circumstances, be supplanted not only by those of Israel but also by U.S. attempts to reestablish relations with Iran. The United States needed to reassert its commitment to the GCC states. However, the wisdom of using the reflagging to achieve this unofficial objective is questionable. The reaction of the GCC states to the Kuwait initiative was ambivalent, and the U.S. action was likely to increase tension in the region, whereas the long term interests of the GCC states would probably be better served by minimizing friction. Kuwait's main objective (shared by other GCC states) was not to protect its exports but to internationalize the war and thereby bring pressure for its termination.

This objective could have been achieved without resorting to reflagging. In addition, the attempt to reassert U.S. commitment to the region could easily go awry if the United States were to abruptly withdraw again, as it did from Lebanon in 1984. The likely cause of such a reversal in policy would be congressional pressure following a disaster, but since U.S. policy makers were well aware of the dangers involved, they would be unlikely to advocate such action.

Finally, in 1986, for the first time in four years, Iraq appeared to be facing the possibility of total collapse. A number of statements by U.S. administration officials indicated that such an outcome would not have been acceptable. For example, a report of the U.S. House of Representatives Armed Services Committee, while discussing the administration's strategy for ending the Iran-Iraq war, claimed that "while the Administration has proclaimed a policy of strict neutrality . . . a minimal requirement of its strategy is to see that Iraq does not collapse. If it did, radical Islamic fundamentalism could well spread to Iraq itself, and quite possibly to the moderate Gulf states and beyond."[34] The U.S. decision to reflag Kuwaiti tankers and its subsequent actions in the gulf could be interpreted, at least in part, as implementing this policy, which was part of a more comprehensive U.S. strategy toward the region. The United States identifies its two key interests in the Persian Gulf as security of oil supplies for itself and its allies and prevention of Soviet use of the strategically located regions.[35]

Since the 1973–74 oil crisis the United States has developed the means to intervene militarily in the region should its interests be threatened. The invasion of Afghanistan and the revolution in Iran prompted President Carter to announce that the area was considered one of "vital interest" to the United States, and U.S. military capabilities to intervene were transformed during the Reagan presidency with the establishment and development of CENTRAL COMMAND.[36]

As is often the case, the public rhetoric used to justify the U.S. decision to reflag was at some variance with its official rationales. The rhetoric was concentrated in four areas.

(1) *Protection of freedom of navigation.* President Reagan, during a television interview, said the purpose of the U.S. presence in the Persian Gulf was "to protect neutral nations' shipping in international

waters that, under international law are supposed to be open to all traffic."[37] However, as pointed out in a U.S. Senate Foreign Relations Committee report, "The decision to reflag only 11 Kuwaiti tankers . . . seems little more than symbolic. With ships of all flags making over 600 monthly transits through the Gulf, it can hardly be argued that reflagging 11 tankers extends a protective umbrella to all Gulf shipping."[38] The "freedom of navigation" argument has to some extent been strengthened by the extension of U.S. naval protection, on a random basis, to all nonbelligerent shipping. However, merchant shipping cannot expect to conduct its operations without some constraints in the region of a major war, and the U.S. position would be more credible if there had been any attempt to stop illegal Iraqi attacks.

(2) *Protection of oil supplies.* In reference to Western dependence on Persian Gulf oil supplies, President Reagan is reported to have said that "the use of the vital sea lanes of the Persian Gulf will not be dictated by the Iranians. These lanes will not be allowed to come under the control of the Soviet Union. I will not permit the Middle East to become a choke point for freedom nor a tinderbox of international conflict."[39] Before the reflagging oil supplies had been disrupted little; thus this sudden concern would appear difficult to justify. Events after the reflagging further undermined the claim to be protecting oil supplies. Iran's response to the reflagging was to target non-U.S., non-Kuwaiti shipping. There were then reports that a quarter of the vessels calling at Kuwaiti ports in December 1987 were targeted and that Kuwait was, for the first time, having difficulty in fulfilling its orders for crude oil.[40] After the U.S.-Iranian clashes in April 1988, shipping and oil commerce in the southern Persian Gulf virtually ceased for two days. U.S. action had precipitated the situation that it was supposed to prevent.

(3) *Silkworm missiles.* When the decision to reflag became public knowledge, much emphasis was placed on the threat to international shipping posed by the Iranian purchase of Silkworm missiles. The heavier payload and longer range of these missiles provided Iran with the theoretical capability to sink, rather than just to damage, tankers passing near the Straits of Hormuz.[41] Concern about the consequences of this capability led to various bellicose statements by the U.S. administration about reprisals for any use of the missiles.[42] This reaction by

the United States was somewhat surprising as the administration had known since the summer of 1986 that Iran was purchasing the weapons but had not previously expressed concern.[43] Further, reports of a shipment of the air-launched version of the Silkworm reaching Iraq in June 1987 received little public attention.[44] The Silkworm issue seems to have been used as rhetoric to justify the sudden change in U.S. policy toward the dangers to international shipping in the Persian Gulf rather than being a major factor in the decision to reflag.

(4) *The U.S. responsibility to protect U.S.-flagged ships.* According to Secretary of Defense Caspar Weinberger, "U.S.-flagged ships have received U.S. protection since the beginning of the U.S. Navy and will continue to have this protection as long as they fly the U.S. flag. U.S. interests, whether they are U.S. ships, facilities, or personnel will continue to be protected by U.S. forces in the region [of the Persian Gulf] or elsewhere in the world, wherever they are threatened."[45] Although the U.S. Navy may have responsibility for protecting U.S. ships, clearly the need to escort the Kuwaiti tankers would not have arisen had they not been reflagged.

Despite these superficial arguments, the majority of the U.S. public accepted the action because people saw it as an opportunity for the United States to reassert itself after the hostage crisis of 1979–80. The intense animosity Americans still felt toward Iran should not be underestimated. The seizure of the U.S. Embassy and the retention of hostages caused not only deep humiliation for a powerless United States but also aroused widespread hostility toward Iran because of its breach of diplomatic norms. This animosity was fed by general ignorance of both the Islamic and Ba'ath regimes and by the media, which consistently presented the Islamic Republic of Iran as fanatical and out of control. Consequently, for example, it was possible for public anger about Iraq's attack on the USS *Stark* to be turned into anti-Iranian rhetoric and action. If Iran is to find the international support that it needs, it is extremely important that it recognizes this domestic reality within the United States and work to rectify the image.

Thus, there was widespread support in the United States from the public, Congress, and the defense establishment for the Reagan administration's decision to reflag the Kuwaiti tankers and for the U.S. "tilt" toward Iraq. According to an opinion poll a few weeks after the Iraqi attack on the *Stark*, 75 percent of Americans believed that the United States "should maintain a military presence in the Persian Gulf to protect our interests in the region," although only 53 percent supported the reflagging of the Kuwaiti tankers.[46] After the United States destroyed Iranian oil platforms in October 1987, a similar poll showed 76 percent approved of the U.S. action.[47] These and other polls indicate clearly that a large majority of the U.S. public perceived the purpose of the U.S. naval presence in the Persian Gulf to be to "keep the oil flowing and the Soviets out" and that it approved of such a policy. Congressional support for the reflagging operation was not uncritical. After the attack on the *Stark*, there was considerable concern about the potential dangers to U.S. forces, and the administration was forced to delay the reflagging operation and produce a report from the secretary of defense on its security implications.[48] After a period of some disarray in both the Senate and House of Representatives, attempts to change administration policy completely became marginalized, and concern was concentrated on specific criticisms of various aspects of the policy and its implementation.

One main element of this criticism was that the United States was allowing itself to be dragged into "another Vietnam," i.e., that policy goals were not clear and that the "mission" was open-ended in terms of both time limits and potential for escalation.

A second concern was that the U.S. allies were the main recipients of oil from the region but that the United States was "being saddled" with the political, military, and financial burden of "protecting the oil." This stance was part of a much broader debate within NATO about "burden sharing," but the strength of feeling on the issue was sufficient to have forced the allies to contribute more than their skepticism about the wisdom the U.S. policy might have warranted.

A third concern was the cost of the operation. The Center for Defense Information has estimated that the United States spent over $400 million on operations in the Persian Gulf between mid-May and mid-September 1987.[49] The official Department of Defense estimate for additional costs (i.e., those that would not have been incurred without the reflagging operation) for approximately the same period was $70 million,[50] but these estimates excluded maintenance, wear and tear, classified operations, the loss of the *Stark*, etc.[51] The DOD announced in September 1987 that the navy's portion of these costs was being absorbed by the existing naval budget rather than extra funds being requested. A number of congressional and military personnel expressed concern about the effect of these unexpected costs on the defense budget, and there were several reports of maintenance programs and the like being delayed as a result.[52]

A fourth concern was the constitutional question of who can involve the United States in a war. Under the U.S. Constitution the responsibility for declaring war lies with Congress, but in practice changes in military capabilities have tended to reduce the role of Congress and transfer that authority to the president. After the Vietnam War an attempt was made to constrain presidential action through the War Powers Act, but it has never been accepted by a U.S. president and the issue remains unresolved. Many members of Congress and the Senate tried to invoke the War Powers Act over the reflagging decision but were not successful.[53] One of the restraining influences on U.S. actions was concern from some sections of the military that the United States might overreach itself.[54] Admiral William Crowe, chairman of the Joint Chiefs of Staff, opposed plans to launch a preemptive strike against Iranian Silkworm missiles[55] and urged caution over plans to retaliate for the missile attack on the *Sea Isle City*.[56] This attitude does not appear to have been shared by the civilian secretaries of defense, first Weinberger and then Frank Carlucci, or then secretary of the navy, James Webb.[57]

Reaction of Iraq

Iraq seemed to have regarded this U.S. decision as a useful development. For example, the Iraqi foreign minister informed a delegation of U.S. officials that "they disagreed with the Soviet demarche for all foreign navies to leave the Gulf, and that reflagging would be of mutual benefit."[58] This was because in some respects Iraq at that time was in a stronger position than either Iran or the United States. As long as it could attack tankers with relative impunity it could determine the tempo of the Tanker War, and therefore the level of Iranian attacks and the U.S. retaliation for them. Thus, Iraq was to some degree controlling U.S. and Iranian actions.

Reaction of Iran

Iran clearly saw the action taken by all the outside powers as partisan, basing its view on three factors. (1) While claiming to be interested in protecting the rights of neutral shipping, no attempt was made by any outside power to prevent Iraq's attacks on tankers serving Iran, despite Iraq's dominant role in the Tanker War and Iran's promises not to attack any ships if Iraq did the same.[59] (2) Iraq's purpose in conducting the Tanker War was to strangle Iran economically. Actions such as the U.S. and French embargoes against Iranian oil furthered Iraqi war aims.[60] The United States, through Operation Staunch[61] and its attempt to follow up Resolution 598, had been promoting an arms embargo against Iran with no comparable initiative directed against Iraq. (3) The action by outside powers was taken only when, for the first time, the total defeat of Iraq was considered a serious possibility.[62] The Soviet Union had a Treaty of Friendship with Iraq, and the Western powers frequently made statements expressing concern about the consequences of an overwhelming victory by Iran.[63]

Reaction of the GCC States

With the possible exception of Saudi Arabia, the GCC states appear to have been taken by surprise by the Kuwaiti initiative,[64] despite the interest Kuwait expressed in superpower protection of gulf shipping at a meeting of the GCC in November 1986.[65] The reactions of the states were initially ambivalent, particularly those of the southern ones (UAE, Oman, and Qatar), which had retained much closer links with the Islamic Republic than the others. But by June 1987 the GCC issued a communiqué expressing support for the steps Kuwait had taken to preserve its "commercial and economic interests."[66] There was concern that Kuwait had effectively issued an open-ended invitation to the superpowers to increase their influence in the Persian Gulf, and statements were made that regional security was an issue for the region rather than for outsiders. Nevertheless, once the decision had been taken and implemented, the GCC states appeared to conclude that it would be more destabilizing for the United States to withdraw suddenly than to remain,[67] and a limited amount of low-level assistance was given to the U.S. forces.[68]

The United States hopes for land bases, initially cited as essential for the effective operation of U.S. forces,[69] were not fulfilled. Even Kuwait refused to allow the establishment of foreign military bases of any type or nationality on its territory, and U.S. naval forces only escorted the reflagged ships beyond the outer limit of Kuwait's territorial waters.[70] Iran repeatedly threatened to attack any bases or ports that the GCC allowed the United States to use.[71] While continuing their varying degrees of support for Iraq, the GCC states basically promoted an end to the gulf war after 1981. However, the incidents surrounding the reflagging (especially the Silkworm attacks on Kuwait and the disturbances in Mecca) and the willingness of the United States to become more involved caused the GCC to harden its position temporarily. Whereas the position of the GCC as a whole was softening again by December 1987, Kuwait and Saudi Arabia remained strongly anti-Iranian, and the breach of diplomatic relations between Saudi Arabia and the Islamic Republic in April 1988 led to speculation that open military conflict was possible.[72]

Reaction of U.S. European Allies and Japan

Initially, the European allies gave little support to the United States—even Margaret Thatcher expressed reservations about the reflagging.[73] Since NATO was formed, there have been transatlantic disputes about threats to NATO security from outside the geographical limits of the treaty. These disputes have been closely related to equally longstanding ones about the equitable division of defense responsibilities—so-called burden-sharing. From 1981 until May 1986, communiqués from NATO's Defense Planning Committee included references to the "Out of Area" (OOA) threats to NATO security and the desirability of individual NATO members protecting NATO as a whole.[74] Even so, the communiqué issued after the May 1987 meeting of NATO's DPC did not include any reference to OOA, despite the fact that, according to reports, Secretary of Defense Weinberger specifically requested both collective and individual support.[75] The United States then made a second attempt to get Western backing at the Venice "Heads of Government" economic summit in June 1987 but succeeded only in obtaining a general statement that "the principle of freedom of navigation in the Gulf is of paramount importance for the U.S. and for others and must be upheld . . . the free flow of oil and other traffic through the Strait of Hormuz must continue unimpeded . . . we pledge to continue to consult on ways to pursue these important goals more effectively."[76]

Individual nations had expressed limited support for the United States, notably the Dutch, but in general there was little enthusiasm. However, a major change in European policy was caused by the discovery of mines outside the Straits of Hormuz. If, as widely assumed, these mines were laid by the Iranian Revolutionary Guards, it was a major tactical error on Iran's part as it caused an immediate reversal of U.K. policy, followed over the next six weeks by similar reversals from France, Italy, the Netherlands, and Belgium. The new policies were welcomed by the United States, and one of the reasons for the continued allied presence, particularly of the smaller European powers, appears to have been pressure from the United States. As critics were quick to point out, the United States normally imports little of its oil from the Persian Gulf. It was therefore difficult for it to justify its policy unless the European powers were seen to be contributing.[77]

Although Japan did not send ships to the region (on the basis that their constitution probably forbids it), it contributed in other ways. For example, it offered to finance a $10 million navigational system that would have assisted the U.S. navy in locating mines and to donate another $10 million toward UN efforts to end the Gulf war.[78]

Reaction of the Soviet Union

The Soviets received a major opening from Kuwait when the suggestion was made that they reflag the tankers. The Soviet navy had been gradually increasing its area of operations since 1945, entering the Indian Ocean for the first time in 1968 and conducting a four-month cruise that included visits to both Iran and Iraq.[79] It was a key component of U.S. policy since World War II to deny the right of the Soviet Union to maintain a presence in these areas, but the United States could not have objected to a Soviet presence in the Persian Gulf if they were there at the express invitation of a littoral state.

The agreement of the Soviet Union to accept the far more limited role of chartering and escorting three vessels to Kuwait was an indication of the considerable significance to them of the original offer. In practice, the situation worked out well for the Soviet Union because it was able to establish patrols in the region quietly while criticizing U.S. handling of the consequences of its high-profile reflagging operation.[80] It used the opportunity to call for withdrawals of all outside naval powers from the region or for the establishment of a UN naval peacekeeping force, knowing that it would be impossible to exclude the Soviet Union from the latter. The low profile it chose to adopt enabled it to further its relations with Iran, at the expense of the United States, not least because of the Soviet ability to veto moves to establish a partisan arms embargo against Iran at the UN Security Council if the Soviets believed it to be in their interests to do so.

Consequences of the U.S. Decision

The political decision to reflag the tankers caused a major change in the military environment of the gulf. The U.S. naval presence in the region was vastly expanded[81] and, given Iran's view that the U.S. action was partisan, clashes between the two forces were inevitable. Below is a brief survey of the main clashes involving the U.S. Navy and Iran in the Persian Gulf in 1987–88. It is not comprehensive and does not consider the merits of each incident in any detail.

Although Iran has never claimed responsibility for the attack, it is widely believed that the mine that damaged the *Bridgeton* during the first convoy of the reflagged tankers was planted by Iran. U.S. reaction was muted on the grounds that the culprit could not be identified, although nearly three weeks after the attack Secretary of Defense Weinberger announced that Iran had been responsible.[82] The attack exposed a major weakness in the U.S. military capability to deal with threats in the gulf,[83] and the United States requested assistance from its allies. This was withheld—until the discovery of mines in the Gulf of Oman. On September 21, the United States attacked an Iranian vessel, *Iran Ajr*, on the grounds that it was laying mines in international waters (it was also near an operating area of the U.S. Navy). A number of Iranians were killed and twenty-six others taken into U.S. naval custody (they were subsequently repatriated via the Red Crescent).[84] The *Iran Ajr* was later sunk by the U.S. Navy. The attack on the *Iran Ajr* occurred the night before President Khamene'i was to make a speech to the UN on Iran's willingness to observe a cease-fire based on a modified version of Resolution 598. Instead, Khamene'i "spent most of his visit answering questions about Iran's attacks on shipping."[85]

In mid-October, at least three Silkworm missiles were fired by Iran from the Faw Peninsula. Two tankers were hit, one U.S. owned and Liberian flagged, the other a Kuwaiti tanker reflagged by the United States. Although the attack on the reflagged tanker occurred in Kuwaiti territorial waters, the United States decided to retaliate for these attacks by destroying two Iranian oil platforms. (At Kuwait's insistence, U.S. protection of the reflagged tankers ceased when the tankers reached Kuwaiti territorial waters, and responsibility for them was transferred to Kuwait.) The platforms were not in use for oil production but, according to the United States, were being used by the Iranians to coordinate attacks on shipping. President Reagan justified the action under Article 51 of the UN Charter, that is, as an action of self-defense.[86] However, Reagan's letter to Congress clearly links the destruction of the oil platforms with the Iranian attack on the reflagged tanker. Hence, the decision to destroy the oil platforms represented a major shift in U.S. policy—from one of direct defense against attack to one of retaliation.

On October 22, an Iranian missile hit Kuwait's main offshore oil terminal, Mina Al-Ahmadi, disabling it for a month, and the speaker of the Iranian Majlis, Hashemi Rafsanjani, made it clear that this action was intended as retaliation for the U.S. attack.[87] The United States did not respond. On April 14, 1988, the USS *Samuel Roberts* hit a mine while in international waters. The frigate very nearly sank and has since been written off.[88] A number of other mines were found in the vicinity. The United States determined that the mines were from the same series as those found on the *Iran Ajr* and therefore concluded that they had been laid by Iran. Consequently, President Reagan "ordered U.S. forces in the Persian Gulf to launch retaliatory strikes against Iranian military units in the Persian Gulf."[89] The destruction of two Iranian oil platforms (previously producing around 150,000 bpd) triggered a major naval battle in which six Iranian ships were sunk or crippled (including two modern frigates), a U.S. helicopter was shot down, and a U.S. resupply vessel was hit. An Iranian vessel also attacked a U.K.-flagged tanker and a U.S.-operated oil field.[90] U.S. naval forces fired ten missiles during the battle and successfully evaded seven fired by Iranian forces.[91] The shipping and oil commerce of the southern Persian Gulf was brought to a virtual halt for two days.[92] British- and French-accompanied convoys were temporarily halted.[93]

On April 29, Secretary of Defense Carlucci announced that U.S. assistance would in the future be provided to "friendly" innocent neutral vessels flying a nonbelligerent flag, outside declared war/exclusion zones, that were not carrying contraband or resisting legitimate visit and search by a Persian Gulf belligerent.[94] Although this extension of the rules of engagement superficially appeared to apply to both belligerents, it was clear from other information given at the DOD press briefing concerning the pattern of tanker attacks that the change in policy was directed against Iranian attacks.[95] The U.S. Navy's presence in the gulf was obviously not capable of offering blanket protection to all ships that met its criteria, and therefore the policy was intended to be applied randomly. The first help known to have been extended under these new rules was to a Danish-registered tanker on July 2, 1988.[96]

Although there are precedents, such as the major conflict between Britain and Argentina in 1982, it seems remarkable that modern warfare has so outpaced traditional laws of war that the United States could destroy a substantial proportion of the active Iranian navy without any declaration of war. Such a declaration was extremely unlikely, not least because for domestic reasons it would have been politically impossible for the United States to commit ground troops to aid Iraq.

By far the biggest tragedy of the Tanker War occurred on July 3, 1988. A U.S. warship, the USS *Vincennes*, shot down an Iranian civilian airliner killing nearly 300 innocent people. Despite having the most modern air defense system at their disposal, the crew of the *Vincennes* mistook the airliner for an F-14 fighter. The reasons for this mistake are unclear. The airliner was flying on a regularly scheduled flight (albeit an hour late) and, contrary to initial claims by the United States, was neither off course nor descending, and even though the crew of the *Vincennes* may have received confusing data from the plane's radar and "Identification Friend or Foe" signals,[97] it is difficult to understand why civilian air traffic control communications were not being monitored.[98] There were apparently no U.S. aircraft or AWACS in the area at the time of the attack because there was no U.S. convoy in need of protection.[99] It is also unexplained why the aircraft was shot down even after its identification as an F-14 because these do not usually have a significant antiship capability and the *Vincennes* had not received any threat warnings that it had been scanned by a missile fire control radar.[100] Iran was criticized by the United States for allowing a civilian airliner to fly into "a war zone," but no more than thirty-five minutes had elapsed between the exchanges of fire between the United States and Iran and the airliner's take-off. It would appear unreasonable to expect Iranian civil air traffic control to have been informed of the incident in such a short time, especially as two of the Iranian gunboats involved were sunk and a third damaged. Civilian flights in the area were very frequent—189 took place the day before the incident—and near accidents had occurred previously.[101]

In sharp contrast to the events following the attack on the USS *Stark*, the United States expressed regret only for the loss of innocent lives and did not make a specific apology to the Iranian government. The United States refused to pay compensation to the government but, more than a week after the incident, stated its intention to compensate the families of the victims.[102] The shooting down of the airliner was also remarkable because of Iranian restraint in calling for retaliation against the United States. Efforts were concentrated instead on calling for volunteers to fight Iraq and on diplomatic initiatives. Iran requested that the UN Security Council hold an emergency meeting to condemn the U.S. action. When this meeting took place on July 14, the Iranian representative, Velayati, urged denouncement of the attack on the grounds that it was "deliberate and pre-meditated," while the United States (represented, unusually, by Vice-President Bush) concentrated on the need to implement Resolution 598 to end the war.[103] A resolution calling for "full observance of the international rules and practices governing civil aviation safety" and rapid settlement of the war following Iran's acceptance of Resolution 598 was unanimously agreed on by the Security Council on July 20.[104]

Implications of the Reflagging

U.S. actions, particularly those of 1987–88, were intended to bring the Iraq-Iran war to an end because the United States feared an Iranian victory, which it did not believe to be in its interests. Despite official denials of this partisanship by the Reagan administration, even Weinberger has acknowledged that what is euphemistically described as a "tilt toward Iraq" occurred.[105]

Examples of the partisan nature of U.S. actions include (1) the political and military intimidation of Iran, such as the reflagging, Operation Staunch, and UN Resolution 598; (2) the signing of a five-year trade agreement with Iraq[106] while instituting a trade embargo against Iran; (3) the provision of military intelligence to Iraq, such as that given in "compensation" for Irangate; (4) assistance to Iraq's regional supporters, such as provision of military hardware, training and advice and pledges of "all necessary diplomatic and, if requested, military assistance" to them.[107]

One of the problems for the United States in adopting such a strategy was that it was extremely inflexible. Whereas in the winter and spring of 1987–88 concern was being expressed about the possibility of a total collapse of the Iraqi war effort, Iran subsequently suffered a number of reversals. Yet the United States was locked into a series of anti-Iranian initiatives such as the reflagging of the Kuwaiti tankers and calls for an arms embargo.

The United States needed to reassess its position in light of the changed circumstances in the Persian Gulf area. In particular, the militancy of the GCC states ebbed with the dampening of fears that they were in danger of becoming directly involved in the war. Although this would have been extremely difficult after the civilian airliner disaster, in order to avoid an embarrassingly isolated position the United States should have lowered the profile of its operations and sought ways to improve relations with the Islamic Republic of Iran. The comparative isolation of Iran posed major problems in its efforts to deal with nonbelligerent nations, especially when they had the military capability of superpowers. It has astutely identified gaps in U.S. policy (e.g., the "anonymous" mining of the *Bridgeton*, attacks in territorial waters, attacks against vessels that had U.S. interests but were not U.S. flagged, etc.), but the United States was able to close these gaps as quickly as they were identified. The overwhelming military superiority of the United States was clearly demonstrated with the destruction of such a large part of the operational Iranian naval forces in one afternoon. Iran could harass the United States in a limited way, but if it attempted anything major it risked total destruction of its navy, and probably more.

Iran should have been wary of drawing parallels with the U.S. withdrawal from Lebanon in 1984. In that instance, U.S. forces had no specific "mission," they were a vulnerable target on land, and there was little public support in the United States. The death of nationals is always a catalyst for public influence on a nation's policy, but even it can be deflected if the public can be convinced that there was a purpose in the deaths. In the case of Lebanon there was no clear purpose; in the case under discussion here the U.S. public had been convinced of the need to maintain oil supplies and that the means to do so was to contain Iran. In addition, the U.S. military have learned from their mistakes in Lebanon, making it more difficult for Iran to emulate the 1983 suicide bombings.

Despite Iran's isolation there were indications that regional support could be nurtured. While the GCC states were willing to make use of U.S. assistance in upgrading their armed forces, they were as concerned as Iran about U.S. policies toward the region and, in general, did not relish dependence on an unpredictable superpower. Thus, for example, Saudi Arabia, which is traditionally the closest of all the GCC states to the United States, began to diversify its sources of arms supplies.[108] The GCC also pursued its own initiatives to enhance its security by promoting an end to the war.

These initiatives began in January 1981 when an "Islamic Mediation Team" was formed.[109] The most recent major peace plan was launched in September 1987, offering Iran reparations and promising GCC neutrality.[110] However, following the missile attacks on Kuwait, the GCC summit meeting in October 1987 issued strong complaints about the behavior of Iran and urged the Arab League to "reconsider its relations with Iran" at its coming summit meeting—the first time that Oman and the UAE had openly expressed criticisms of their neighbor.[111] The unanimous declaration issued after the Arab summit, although rapidly buried, was another indication of the isolation of the Islamic Republic.[112] Criticisms from the GCC were more muted again by December,[113] and in February 1988 the secretary-general of the GCC urged the United States to return to a "low profile" in the gulf.[114]

Conclusions

Despite popular impressions to the contrary, the main responsibility for the Tanker War rested with Iraq, not Iran. Iraq conducted the Tanker War with the specific objectives of involving outside powers in the Iran-Iraq war and of damaging Iran's economy. Iranian attacks were largely retaliatory and, until 1987, were considerably less frequent than those of Iraq. Because there were no Iraqi tankers in the gulf for Iran to attack, Iran concentrated mostly on shipping connected with Kuwait and Saudi Arabia. The purposes of these attacks were to encourage Kuwait and Saudi Arabia to persuade Iraq to cease its tanker attacks and to warn Kuwait against supporting Iraq too overtly. Due to geographical asymmetry, the types of attacks conducted by Iran and

Iraq—and their locations and targets—were different, but both sides were in clear breach of traditional international law.

Arguments used by outside powers to justify their actions on the grounds of ensuring freedom of navigation and protection for oil supplies were superficial. It is reasonable to expect that civilian shipping will be disrupted near a major war zone—both Iran and Iraq exceeded these "reasonable limits," not just Iran. Since only about 1 percent of gulf shipping had been attacked before the Kuwaiti request for reflagging, oil supplies were clearly not suffering major disruption. Kuwait's chief objective in requesting assistance for protection of its tankers was to draw international attention to the Iran-Iraq war. It was successful. U.S. reluctance to increase its involvement in the war was overcome when Kuwait demonstrated that it was willing to involve the Soviet Union in Persian Gulf affairs. This, combined with a desire by the United States to reassert its commitment to the security of Arab states in the region following the revelations of Irangate, and concern that Iraq could be facing total collapse in the war, were the main factors prompting U.S. agreement to reflag the tankers. It was also hoped that the action would facilitate greater U.S. access to the region.

Since the announcement of the Carter doctrine, and the development of CENTRAL COMMAND to implement it, the reluctance of the Arab gulf states to involve themselves publicly with the United States has been a major impediment to U.S. plans to intervene in the region should its interests be threatened. These hopes have not been entirely fulfilled. Some support has been proffered, contingent on strict secrecy, but even this has been considerably more limited than the United States called for. In agreeing to the reflagging, the United States did not take sufficient account of the potential costs to Iranian-GCC relations. Whereas the position of the southern GCC states was ambivalent, the hostilities surrounding the reflagging considerably worsened relations between Iran and both Saudi Arabia and Kuwait. If the United States is seriously interested in the long-term stability of the region it cannot expect to promote it without the cooperation, or at least acquiescence, of the most powerful actor in the region—Iran. Increasing friction between Iran and its neighbors is unlikely to encourage this attitude.

The decision by the United States to reflag the tankers, particularly when considered in the context of its other actions, can reasonably be considered partisan as it seriously constrained Iran's ability to conduct the war. Iraq was able to continue attacking tankers with impunity while increasingly severe penalties were imposed on Iran. In addition, the U.S. oil embargo, pressure—particularly applied to China—to cease supplying arms to Iran, and U.S. actions in the UN Security Council all had a combined adverse effect on Iran. The United States generally received more support for its policy than might have been expected—in part because of Iranian tactics, for example (assuming Iranian Revolutionary Guards were responsible), the mining of the Gulf of Oman but in part because of the vested interests of other powers.

Notes

1. R. King, "The Iraq-Iran War: The Political Implications," *Adelphi Papers*, 219 (Spring 1987): 18.
2. E. Karsh, "The Iraq-Iran War: A Military Analysis," *Adelphi Papers*, 220 (Spring 1987): 29.
3. *Daily Telegraph*, February 3, 1984, p. 5a; *Philadelphia Inquirer*, February 24, 1984, p. 1.
4. Karsh, "Iraq-Iran War," 30.
5. J. Glenn and J. Warner, "Persian Gulf," report to the majority leader of the U.S. Senate on their trip to the Persian Gulf May 27–June 4, 1987, S PRT 100–38, June 1987 (hereafter Glenn/Warner, "Persian Gulf,"), p. 26.
6. "The Persian Gulf Controversy," Democratic Study Group, U.S. House of Representatives, S PRT 100–9, June, 1987 (hereafter "The Persian Gulf Controversy"), p. 11; R. O'Rourke, "The Tanker War," U.S. Naval Institute Proceedings, *Naval Review* (1988): 34.
7. O'Rourke, "The Tanker War," 30. U.S. Center for Defense Information (hereafter CDI) Press Release 129 quotes figures of eleven and seven attacks by October 1987 on Kuwaiti- and Saudi-flagged ships, respectively.
8. U.S. Under Secretary Michael Armacost, "U.S. Policy in the Persian Gulf and Kuwaiti Reflagging," Department of State, Current Policy No. 978, June 1987.
9. *Guardian*, July 22, 1987, 2. According to Ted Stevens et al., "U.S. Presence in the Persian Gulf: Cost and Policy Implications," report to U.S. Senate Committee on Appropriations, S PRT 100–76, January 1988, p. 12, these eleven ships carry approximately 5 percent (by volume) of the total Kuwaiti exports and approximately the same percent by value. However, "National Security Policy Implications

of U.S. Operations in the Persian Gulf," report of the Defense Policy Panel and Investigations Subcommittee of the Committee on Armed Services, U.S. House of Representatives, July 1987 (hereafter "National Security Policy Implications"), 13, quotes 35 percent and CDI press release no. 133 estimates that before the reflagging, the eleven tankers carried 33 percent of Kuwait's crude exports and have carried less than 10 percent since.

10. A.H. Cordesman, *The Iran-Iraq War and Western Security 1984–1987* (Janes, 1987), chap. 5.

11. Ibid.

12. Ibid.

13. "War in the Persian Gulf: The U.S. Takes Sides," staff report to the Committee on Foreign Relations, U.S. Senate, S PRT 100–60, November 1987 (hereafter "War in the Persian Gulf," 37. Most sources give December 1987 as the initial date of approach.

14. Ibid.

15. C. Weinberger, "A Report to Congress on Security Arrangements in the Persian Gulf," Department of Defense report, June 15, 1987, table 1.

16. Personal interview with DOD official, April 1988. Confirmed by, e.g., "U.S. Military Forces to Protect 'Reflagged' Kuwaiti Oil Tankers," hearings before the U.S. Senate Committee on Armed Services, S HRG 100–269, June 5, 11, 16, 1987, p. 48; *New York Times*, August 23, 1987, p. A12.

17. "National Security Policy Implications," 10.

18. Until September 1985, Kuwait was the only GCC state to have diplomatic relations with the Soviet Union and the first to sign a major arms equipment deal with it. See E. Nakhleh, *The GCC: Policies, Problems and Prospects* (New York: Praeger, 1986), 41 and 39, respectively.

19. *Washington Times*, June 10, 1987.

20. *Guardian*, June 18, 1987.

21. Ibid., July 13, 1987.

22. Ibid., July 16, 1987.

23. Ibid., October 20, 1987.

24. Weinberger, "Security Arrangements"; Glenn/Warner, "Persian Gulf," 11.

25. "War in the Persian Gulf," 38. In June 1987, the United States planned to deploy three AAW warships in addition to the force levels at the time of the attack on the USS *Stark* and were considering deploying a battleship surface action group in the North Arabian Sea. See S HRG 100–269, " 'Reflagged' Kuwaiti Tankers," 101.

26. *Washington Post*, July 5, 1987, p. 13. The impression given in a number of reports that the danger of mines had not been considered at all is incorrect. Mines were one of the four major threats identified (see *New York Times*, May 29, 1987), and a team of experts went to Kuwait. Working with Kuwaiti, Saudi Arabian, and Dutch experts, they cleared between twelve and twenty mines from Kuwait's shipping lanes. See *Washington Times*, July 2, 1987, and *Guardian*, July 3, 1987.

27. *Washington Post*, July 5, 1987; "National Security Policy Implications," 37.

28. Armacost, "U.S. Policy."

29. R. Murphy, "International Shipping and the Iran-Iraq War," U.S. Department of State, Current Policy No. 958, May 19, 1987, p. 1.
30. "National Security Policy, Implications," 25.
31. R. Ciarrocchi, "U.S., Soviet and Western European Naval Forces in the Persian Gulf Region," U.S. Congressional Research Service Report 87–956 F, December 8, 1987, p. 11.
32. *Washington Times*, December 30, 1987.
33. *Guardian*, August 25, 1987.
34. "National Security Policy Implications," 25.
35. T. McNaugher, *Arms and Oil: U.S. Military Strategy and the Persian Gulf* (Washington, D.C.: The Brookings Institution, 1985).
36. Annual statements to Congress by the commander-in-chief, U.S. Central Command, and the secretary of defense.
37. *Baltimore Sun*, October 23, 1987, p. 2.
38. "War in the Persian Gulf," 43.
39. *Washington Times*, June 1, 1987, p. 3.
40. *Washington Post*, January 15, 1988.
41. *Aviation Week and Space Technology*, June 22, 1987.
42. *New York Times*, June 8 and 15, 1987. The missiles have, in fact, been fired on several occasions from Faw and may also have been fired in the Straits of Hormuz in April 1988. See *Washington Post*, April 20, 1988, and *Baltimore Sun*, April 29, 1988.
43. *Guardian*, June 17, 1987.
44. *Washington Post*, June 27, 1987.
45. Weinberger, "Security Arrangements."
46. *Washington Post*, June 3, 1987, p. 1.
47. *Guardian*, October 22, 1987.
48. Weinberger, "Security Arrangements."
49. CDI press release no. 127, September 13, 1987.
50. Ibid.
51. *Jane's Defence Weekly*, November 28, 1987.
52. "The Persian Gulf Controversy," 27.
53. Ibid.
54. Reports of naval unease ("Unease of Senior Staff at the Pentagon," *Guardian*, June 30, 1987).
55. *Washington Post*, June 8, 1987, p. 5.
56. *Guardian*, October 19, 1987, p. 7.
57. *Washington Times*, November 3, 1987.
58. "National Security Policy Implications," 63.
59. *Guardian*, July 21, 1987.
60. Ibid., December 23, 1987.
61. G. Shultz, "U.S. Interests in the Persian Gulf," Department of State, Current Policy No. 911, January 27, 1987.
62. "War in the Persian Gulf," 23.
63. For example, "National Security Policy Implications," 25; U.K. Foreign Affairs Committee Report, cited in *Guardian*, July 1, 1988, p. 22.

64. "War in the Persian Gulf," 29.

65. *New York Times*, June 15, 1987.

66. *Guardian*, June 10, 1987; *New York Times*, June 15, 1987; "National Security Policy Implications," 62.

67. "War in the Persian Gulf," 29.

68. Weinberger, "Security Arrangements," 19.

69. *New York Times*, May 25, 1987; *Guardian*, May 25, 1987; *Washington Post*, May 29, 1987.

70. *Al Yaqahda*, October 21, 1987, cited in *Pentagon Current News*, October 23, 1987; *Washington Post*, October 16, 1987.

71. *Philadelphia Inquirer*, June 6, 1987, p. 8.

72. Personal interviews in the United States, April 1988.

73. *Guardian*, August 4, 1987.

74. *NATO Review*, various issues. The term "Out of Area" (OOA) is almost invariably used synonymously to mean the Persian Gulf region in NATO debates.

75. *Washington Post*, May 31, 1987.

76. *New York Times*, June 10, 1987; *Guardian*, June 10, 1987.

77. *Guardian*, May 25, 1987.

78. *Washington Post*, September 26, 1987.

79. J.L. George, *U.S. Navy: View from the Mid-1980s* (Boulder, CO: Westview Press, 1985), 288.

80. *Janes Defence Weekly*, November 28, 1987.

81. For thirty years after its establishment in 1979, the U.S. Middle East Force consisted of "2 small warships and a command vessel" (Ciarrochi, "Naval Forces," 3). After the withdrawal of Britain from "East of Suez" in 1971, regular deployments of U.S. naval aircraft carrier and cruiser task forces began in the Indian Ocean/North Arabian Sea. In February 1979, in response to the seizure of the U.S. Embassy, the Middle East Force was enlarged to five warships and a command ship (ibid., 30). At the time of the attack on the USS *Stark* there were seven warships present in the Persian Gulf. The U.S. naval presence in the North Arabian Sea/Indian Ocean is constantly changing. At its peak, in 1987, the Middle East Force was expanded to at least twenty-five warships (*Washington Post*, November 17, 1987), plus a number of other smaller vessels, e.g., those of Special Operations Forces, and at least one aircraft carrier and one battleship group just outside. CDI estimated that a total of forty-eight U.S. naval combat ships and their support vessels were in the region (*National Journal*, January 23, 1988). The Pentagon's highest estimates were of thirty-two warships being in the region (*Washington Post*, October 24, 1987, January 7, 1988). This discrepancy is presumably accounted for by different use of the term "warship."

82. *New York Times*, August 10, 1987.

83. "Department of Defense Annual Report to Congress, Fiscal Year 1988/9," p. 182.

84. *Washington Post*, September 23 and 25, 1987.

85. G. Sick, "The Internationalization of the Iraq-Iran War," in *Neither East nor West: Iran, the Soviet Union and the United States*, ed. N. Keddie and M. Ga-

siorowski (New Haven and London: Yale University Press, 1990); *Guardian*, September 23, 1987, p. 8.

86. R. Reagan, "Letter to the Speaker of the U.S. House of Representatives," October 20, 1987.

87. *New York Times*, October 23, 1987.

88. *Guardian*, June 23, 1988.

89. Admiral W. Crowe, Pentagon news briefing, April 18, 1988.

90. *Washington Post*, April 19, 1988.

91. UPI report, cited in *Pentagon Current News*, April 22, 1988.

92. *Washington Post*, April 20, 1988; *New York Times*, April 21, 1988.

93. "London Press Association Report," cited in *Pentagon Current News*, April 20, 1988.

94. F. Carlucci, Pentagon press release, April 29, 1988.

95. D. Howard, Department of Defense news briefing, May 3, 1988.

96. *Guardian*, July 4, 1988.

97. Ibid., July 6, 1988, p. 9.

98. *Aviation Week and Space Technology*, July 11, 1988.

99. Ibid., 17.

100. Ibid., 16.

101. Ibid., 17; *Guardian*, July 5, 1988, p. 1, July 6, 1988, p. 9.

102. *Guardian*, July 12, 1988, p. 8.

103. Ibid., July 15, 1988, p. 1.

104. Ibid., July 21, 1988, p. 8.

105. *Washington Post*, October 24, 1987.

106. *Guardian*, August 27, 1987, p. 26.

107. Ibid., October 23, 1987.

108. For example, in March 1988 it was revealed that Saudi Arabia had secretly purchased Chinese ballistic missiles (*Washington Post*, March 29, 1988, p. 1), and in July 1988 a multibillion-pound deal with Britain was announced (*Guardian*, July 9, 1988, p. 1).

109. A. Rubinstein, *The Great Game: Rivalry in the Persian Gulf and South Asia* (New York: Praeger, 1983), chap. 1.

110. *Observer*, September 20, 1987.

111. *Guardian*, October 27, 1987.

112. Ibid., November 12, 1987.

113. Ibid., December 30, 1987.

114. *Washington Post*, February 24, 1988, p. 20.

11

International Law: Observations and Violations

BAHMAN BAKTIARI

Since the days of antiquity, sovereign political units have sought to regulate their relations by adopting rules and institutions designed to replace self-help and violence as prevalent methods for settling disputes. Historically, international law is a set of rules and principles of action that are binding on civilized states in their relations with one another. Rules of international law have existed since humans began to organize into political communities, where they felt the need of some system of rules, however rudimentary, to regulate their intercommunity relations. Thus, the adequacy of international law is a function of its acceptability.

Beginning in the sixteenth century, the writings of great scholars of international law refined its context and purpose so that it could become a major source of identification among states. Francisco de Vitoria wrote about the justice of Spanish conquests in America in 1557. Alberico Gentili (1598) and Francisco Suárez (1612) elaborated on the doctrines of just and unjust war, maintaining that a war was considered just if it was fought in self-defense, that is, against external attack, or if its purpose was to punish wrongdoers. They further differentiated natural law (*jus naturale*) from the law practiced by nations (*jus gentium*). Dutchman Hugo Grotius established himself as the "father of international law" with the publication of his famous book *De Jure Belli ac Pacis* (Law of War and Peace) in 1625.[1]

Thus, since its modern inception, the central focus of international law has been to limit or justify war and violence in international relations.[2] In the nineteenth century, new laws of neutrality established definite rights and obligations for both belligerents and neutrals, helping prevent the extension of bilateral military confrontations into continental or regional arenas. Series of multilateral conventions and codes were also drafted to prevent undue suffering among troops and civilians alike. Most of these rules were incorporated into voluminous codes of war during the Hague conferences of 1899 and 1907.[3]

Nineteenth-century attitudes and doctrines toward war as an instrument of policy to be unleashed by any government solely at its own discretion have been replaced by the prohibitions in the covenant of the League of Nations and the charter of the United Nations. The old laws of neutrality have been superseded by the obligation of all states to assist victims of aggression. As an outcome of the Nuremberg trials of Nazi war criminals and the genocide convention, personal criminal liability can be imposed against those who launch wars of aggression. Under the new international law, as Quincy Wright points out, war is no longer viewed as a duel between legal belligerents to be regulated only in scope but rather as a crime against all nations that must be prevented.[4] It is within three areas that these documents are relevant to the Iraq-Iran war: the definition of aggression, the status and interpretation of treaties among nation-states, and the question of war reparations.

The Definition of Aggression

Both in the days of the League of Nations and under the United Nations there has been much interest in attempts to define "aggression." From the point of view of form, three categories of definitions may be distinguished: enumerative, general, and combined.[5]

The enumerative definitions list acts of aggression. In 1956 the Soviet Union proposed, in the Special Committee on the Question of Defining Aggression, that the General Assembly adopt a resolution that states, "In an international conflict that state shall be declared the attacker that first commits one of the following acts":

(1) declaration of war against another state;
(2) invasion by its armed forces, even without a declaration of war, of the territory of another state;

(3) bombardment by its land, sea or air forces of the territory of another state or carrying out a deliberate attack on the ships or aircraft of the latter;
(4) the landing or leading of its land, sea or air forces inside the boundaries of another state without the permission of the government of the latter, or the violation or the conditions of such permission, particularly as regards the length of their stay or the extent of the area in which they may stay;
(5) naval blockade of the coasts or ports of another state;
(6) support of armed bands organized in its territory which invade the territory of another state, or refusal, on being requested by the invaded state, to take in its own territory any action within its power to deny such bands any aid or protection.[6]

Instead of listing the acts of aggression, the general definitions are couched in general terms that cover the entire class of cases to be included. The General Assembly empowers international organs to determine the scope of the terms when specific cases are brought before them. An example of this type of definition can be found in Article 9 of the Inter-American Treaty of Reciprocal Assistance dated September 2, 1947:

(1) unprovoked armed attack by a state against the territory, the people, or the land, sea or air forces of another state;
(2) invasion by the armed forces of a state, of the territory of an American state, through the trespassing of boundaries demarcated in accordance with a treaty, judicial decision, or arbitral award, or, in the absence of frontiers thus demarcated, invasion affecting a region which is under effective jurisdiction of another state.[7]

The combined definitions are a combination of the two preceding types. They contain both general terms and a list, but a list that is not exhaustive. The combined definitions describe the principal forms of aggression. After grappling with the issue for over two decades, the United Nations finally adopted a resolution on December 14, 1974, in which the acts of aggression were defined as follows:

(1) the first use of armed force in contravention of the charter (unless the Security Council concludes that such a determination would not be justified in the light of prevailing circumstances);

(2) the invasion or attack by the armed forces of a state of the territory of another state;
(3) bombardment . . . or the use of any weapon against the territory of another state;
(4) blockade of the ports or coasts of a state;
(5) an attack by the armed forces of a state on the land, sea or air forces, marine and air fleet of another state;
(6) the use of armed forces stationed in another country with its consent in contravention of the conditions provided for in the agreement or any extension of their presence . . . beyond the termination of the agreement;
(7) the action of a state that has placed its territory at the disposal of another state to be used by that other state for perpetrating an act of aggression;
(8) the sending by or on behalf of a state of armed bands, groups, irregulars or mercenaries, that carry out acts of armed force against another state of such gravity as to amount to the acts listed above.[8]

The resolution also states that the Security Council may determine that other acts constitute aggression. On the whole, the UN attempts to define aggression have to be considered within the overall purposes of the UN, specifically, its intention of seeking pacific settlements of disputes between member states. If the Nuremberg trials sought to define aggression by addressing the criminal nature of "aggressive acts," the UN insists on developing, institutionalizing, and persuading states to use peaceful methods to solve their differences.[9]

The Status and Interpretation of Treaties

Considerable controversy has also arisen regarding the status and interpretation of treaties among nation-states. Two important principles in international law have provided continuity in the international system with respect to treaties. The first principle, *pacta sunt servanda*, holds that treaties are not to be violated. The second, *rebus sic stantibus*, offers an escape clause by positing that treaties can be revised when the conditions that led to their initiation and adoption have been altered. However, it is important to note that the second principle is utilized in rare cases when the original treaty did not provide the means with which to seek necessary adjustments.[10]

The Vienna Convention on the Law of Treaties is a convenient starting point for discussing treaties. Specifically, what are the obligations of a state once it enters into a treaty with another state? Article 18 of the Vienna Convention says, "A state is obliged to refrain from acts which would defeat the object and purpose of a treaty when: (a) it has signed the treaty or has exchanged instruments constituting the treaty; (b) it has expressed its consent to be bound by the treaty."

Furthermore, Article 42 (1) of the Vienna Convention provides that "the validity of a treaty or of the consent of a state to be bound by a treaty may be impeached only through the application of the present convention." This is to prevent states from attempting to evade inconvenient treaty obligations by making far-fetched allegations that the treaty is invalid.

Article 26 of the Vienna Convention states unequivocally that "every treaty in force is binding upon the parties to it and must be performed by them in good faith." In other words, a state cannot release itself from its treaty obligations whenever it feels like it; if it could, legal relations would become hopelessly insecure. And, according to Article 54, "The termination of a treaty or the withdrawal of a party may take place in conformity with the provisions of the treaty."

Article 62 of the convention is of particular significance to my discussion. It declares that "a fundamental change of circumstance may not be invoked as a ground for terminating or withdrawing from the treaty *if the treaty established a boundary*" (emphasis added).

No doubt treaties often need to be altered, to bring them into line with changing conditions. But the *rebus sic stantibus* rule is an unsuitable method for achieving this end. Alterations, as opposed to termination, can only be brought about by agreement. Moreover, the fact that the UN General Assembly has power to recommend alterations of treaties is often overlooked. Under Article 14 of the charter, "the General Assembly may recommend measures for the peaceful adjustment of any situation, regardless of origin, which it deems likely to impair the general welfare or friendly relations among nations."

Does the outbreak of war terminate all treaties between belligerent states? Not necessarily. First, the Vienna Convention does not deal with the effects of war on treaties, apart from stating that "provisions of the present convention shall not prejudge any question that may arise in regard to a treaty . . . from the outbreak of hostilities between states" (Article 73). Second, when states are engaged in hostilities nowadays, they seldom admit that they are in a state of war in the technical sense; and unlike war, hostilities falling short of war do not generally terminate treaties between hostile states.[11]

War Reparations

The international law relating to war claims appears to be one of the least satisfactory parts of the law of state responsibility and international claims. Wars entail extensive destruction of property and widespread personal injury and violent death. The situation is complicated by the fact that any recovery for war claims is governed by particular agreements made for each particular situation, and it is only with the greatest difficulty that one can assert that certain rules or practices have become established as "international law." What follows in this section is a summary of relevant conventions and "norms" that have been adopted in the absence of specific agreement.

The Fourth Hague Convention of 1907 says with respect to the Regulations Governing Land Warfare annexed thereto: "A belligerent party which violates the provisions of the said regulations shall, if the case demands, be liable to pay compensation. It shall be responsible for all acts committed by persons forming part of its armed forces."[12] Insofar as the Hague Convention is applicable as a treaty or represents the general customary rule of international law (and it is believed to do so on this point), it may be said that under international law there is responsibility for war losses caused by conduct that violates that law.

Under Article 231 of the Treaty of Versailles (1919), "The Allied and Associated Governments affirm and Germany accepts the responsibility of Germany and her allies for causing all the loss and damage to which the Allied and Associated Governments and their nationals have been subjected as a consequence of the war imposed upon them by the aggression of Germany and her allies."[13] Under Article 232, "The Allied and Associated Governments . . . require, and Germany undertakes, that she will make compensation for all damages done to the civilian population of the Allied and Associated Powers and to their property during the period of the belligerency of each . . . against Germany by such aggression by land, by sea and from the air."[14]

Following the cessation of hostilities in World War II, war reparations were sought more stringently than ever before. In the United States, attempts to redress some forms of war claims were made by Congress in separate bills even in anticipation of the country's entry into the war. With the great number and variety of claims requiring its attention, Congress enacted the War Claims Act of 1948.[15] War reparations were sought under four general categories: (1) loss or destruction of, or physical damage to, property located in certain European countries and in areas attacked by the Japanese resulting from military operations of war or from special measures directed against property in such countries or territories because of the enemy or alleged enemy character of the owner; (2) damage to or destruction of ships and ship cargoes as a result of military action by Germany and Japan; (3) net losses of insurers under war-risk insurance contracts covering ships; (4) loss or damage on account of the death, injury or permanent disability of civilians.[16] (See Appendix I.)

In arranging peace terms after various modern wars, the victors have demanded certain payments from the vanquished. Whether termed indemnities, reparations, compensation, or other names, these payments have been associated with losses incurred by the victors or the expenses to which the victors have been put.

Legal Dimensions of the Iran-Iraq War

It is now appropriate to see whether this discussion of the basic principles of international law with respect to the questions of aggression, treaty violation, and war reparations can assist us in evaluating some of the major legal contentions relating to the Iran-Iraq war. The Islamic Republic of Iran has raised various legal questions. Does the Iraqi invasion of Iran on September 22, 1980, constitute an act of aggression under international law? Who is responsible for the abrogation of the 1975 Algiers Treaty?

On September 22, 1980, Iraq launched "air raids on at least 10 major Iranian cities, thus widening the theater of operations in its conflict with Iran and expanding the border fighting between the two states into an undeclared war." According to Arab diplomatic reports, Iraq had been planning the invasion for about six months, during which time it mobilized 50,000 troops.[17] Within two months, the Iraqi army had encircled the cities of Khorramshahr, Abadan, Dezful, Ahvaz, Qasr-e-Shirin, and Mehran. Instead of moving into the cities, the Iraqi regime sought to cause their surrender primarily through artillery and rocket bombardment, supplemented by air attacks. Clearly, the Iraqi invasion violated two articles of the United Nations Charter:

> Article II (sec. 3): All members shall settle their international disputes by peaceful means in such a manner that international peace and security, and justice, are not endangered.
>
> Article II (sec. 4): All members shall refrain in their international relations from the threat or use of force against the territorial integrity or political independence of any state.

Moreover, according to the definition of aggression adopted by the General Assembly in 1974, the Iraqi invasion of Iran constituted an act of aggression. Nevertheless, the Iraqi regime steadfastly argued in international forums that it did not commit aggression against Iran. It based its contentions on the well-known *Caroline* case, claiming that its "direct preventive strikes against military targets in Iran were a necessity of self-defense, instant, overwhelming, leaving no choice of means and no moment of deliberations."[18] This is a highly dubious interpretation of the *Caroline* case because, according to Arab sources, Iraq had planned the border attack in April 1980.[19] Even if one accepts alleged provocations by Iran, the Iraqi argument for "self-defense" fails to pass the test of "proportionality."

Another element in the Iraqi contention is based on invoking the United Nations Charter as giving Iraq "the right to self-defense."[20] This is again a one-sided interpretation. Article 51 of the charter emphasizes the "inherent right of individual or collective self-defense *if an armed attack occurs against a member of the United Nations*" (emphasis added). International law experts have interpreted this to mean *if an invasion* of a member state territory has taken place, then the latter is obligated to defend itself. Hostile propaganda and hit-and-run attacks are not sufficient justification for retaliation with *sustained force*. Iraq's argument is not dissimilar from those mounted from time to time in support of Israel when it initiates attacks on Arab countries. In the 1956 Suez war, in which Israel, France, and Great Britain attacked Egypt, the Israeli government justified its involvement by arguing that Nasser's Egypt was guilty of "indirect aggression" because it gave support to Palestinian operations. Even the United States condemned the Israeli action as a violation of the territorial integrity of Egypt.[21]

Further complicating the Iraqi argument for "self-defense" is the fact that Iraq unilaterally abrogated two articles of the 1975 Algiers Treaty. Article 4 states that the provisions of the three protocols concerning demarcation of land and river frontiers, as well as the establishment of security along the common borders between the two countries, are indivisible and constitute an integral part of the treaty. Article 6 enumerates the detailed procedures to be followed in case of differences between the two contracting parties over the interpretation or the application of the treaty, namely, direct bilateral negotiation between the parties. In case of nonagreement, the parties have to resort within a period of three months to the good offices of a third friendly state. If one of the parties refuses to resort to the good offices or the good offices fail within a period not exceeding one month beginning from the date of refusal or failure, the disagreement will be solved by arbitration. If the parties disagree on the procedure of arbitration, any one of them can resort within fifteen days following the date of disagreement to an arbitration tribunal.

President Saddam Hussein of Iraq explained the decision to abrogate the Algiers Treaty in an address before the Iraqi National Assembly on September 17, 1980: "Since the rulers of Iran have violated this agreement as of the beginning of their reign by blatantly and deliberately intervening in Iraq's domestic affairs . . . , and by refusing to return Iraqi territories, I announce before you that we consider the 6 March 1975 agreement as abrogated from our side. . . . Thus, the legal relationship concerning Shatt al-Arab should return to what it was before 6 March 1975. The Shatt shall again be, as it has been throughout history, Iraqi and Arab in name and reality, with all rights of full sovereignty over it."[22]

Besides the fact that Iraq never sought to invoke Article 6 of the Algiers Treaty to redress its grievances, it seemed to ignore the fact that, following the signing of this treaty, the Iraqi government issued a statement expressing its satisfaction and had not issued any complaints for six years. Furthermore, Saddam Hussein himself had stated just weeks before his troops invaded Iran that Iraq had recovered the territories "by force." His staff general, Adnan Khayrallah, had declared: "On 7 September, we regained the first area, called Zayn al-Qaws. On 10 September, we regained the second area, that of Sayf Sa'd. . . . I believe that on 12 or 13 September we regained five border posts which had been trespassed upon. *Thus we have regained all the land areas which have been trespassed upon by the Iranian side and have settled our dispute with Iran concerning the land differences*" (emphasis added).[23] If this is the case, then how could the territorial claim be a valid basis for the abrogation of the Algiers Treaty four days later? How could it be bona fide basis for escalating hostilities to a full-scale invasion of Iran ten days subsequent to the recovery of all the lands that Iraq had claimed?

The Iraqi interpretation introduces another element into the treaty that is contrary to its spirit and to the Vienna Convention on the Law of Treaties. Iraq argued that a particular article of the treaty has a higher priority than others. Here it referred to Article 3 of the Algiers agreement that calls on the two nations to "exercise strict and effective permanent control over the frontier in order to put an end to any infiltration of a subversive nature from any source." Iraq has erroneously argued that Iran violated this article and that therefore it was Iran that had abrogated its obligations under the 1975 Algiers Treaty. The invalidity of such an argument is clear both in terms of the Vienna Convention and the 1975 Treaty itself (see The Status and Interpretation of Treaties, above).

Article 6 had been drafted into the treaty in order to prevent such rationalizations by either of the two parties. In fact, the Iraqi interpretation not only rendered Article 6 of the treaty pointless; it also implied an illogical application of the principle *rebus sic stantibus*. If a state can release itself from its treaty obligations whenever it wishes to, what is the purpose of signing a treaty in the first place? Self-releases from treaties could make legal relations hopelessly insecure. If Iraq wanted to reserve its rights to abrogate its obligations, it should not have agreed to the inclusion of Article 6 in the text of the treaty. Moreover, the principle of *rebus sic stantibus* is not to be invoked if the treaty has established a boundary.[24]

It is interesting to note that this view had been shared by the Iraqi regime until it invaded Iran in 1980. The acting permanent representative of Iraq to the United Nations had circulated a document in 1969 that stated that "the rules of international law generally are obligatory with regard to the respect of treaties, and do not particularly sanction the unilateral abrogation or amendment of boundary treaties under any circumstances. The rule is absolute even if a war exists between the two States which are bound by a boundary treaty."[25] Therefore, the Iraqi abrogation of the Algiers Treaty is difficult to defend in legal terms, and Iran undoubtedly has a strong case in emphasizing the fact that the 1975 Treaty included options for avoiding unilateral abrogation or suspension.

How legitimate is Iran's claim that under international law Iraq must pay war reparations? To examine this question more comprehensively, we should first look at a number of relevant international cases and agreements. Because international law theorizes that the state is responsible for its own acts, it follows logically that its own delinquency (in this case, the acts of aggression committed by Iraq) should be the criterion for determining responsibilities for reparations. According to Article 3 of the Hague Codification Conference of 1930, "The international responsibility of a state imports the duty to make reparation for the damage sustained insofar as it results from failure to comply with its international obligations." In the case in point, the Iraqi regime failed to comply with the UN Charter and the 1975 Algiers Treaty when it invaded Iran. A case in international law clearly makes Iraq responsible for war reparations. It concerned the factory at Chorzow, and the Permanent Court of International Justice, 1928, Ser. A, No. 17 ruled that "as regards the first point (the existence of the obligation to make reparation), the Court observes that it is a principle of international law, and even a general conception of law, that any breach of an engagement involves an obligation to make reparations. . . . The reparations of a wrong may consist in an indemnity corresponding to the damage which the nationals of the injured state have suffered as a result of the act which is contrary to international law."[26]

Although there is no standard format for reparations of war damages, some suggestions may be helpful for making a coherent presentation.

(1) An international commission or tribunal must be established to gather and examine documents submitted by the aggrieved state.[27]

(2) A distinction must be made between proper war claims and those that are otherwise "war losses." The latter require special agreements and should be assessed separately.

(3). Measuring war damages must follow two phases: (a) Damages incurred by Iran while Iraq occupied Iranian territory, which include industrial, civilian, and other nonmilitary structures destroyed by the Iraqi armed forces; and (b) damages incurred because of reckless disregard of the rules of warfare, such as bombardment of cities located outside the battle areas, use of chemical gas, which is banned by the Geneva Convention of 1925, etc.

(4) There are two methods of dealing with war claims: a lump-sum settlement and the Foreign Claims Settlement Commission. The first involves negotiating a lump-sum settlement and then distributing it to the state or individuals through a neutral agency. The other occurs under the Foreign Settlement Commission of the United States (a domestic agency created in 1954 that replaced the International Claims Commission of 1949): The government of a state seeking reparations establishes a permanent body (usually three or four persons appointed by the head of state) to which there can be assigned jurisdiction over claims of the state and its nationals.[28] In selecting these methods, some important considerations must be taken into account. Does the lump-sum settle-

ment process bring about a quicker and fairer settlement than the process of international adjudication or arbitration? Is it less expensive and politically more expedient? Which method would facilitate overall process of negotiation in other areas of dispute?

In light of this discussion, we must bear in mind that in most cases of war claims the situation is ultimately governed by agreements specific to each particular situation and that the parties are likely to be guided by consideration of politics, of who won and who lost, or by the "moral climate of opinion" incident to the termination of the hostilities. The Iran-Iraq war is no different from any other wars in which the questions of international law would be subjected to political negotiations. In arranging peace terms after various modern wars, states have found it expedient to include the issue of war claims on the negotiation agenda along with other strategic considerations.

Iranian calculations of the sums owed to it as reparations run into billions of dollars. By 1986, figures as high as $400 billion were being mentioned in Tehran, although the Planning Ministry claimed only $309 billion in midyear.[29] Clearly, Iraq is responsible for the damages inflicted on Iranian installations and cities. Furthermore, population displacement by the war (estimated to involve upward of one million people) has been a major burden on the Iranian government and should be part of any negotiations for war reparations.

Under international law, both Iran and Iraq are obliged to refrain from the use of force and to settle their disputes by peaceful means. As the demarcation of land and offshore boundaries has been clearly outlined in the 1975 Algiers Treaty, Iraq violated this treaty by invading Iranian territory.[30]

If both countries want to achieve a just settlement, they must actively support the endeavors of the United Nations to guarantee peace in the region. The UN was successful in arranging cease-fires in the Korean conflict of 1952, and in the Arab-Israeli conflict and has consistently provided a forum for member nations to argue their cases and persuade other countries of their position. The Islamic Republic of Iran has a strong legal case on who started the war. There is every reason to believe that an impartial body will identify Iraq as the aggressor.

Notes

1. For a good overview of the history of international law, see Arthur Nussbaum, *A Concise History of the Law of Nations* (New York: Macmillan, 1954), and M. H. Keene, *The Laws of War in the Late Middle Ages* (Toronto: University of Toronto Press, 1965).
2. Richard Falk, "Revolutionary Nations and the Quality of International Legal Order," in *The Revolution in World Politics*, ed. Morton Kaplan (New York: John Wiley, 1962), 320.
3. Quincy Wright, *The Role of International Law in the Elimination of War* (Manchester, U. K.: Manchester University Press, 1961).
4. Ibid., 27–28.
5. Secretary-general of the United Nations, "Report on the Question of Defining Aggression," October 3, 1952.
6. United Nations Document, International Legal Materials, no. 661, A/AC 134/L.12, 1969.
7. William W. Bishop, Jr., *International Law: Cases and Materials*, 3d ed. (Boston: Little, Brown and Company, 1962), 924.
8. United Nations General Assembly Resolution 3314, vol. 24, December 14, 1974.
9. Inis L. Claude, Jr., *Swords into Plowshares: The Problems and Progress of International Organizations*, 4th ed. (New York: Random House, 1971), 218.
10. Bishop, *International Law*, 173.
11. J.L. Brierly, *The Law of Nations*, 6th ed. (Oxford: The Clarendon Press, 1978), 327–29.
12. Herbert W. Briggs, *The Law of Nations: Cases, Documents and Notes* (New York: Appleton-Century-Crofts, 1952), 1004–5.
13. Bishop, *International Law*, 798.
14. Ibid.
15. U.S. House of Representatives, Doc. 580, 81st Cong., 2d sess.
16. Lester B. Orfield and Edward D. Re, *International Law* (New York: The Bobbs-Merrill Company, 1965), 1059–60.
17. *New York Times*, September 23, 1980.
18. Ministry of Foreign Affairs of the Republic of Iraq, *Origins of the Iran-Iraq Conflict*, 1987.
19. *New York Times*, September 23, 1980.
20. *Origins of the Iran-Iraq Conflict.*
21. See the General Assembly Resolution, November 2, 1956, UN Doc. A/3256.
22. Foreign Broadcasting Information Service, *Middle East and North Africa*, 5, no. 183, September 20, 1980.
23. Ibid., 5, no. 189, September 26, 1980.
24. See Article 62 of the Vienna Convention on the Law of Treaties.

25. Security Council Doc. S/9185, May 9, 1969.

26. Briggs, *Law of Nations*, 742.

27. An international tribunal can be composed of either individuals who have achieved stature and acceptability to act as arbitrators in international legal claims or of selected members of the United Nations. A list of countries to be approached may include the following: Algeria, Romania, the Federal Republic of Germany, Costa Rica, Brazil, Mexico, Yugoslavia, India, Indonesia, and Zambia.

28. Concerning lump-sum settlements of international claims, see *Yearbook of the International Law Commission*, 2 (1958): 66–67; George Joffe and Keith McLachlan, "Foreign Claims Settlement Commission: Its Functions and Jurisdiction," *Michigan Law Review*, 60, no. 1078 (1962).

29. The Economist Intelligence Unit, "Iran and Iraq: The Next Five Years," Special Report No. 1083.

30. For a comprehensive discussion of the boundary dispute, see S.H. Amin, "The Iran-Iraq War: Legal Implications," *Marine Policy*, 6, no. 3 (July 1982).

12

The UN Secretary-General: Attitudes and Latitudes

PAUL TAVERNIER

The lines "Since 1946 a new actor has appeared on the international scene: The United Nations Secretary-General. Nevertheless, no one is able to say exactly what is expected of the UN Secretary-General and what is his role in resolution of conflicts and his role in maintenance and establishment of peace," written in 1971, continued to be valid in 1988.[1] The secretary-general was active during the Iran-Iraq war, and from the first day offered his good offices for mediation. Later in the war, he attempted to achieve a comprehensive settlement of the conflict and to resolve certain of its aspects, such as the use of chemical weapons by Iraq or the war of the cities.

Nevertheless, the secretary-general's actions were limited because they were taken within the legal constraints of the UN Charter. Taking these conditions into account, the secretary-general used his imagination and gave a broad interpretation of his powers. Given limited space, I will just refer to the provisions of the charter that determine the powers of the secretary-general in dealing with threats to peace and international security. This will allow us to find out the extent of the secretary-general's competence in the Iran-Iraq war and to determine whether he could have done more.

The Legal Constraints of the United Nations

Chapter 15 of the United Nations Charter specifically deals with the Secretariat (Articles 97–101). Here, I refer only to Articles 97, 98, and

99. I should also mention Article 7, which refers to the Secretariat as the principal organ of the United Nations. It can be construed from the texts of these articles that the secretary-general is essentially a subordinate organ with limited powers. Nonetheless, certain provisions of the charter recognize independent status for the secretary-general, with authority to take initiatives—particularly for the maintenance of peace.

The Secretary-General as a Subordinate Organ

The UN secretary-general, whether in his status or in accordance with his functions, is in many regards like most of his counterparts in other international organizations, namely, a subordinate official. Accordingly, he has little power to use his personal initiatives to maintain peace and international security, especially in the case of armed conflicts between member states.

The status of the secretary-general.—The secretary-general is without any doubt "The chief administrative officer of the Organization" (Article 97 of the charter). Moreover, he is appointed by the General Assembly on the recommendation of the Security Council. Therefore, he is politically dependent on two principal bodies in the organization, and in this way he depends on the will of governments, particularly the five permanent members of the Security Council with veto power (Article 27). This dependence is not merely theoretical, and the Security Council's power is fully exercised at the time of the nomination of the secretary-general, as the procedures in 1971, 1976, and 1981 make clear.[2] The dependence has been manifested abundantly during the tenure of the secretary-general. Because of this double dependence on the Security Council (particularly its permanent members) and on the General Assembly, the secretary-general faces certain difficulties, though on some occasions he takes advantage of the rivalries between the two organs. The subordinate character of the secretary-general can also be seen in the functions entrusted to him.

Functions of the secretary-general.—The functions of the secretary-general are essentially administrative and related to the execution of the decisions of other organs of the United Nations. Thus, his ability to take initiatives is limited. Against this background, Article 98 of the charter provides that "the Secretary-General shall act in that capacity in all meetings of the General Assembly, of the Security Council, of the Economic and Social Council, and of the Trusteeship Council" and "he shall perform such other functions as are entrusted to him by these organs." These provisions entrust to the secretary-general executive functions: he convokes the meetings of the principal organs of the organization and applies their decisions. There has been much discussion about the legal scope and obligatory and nonobligatory character of the Security Council and General Assembly resolutions. It is certain, however, that these resolutions must be implemented by the secretary-general, even if they contain nonimperative terms such as "request" or "urge."

Although the secretary-general is obligated to implement the directives of the other principal organs of the United Nations, particularly the Security Council and the General Assembly, in practice these resolutions allow a more important role that goes far beyond simple execution. Certain directives addressed to the secretary-general are imprecise and allow him a large margin in which to maneuver. The UN peacekeeping operations in the Middle East, the Congo, and other areas, which were carried out in accordance with the Security Council or General Assembly resolutions, are good examples.

Despite the fact that the imprecision of the General Assembly and Security Council resolutions may favor his initiatives with respect to the maintenance of peace, the secretary-general may face difficulties because of a lack of consensus among states. He must always keep his instructions in mind because he is a subordinate official, but at the same time he can use personal initiatives as an independent organ; this is one of the innovations of the charter.

The Secretary-General as an Independent Organ

The San Francisco Charter contains provisions that appear simple but are inconsistent with Articles 97 and 98. These provisions present the secretary-general as an independent organ empowered to assume political and diplomatic roles and initiatives with respect to questions of peace and international security. The charter has described the Secretariat as a principal organ of the United Nations, with the same stature as that of the General Assembly or the Security Council. This can be construed from Article 7. Although the Secretariat is mentioned in the sixth position after the General Assembly, the Security Council, the Economic and Social Council, the Trusteeship Council, and the International Court of Justice, the high position of the Secretariat is clear.[3]

Article 99 requires more attention and is generally considered the basis for the political role of the secretary-general.[4] According to this article, "The Secretary-General may bring to the attention of the Security Council any matter which in his opinion may threaten the maintenance of international peace and security." This is not merely a simple text on procedure permitting the secretary-general to convoke the meeting of the Security Council. On the contrary, it gives him considerable power, something that the secretary-general of the League of Nations did not possess. This power is entrusted to him on an equal footing with the member states, and he exercises it with complete independence.

Except on rare occasions (e.g., the 1960 Congo crisis) the secretary-general has not used this power. But Article 99 appears to have been used as the basis of the secretary-general's actions in various cases, most notably in 1971 concerning the East Pakistan question and in 1979 for the American hostages in Tehran.[5] In addition, the provisions of Article 99 have been used on many other occasions,[6] allowing the Secretariat to take independent measures with respect to maintenance of peace, without relying on the directives or instructions of the General Assembly or the Security Council. Thus, the secretary-general can, by relying on the "spirit" of Article 99 and the responsibilities entrusted to him by the charter, justify his "quiet diplomacy," which is sometimes referred to as "discrete" or "private" diplomacy.

The secretary-general's independence is further reinforced in Article 100 of the charter, which provides, "In the performance of their duties the Secretary-General and the staff shall not seek or receive instructions from any government or from any authority external to the organization." Nevertheless, this does not prevent the secretary-general from taking action, on the request of two governments or based on their expressed agreement, with respect to the maintenance of peace, without explicitly invoking any of the provisions of the charter. This happened in the *Rainbow Warrior* case between France and New Zealand.[7]

The combination of Articles 99 and 33 of the charter offers broader possibilities, especially in the field of providing "good offices." Consequently, the secretary-general should reconcile provisions that are at odds with each other; some are restrictive and others permit great flexibility of action and interpretation for using the instrument of initiatives in international conflicts, particularly since interpretation of these texts has shown extensive authority for the secretary-general. Thus, the highest official of the United Nations is obliged to abide by different and often contradictory regulations, as demonstrated in the Iran-Iraq war.

Various Initiatives in the Iran-Iraq War

From the first day of the war in 1980, Secretary-General Kurt Waldheim intervened actively, as did his successor, Javier Pérez de Cuellar. The actions of the secretary-general in this regard have received different assessments, both by the two warring states and by outsiders. Some say that these actions should have been expedited, at least in the beginning of the war, when there was no direct interference from major powers. On the other hand, it was not a civil war, which could have made the efforts of the secretary-general more difficult. In any case, the actions of both secretaries-general were cautious and delicate.

Certain initiatives of the secretary-general, at the beginning of the conflict and afterward, relate to Article 99. Other initiatives, concerning the implementation of the resolutions of the Security Council or the General Assembly, relate to Articles 97 and 98. The secretary-general, however, rarely explains the reason for his interventions, and it can be said that he usually acts on the basis of the charter as a whole. Some of his initiatives are general in scope, concerning all aspects of the war (these have had limited effect), while others have more limited objectives dealing with particular aspects. Although this distinction may appear slightly artificial, a review enables us to look at the activities of the secretary-general, without pretending to be exhaustive.

The Initiatives of General Scope

Even if not expressly linked, these initiatives are basically related to Article 99 of the charter and confirm the political and diplomatic role of the secretary-general on the basis of Article 98. In fact, the implementation of resolutions from the General Assembly (only one in 1982) and the Security Council (eight from 1980 to 1988) generally required important, sometimes complex, negotiations with the interested states.

Starting on September 22, 1980, Secretary-General Waldheim proffered his good offices to Iran and Iraq, and the president of the Security Council approved these initiatives.[8] Before Mexico and Norway brought the case to the attention of the council,[9] the secretary-general sent two letters to the president of the council. In the first, he mentioned that the war between Iran and Iraq might become a serious threat to peace, and he called on the members of the council for urgent consultation.[10] In the second, he was more explicit and offered further explanation: "I therefore feel obliged, in the exercise of my responsibilities as the Secretary-General of the United Nations, to suggest that the Security Council consider this matter with the utmost urgency."[11] Reference to Article 99 was not explicit but can be understood from the terms used. In the framework of these responsibilities, Waldheim could have drawn the attention of the Security Council to the issue but, of course, could not have taken the place of the council for determining the aggressor. According to Article 39 of the charter, this lies within the council's scope.

In Resolution 479 of September 1980, the Security Council acknowledged that Article 24 entrusted to the council the primary responsibility for the maintenance of international peace and security, but the aggressor was not named in this resolution. Nevertheless, the council approved the mediation efforts of the secretary-general. The latter, after consulting with Iran and Iraq, appointed Olaf Palme as his special envoy.[12] Palme visited Tehran and Baghdad and managed to get an agreement in principle for the free passage of commercial ships that were blocked in the Shatt al-Arab waterway. This agreement failed because of Iraq's refusal to accept hoisting the UN or ICRC flag on the ships.[13] After eight years of war, these ships were still stranded.

Thus, though he persevered for a number of years, Palme's mission failed. However, on July 12, 1982, when Iran was in a better military position, the Security Council in Resolution 514 asked the secretary-general to coordinate mediation efforts by other organizations, namely, the Non-Aligned Movement and the Organization of Islamic Countries.

These efforts failed to produce any concrete results. There were similar failures with other Security Council resolutions, e.g., that of July 12, 1982, to send observers to investigate a cease-fire and withdrawal of forces.[14]

Despite these failures, the secretary-general did not abandon his efforts throughout the war, paying a number of visits to Tehran and Baghdad. In the wake of these consultations, Secretary-General Pérez de Cuellar came up with an eight-point proposal for the settlement of disputes. This proposal was reviewed by the Security Council on March 18, 1989. Pérez de Cuellar, in his report on his visit to Iran and Iraq, emphasized that "the underlying premise of the proposals is that, as Secretary-General of the United Nations, my overriding constitutional responsibility under the Charter is to seek to end the conflict."[15] This is implicitly referring to Article 99 of the charter. The eight-point proposal was never officially publicized.

In 1986, after the passage of Resolutions 581 and 588, the secretary-general suggested the revival of his eight-point proposal. While Iran was of the opinion that the proposal might constitute a useful basis for future efforts, Iraq believed that it was not a balanced and practical instrument for initiating a process leading to a global settlement of the conflict on the basis of Resolution 582. Under these conditions, Pérez de Cuellar was forced to concede his failure: "As is clearly evident from the positions of the two parties described above, at present they show no degree of coincidence which would provide a basis for the presentation of specific proposals designed to give effect to Resolution 582 (1986)."[16] Thus, we can see that the secretary-general's initiatives are carried out within a limited margin for maneuver. He must not only take into consideration the instructions of the Security Council but also the positions of the two belligerents.

The secretary-general's limited room for maneuvering was demonstrated again after Resolution 598 was adopted on July 20, 1987. It was adopted through the initiative of Secretary-General Pérez de Cuellar, who always insisted on the responsibilities of the permanent members of the Security Council in his annual reports on the activities of the United Nations.[17] Many delegations emphasized the secretary-general's role in elaboration of the text. The Soviet Union's delegate particularly thanked Pérez de Cuellar "who has undertaken considerable effort to make today's meeting of the Council possible and has put forward a number of valuable ideas which are reflected in the resolution adopted by the Council."[18] Despite this commendation, the secretary-general encountered many difficulties in implementing the resolution. For example, he suggested that the position of Iran be taken into account, but Iraq opposed any changes in the 1987 text and the sequence of its articles.[19] The core of these difficulties lay in paragraph 6 of the resolution, which "requests the Secretary-General to explore, in consultation with Iran and Iraq, the question of entrusting an impartial body with inquiring into responsibility for the conflict and report to the Council as soon as possible." Considering the position of the two parties, it was almost impossible for the secretary-general to accomplish the mission.

The Iranian government again referred to the secretary-general's eight-point plan,[20] but Iraq never mentioned it. That meant numerous obstacles for the secretary-general's initiatives that were general in scope, and thus he chose initiatives with more limited scope.

The Initiatives Concerning Particular Aspects of the War

In his report of April 12, 1985, on his visit to Iran and Iraq, the secretary-general not only underlined his constitutional responsibilities, which are implicitly based on Article 99, but also emphasized his humanitarian responsibilities. He stressed that as long as the objective of bringing an end to the war was not reached, "I am also legally obliged under recognized international humanitarian laws to try to mitigate its effects in areas such as attacks on civilian population centers, use of chemical weapons, treatment of prisoners of war, and the safety of navigation and civil aviation."[21] He was not idle with respect to these matters but, on the contrary, was very active indeed.[22]

The war of the cities and the June 12, 1984, agreement.—The bombardment of civilian and residential areas preoccupied the secretary-general from 1983 on. At the request of Iran, and after consultations with Iraq, he sent a team to evaluate the damage to civilian targets. On June 20, 1983, he submitted to the Security Council a report on the subject.[23] The mandate of the inspection team was limited, falling within the offers of "good offices" at the beginning of the war.

Iran, once again, asked the secretary-general to dispatch another investigation team to the region in order to supplement the previous report, but Iraq said the team could not serve any purpose. The discussions ran into many difficulties because of the introduction of matters relating to the use of chemical weapons. In June 1984, Secretary-General Pérez de Cuellar received the agreement of the two belligerent states for "an end to deliberate attacks by bombardment, missiles or any other means against residential and purely civilian centers."[24] This agreement, concluded through a complex procedure, was an undeniable success for Pérez de Cuellar's diplomatic efforts. A control mechanism was envisaged in the agreement that worked through the two offices of the United Nations in Tehran and Baghdad to investigate violations of the agreement. The two teams started work in the latter part of 1984, and the reports of the inspectors were published. Afterward, however, despite the frequent resumption of the war of the cities with great intensity, especially in 1988, no report was published. Nevertheless, the government of Iran insisted that the work of the two investigation teams be intensified.

The use of chemical weapons.—Iran first told of Iraq's use of chemical weapons in 1983,[25] but apparently the use of such weapons started in April 1981.[26] In fact, according to a new document submitted by Iran to the secretary-general, they were used as early as January 13, 1981.[27] Iran persuaded Pérez de Cuellar to send various envoys to investigate. Pérez de Cuellar particularly referred to Resolution 37/98 D, giving the secretary-general the authority to investigate the matter, but he preferred to rely on his general competence for humanitarian principles and to avoid entering into legal arguments of an extremely complex nature.[28]

This example shows that the secretary-general had to use great prudence in his actions in order to attain greater efficacy. Along these lines, he published various reports in 1984, 1985, 1986, 1987, and 1988.[29] These reports, along with declarations of the president of the Security Council[30] and certain resolutions condemning violation of the 1925 protocol, contained no explicit mention of the country that was not respecting its obligations, except for the 1986 and 1987 declarations. Failure to name the country can also be seen in the Security Council Resolution of May 9, 1988.[31] Nevertheless, the secretary-general preferred to rely on his ambiguous positions rather than the precise controversial texts of the General Assembly.[32] Restrictions and the limited possibilities for the secretary-general's initiatives also appear in other domains.

The problem of prisoners of war.—The implementation of the Third Geneva Convention lies essentially within the competence of governments and the International Committee of the Red Cross, but the secretary-general has not hesitated to intervene on certain occasions. He dispatched envoys to both Iran and Iraq on their request. The report of this team was examined by the Security Council on March 4, 1985,[33] but did not lead to any official position on the part of the council. The council, like the secretary-general, faced extremely complex problems that limited its intervention.

Freedom of navigation.—The problem of freedom of navigation arose in the beginning of the hostilities, but, as mentioned, Secretary-General Waldheim and his special envoy, Olaf Palme, failed to obtain an agreement for the passage of the ships stranded in the Shatt al-Arab waterway.

Freedom of navigation in the Persian Gulf was again raised in the wake of Iraq's bombardment of Kharg Island. The Security Council adopted a number of resolutions that reaffirmed the principle of free navigation, e.g. Resolutions 540 and 552 of October 31, 1983, and June 1, 1984, respectively. The latter called on the secretary-general to report to the Security Council on the implementation of the resolution. The secretary-general addressed this subject in his report of December 31, 1984, and the matter was raised regularly every year thereafter.[34]

These documents were prepared on the basis of information from the governments and international maritime organizations and do not contain any initiatives on the part of the secretary-general. But the documents mentioned that shipping organizations had requested that the secretary-general intervene. In response to this request, Pérez de Cuellar addressed the foreign ministers of the belligerent countries on June 12, 1986. He told them of the shipping organizations' concern about the increase in cases of violation of the freedom of navigation and about the extension of the zone in which commercial shipping came under attack.[35] In 1987 and early 1988 there was a considerable increase in the number of incidents and in superpower interventions—another element that further limited the secretary-general's scope of action.

Nevertheless, the secretary-general, in addition to his intervention with the two belligerents, repeated some of the Soviet Union's suggestions that the United Nations form a naval force to guarantee freedom of navigation in the Persian Gulf. In his annual report of 1987, the secretary-general proposed that plans for "peacekeeping operations at sea" should be prepared and studies for its possible establishment must be carried out. Thus, Pérez de Cuellar used his imagination, but it seems that these proposals will not produce concrete results soon.

Conclusion

It is difficult to present a balance sheet for the secretary-general's initiatives with respect to peace and international security. Should it be considered defeat or success? The answer is not readily apparent.

Considering the limited legal constraints that the secretary-general must comply with and the present situation of the international community, the secretary-general's initiatives vis-à-vis the belligerents were useful. The secretary-general's actions made possible contacts between two adversaries who otherwise would only have met on the war fronts. Furthermore, these initiatives enabled the United Nations to be active while its particular parts were considered unqualified by Iran (the Security Council) or deliberately stayed silent (the General Assembly). The interventions of the secretary-general also remedied the lack of action by other organizations, such as the International Committee of the Red Cross.

Under such conditions, recourse to the secretary-general was fully justifiable. No doubt, he did not explore all possibilities and powers available to him, but his actions with respect to certain recent conflicts showed that he can play an effective role for the maintenance of peace, provided that the consent of the interested parties is obtained.

Notes

1. M.Cl. Smouts, *Le Sécretaire Général des Nations Unies* (The UN Secretary-General) (Paris: Armand Colin, 1971), 11.

2. P. Tavernier, "L'année des Nations Unies. Questions juridiques" (Legal Points on UN Activities), *Annuaire Français de Droit International* (1971): 560; (1976): 341; (1981): 403.

3. Article 2 of the League of Nations Covenant provided that the league should be active, as specified in this covenant, through an assembly and a council assisted by a permanent Secretariat. This provision shows the subordinate character of the Secretariat.

4. See commentaries of Articles 98 and 99 by Smouts in *La Charte des Nations Unies*, ed. J.P. Cot, A. Pellet, Tavernier et al. (Paris/Brussels: Economica/Bruylant, 1985), 1309–17. An English version is in press.

5. Tavernier, "Questions juridiques" (1971): 593, (1979): 479, respectively.

6. See, e.g., ibid., (1972): 530; (1974): 510; (1976): 353–54; (1978): 536 (the Lebanese crisis).

7. Ibid. (1986): 517–18; G. Apollis, "Le règlement de l'affaire du *Rainbow Warrior*" (The Settlement of the *Rainbow Warrior* Case), *Revue Générale de Droit International Public*, no. 1 (1987): 9–43.

8. UN document S/14190 (hereafter UN documents will be cited by number and letter only).

9. S/14198.

10. S/14196, September 23, 1980.

11. S/14197, September 25, 1980.

12. S/14251 and S/14252, letter from the secretary-general and answer from the Security Council's president November 11, 1980).

13. See Tavernier, "Le conflict frontalier entre l'Irak et l'Iran et la querre du Chatt-el-Arab" (The Boundary Conflict between Iraq and Iran and the Chatt-Al Arab War), *ARES* (1981): 333–70, esp. 342–43.

14. S/15293, report of the secretary-general.

15. S/17097, April 12, 1985.

16. S/18480, report of the secretary-general, November 26, 1986.

17. See Tavernier, "La Résolution 598 du 20 juillet 1987 et le rôle du Conseil de Sécurité dans la guerre entre l'Irak et l'Iran" (The 598 Resolution of July 20, 1987, and the Security Council's Role in the Iran-Iraq War), *ARES* (1988/2): 209–23.

18. S/PV 2750 of July 20, 1987.

19. Iraq made clear its position in a letter dated July 23, 1987, published in document S/19045 of August 14, 1987. The official point of view of the Islamic Republic of Iran was expressed on August 11, 1987, in S/19031.

20. As Iran pointed out, "The eight-point plan of March 1985 of the Secretary-General has been the only practical plan thus far taking various aspects of the war in to account which has not been in force due to Iraqi opposition. This plan is still a suitable ground for future efforts of the Secretary-General" (S/19031).

21. S/17097 of April 12, 1985.

22. See Tavernier, "La guerre du Golfe: Quelques aspects de l'application du droit des conflits armes et du droit humanitaire" (The Gulf War: Some Points about the Application of the Laws of Armed Conflicts and Humanitarian Law), *Annuaire Français de Droit International* (1984): 43–64.

23. S/15834.

24. S/16611, message dated June 9, 1984 from the secretary-general to the presidents of the Islamic Republic of Iran and the Republic of Iraq; S/16609 and S/16610, letters dated June 10, 1984, containing Iran and Iraq's agreement; S/16614 and S/16615, message dated June 11, 1984, from the secretary-general taking note of both governments' agreement: "Consequently, it is now understood that the Government of the Islamic Republic of Iran and the Government of the Republic of Iraq have given undertakings to the Secretary-General of the United Nations that all deliberate military attacks by any means on purely civilian population centers in either country will cease, effective 0001 GMT on 12 June 1984" (S/16627); letter dated June 14, 1984, from the secretary-general to the president of the Security Council pointing out what arrangements he made; S/16628, answer dated June 15, 1984, from the president of the council pointing out that the members of the council agreed with these arrangements. It is worth noting that Iraq claimed all the merit for the first idea that led to the agreement of June 12, 1984: Baghdad would have put forward such an agreement, but Tehran would have rejected it. To accept such an interpretation would lead to improperly diminishing the role of the secretary-general.

25. A/38/650–S/16693 of November 30, 1983.

26. "A Review of the Imposed War," Tehran, February 1983, p. 67.

27. S/19816, of April 21, 1988, letter from Iran transmitting "a chart of chemical attacks by Iraq since the inception of the imposed war." This chart lists 249 chemical attacks before April 18, 1988.

28. See Tavernier, "Questions juridiques" (1984): 52–53.

29. S/16433 (March 26, 1984); S/17127 and Add. 1 (April 17, 1985); S/17911 and Add. 1 (March 12, 1986); S/18852 and Add. 1 (May 8, 1987); S/19823 and Add. 1 (April 25, 1988). In 1987, the secretary-general's mission went to Iraq for the first time.

30. S/PV.2524 of March 30, 1984; S/PV2576 of April 25, 1985; S/PV2667 of March 21, 1986; S/18863 of May 14, 1987.

31. The 612 Resolution was drafted by the Federal Republic of Germany, Italy, and Japan: S/19869. For the first time, the Security Council took up a position in a resolution on the substance of the secretary-general's reports and did not issue merely a presidential declaration. Iran expressed its displeasure about the 612 Resolution: S/19886 of May 16, 1988.

32. The April 25, 1988 report (S/19823) refers to 598 Resolution, passed on July 20, 1987 by the Security Council. This text only deplores in the preamble, "the use of chemical weapons contrary to obligations under the 1925 Geneva Protocol."

33. S/PV.2569. See *Annuaire Français de Droit International* (1985), 551.

34. S/16877 and Add. 1 and 2 (1985), Add. 3 (1986), Add. 4 and 5 (1987), and Add. 6 (1988).

35. S/18480, secretary-general's report (November 26, 1986) with the appended text of a cable sent to the secretary-general by the chief executives of maritime organizations on November 3, 1986, of the message sent by the secretary-general to Iraq and Iran on June 12, 1986, and their answers. On these matters, see Tavernier, "La guerre entre l'Irak et l'Iran et la navigation dans le Golfe" (The Iran-Iraq War and Navigation Through the Persian Gulf), *Annuaire 1987 de l'Association Droit, Littoral et Mer*, 6–21.

Part III

Theoretical Aspects and Meaning

13

The Inherent Right of Individual Self-Defense in the Iran-Iraq War

DJAMCHID MOMTAZ

On September 22, 1980, Iraq launched a large-scale attack against Iran. As a result of their surprise attack, the Iraqi forces were able to cross international boundaries without much difficulty[1] and, after a few days of fighting, occupied 30,000 square kilometers of Iranian territory.[2] To justify its action, Iraq resorted to the concept of "legitimate preventive defense."[3] Below, I shall reject the validity and credibility of Iraq's recourse to this concept. In my opinion and that of my colleagues, Iraq, by violating the provisions of the United Nations Charter, resorted to force, and we believe Iraq's action has all the characteristics of an act of aggression as defined in the annex of UN General Assembly Resolution 3314.[4]

Faced with armed aggression, Iran reacted immediately and spontaneously in order to exercise its right of individual self-defense in accordance with Article 51 of the UN Charter.[5] There is no doubt that in this case we are talking about subsidiary and provisional competence that cannot be exercised, in accordance with Article 51 of the charter. This article provides for such action until the Security Council has taken the measures necessary to maintain international peace and security. Accordingly, the negligence and incapability of the Security Council to assume its responsibility can be taken by Iran as a legal basis for pursuing military operations.

Until July 1982, Iran's decision to pursue military operations did not cause any problem, because the Security Council had not taken any effective measure and merely called on the two parties to refrain from resorting to force,[6] even as the aggressor state continued to occupy large portions of Iranian territory. Then Iranian forces succeeded in pushing back the aggressor, liberated much of their territory, and began to pursue military operations inside Iraq. Therefore, after this date, the question should be studied from a different angle. The Security Council finally adopted a series of resolutions to bring about a cease-fire, withdrawal of aggressor forces to the established international boundaries,[7] and comprehensive resolution of the conflict. Finding the measures of the Security Council ineffective, Iran persisted in its decision to continue the war as a legitimate defense.

From this point on, the question arose of when legitimate defense would cease. It is generally accepted that a state that resorts to legitimate defense has two specific objectives: (1) repulsing the aggressor forces from its territory, thereby guaranteeing the return of its seized territory, and (2) diminishing the danger of new aggression. Because it has the prerogative to use force against the aggressor state, the violated state may continue with its legitimate defense as long as it has not received sufficient assurance from the Security Council as to the realization of its objectives.

Return to the Territorial Status before Aggression

The inviolability of national territory, no doubt, is as much a cardinal principle in international relations as the political independence of states. For this reason, the principle has been a point of departure for a series of proposals to define aggression.[8] In the definition accepted by the General Assembly, "invasion or attack against the territory of a state by the armed forces of another state" is sufficient reason for such an act to be considered one of aggression.[9] Moreover, the violation of borders and subsequent occupation of Iran's territory, in our judgment, is a basic element in qualifying Iraq's attack as an act of aggression. Therefore, the spontaneous and immediate reaction of Iranian forces was a legitimate defense. Iran repulsed the aggressor to the international boundaries as established by the Treaty of International Boundaries and Good Neighborliness between Iran and Iraq signed on June 13, 1975, in Baghdad, especially the Protocol Concerning the Delimitation of the River Frontier between Iran and Iraq.[10] As long as there is ambiguity in the position of Iraq and the Security Council with respect to the borders of the two countries, Iran can continue with its actions until it achieves its rights.

On September 17, 1980, Iraq unilaterally abrogated the treaty and its protocols. On October 26, 1982, Iraq announced that it accepted the border lines as defined in the joint communiqué of March 6, 1975, generally known as Algiers Communiqué.[11] In my view, this position does not at all signify the recognition of the redemarcation of the border lines resulting from the protocol concerning state land frontiers annexed to the 1975 treaty. According to the first paragraph of the joint communiqué, Iran and Iraq undertook to engage in "a process of definitive demarcation of their frontiers on the basis of the Constantinople Protocol of 1913 and the 1914 Procès-Verbaux of the Commission on the Delimitation of Frontiers."

It is clear that at an opportune time Iraq intended to renegotiate the definitive redemarcation of its land borders with Iran and refused to recognize the lines resulting from the protocol annexed to the 1975 treaty. Iraq's actions from the first day the treaty came into force proved the accuracy of this claim. In fact, after the definitive redemarcation of land borders by the mixed committee of Iran, Iraq, and Algeria,[12] Iraq questioned the accuracy of twenty-one border marks.[13] Iran invoked the principle of the inviolability of borders resulting from Article 5 of the 1975 treaty and opposed new demarcation of borders.[14] In any case, parts of Iranian territory remained under the control of Iraqi forces, as was the case for the regions of Talae, Nossoud, and oil-rich Naft Shahr. The military occupation of a state's territory by force constitutes aggression, comparable to a violation of its borders; thus Iraq's refusal to evacuate such territory was by itself, an adequate legal basis for pursuing legitimate defense.[15]

Under these circumstances, the Security Council's numerous calls on the two belligerents to withdraw their forces to the internationally recognized boundaries[16] cannot be considered a sufficient guarantee for Iran. Instead, the Security Council should have explicitly referred to the 1975 treaty and redemarcation of frontiers between Iran and Iraq resulting from the protocol concerning redemarcation. Such a reference would have ended all possibilities of contesting border lines during withdrawal subsequent to a cease-fire.

It is appropriate to ask what happened to the public and private property located in territories where their national ownership changed after borders in the Zainal Qaws and Maimak regions were redemarcated. The parties assigned the settlement of this question to a mixed commission to resolve the matter by compensation, repurchase, or any other appropriate formula.[17] Iraq demanded that the commission also be charged with investigating the question concerning the accuracy of certain border posts. Iran's refusal caused Iraq to abandon the commission, leaving its work unfinished. A few days before the start of the war, Iraq used Iran's refusal to return territories that belonged to it in accordance with the 1975 treaty as an excuse to resort to force and occupy Zayn al-Qaws and Maimak. Taking all of these conditions into account, some emphasized that the return to territorial states existing previously meant that Iraqi forces had to withdraw from these territories so that the mixed commission could carry out its assigned duties under more favorable conditions.

Removing the Danger of New Aggression

It is generally accepted that as soon as a state becomes the victim of aggression, legitimate defense may be pursued in the aggressor's territory and continued until the aggressor's war machinery is destroyed and responsible parties are punished. The question of pursuit of legitimate defense in the territory of the aggressor was raised after World War II. The proponents of this doctrine referred to the concept of legitimate defense in order to justify military operations by the Allied forces until unconditional surrender of the aggressor Nazi state.

It has been stressed that "in case of a premeditated aggression, the legitimate defense may be prolonged, even if the aggressor is forced to retreat beyond the boundaries of the occupied state, and under certain exceptional conditions until total annihilation of the armed forces of the aggressor state,"[18] leading to an "imposition of a peace treaty."[19] It is apparent that within the framework of the United Nations, which is indisputably an effort for tentative centralization of force, legitimate defense may continue as long as the Security Council fails to take effective measures to suppress aggression and restore peace and international security, and the victimized state is the sole judge for the efficacy of these measures.[20]

I contend that the means used by Iran were necessary and adequate to remove the danger of further aggression by Iraq.[21] The repeated use of chemical weapons and bombardment of residential areas by Iraq proved that its aggressive capacity had not diminished. Therefore, Iran pursued military operations inside Iraq to secure its rights. It is interesting to note that in order to justify its aggression, Iraq had claimed that its armed forces wanted to inflict heavy damages on Iran in order to force Iran to guarantee Iraqi rights to resolve differences in a definitive and permanent manner.[22]

Punishment of Individuals Responsible for Aggression

The protocol concerning pacific settlement of international disputes that was unanimously approved by the League of Nations in 1924 qualified a war of aggression as an infraction of solidarity and an international crime.[23] On many occasions thereafter, the international community,[24] within the framework of the General Assembly resolution on the definition of aggression, underlined its intention to consider any kind of war of aggression a crime and to designate it "a crime against international peace."[25] According to the Commission of International Law "a state crime means failure to recognize the obligations that the entire international community considers essential for safeguarding fundamental interests."[26] In this regard, the commission declares that "aggression is a violation of peace or threat to peace and represents a fundamental violation of law and an international crime."[27] Precisely for this reason, the charter of the United Nations (Chapter VII) provides for measures not involving the use of force against a state that has launched a war of aggression.

Under these conditions, if there is inaction or weakness on the part of the Security Council, the measures taken by the victim of aggression may have punitive objectives as the victim exercises its right of legitimate defense. Because the crime against peace and international security is generally attributable to state authorities who have waged a war of aggression, Iran had the right to invoke penal responsibility on the Iraqi authorities and to express clearly its intention for their punishment.[28] To this end, the pursuance of military operations by Iran, while expecting the international community to impose necessary measures, constituted a guarantee. This position was also valid with respect to the civil and penal responsibility of Iraq until it acquitted itself from the obligation for the payment of war damages.

The right of legitimate defense, as provided in the United Nations Charter, demonstrated that the confidence of the redactors of the text was limited as to the efficacy of the collective security system. The future, unfortunately, showed that they were right. The tension between the East and the West, and the conflicts in the Third World that made the colonial powers oppose each other, inflicted the final blow on the system of collective security. This clear defeat caused states to interpret the right of legitimate defense in light of the new circumstances and increasingly extensive interpretation of Article 51 of the UN Charter. I believe this attitude will only increase the tendency of states to resort to confrontation, force, and even war in order to satisfy their perceived vital interests, claims, and aspirations.[29] Thus, Iraq used the concept of legitimate defense for the purpose of "camouflaging the aggression" against Iran.[30]

Notes

1. Letter of the Iraqi minister of foreign affairs to the United Nations secretary-general, dated October 24, 1980 (S/14236).

2. Tareq Aziz, *Iraq-Iran Conflict, Questions and Discussions* (London: Third World Center for Research and Publishing, 1981), 28–29; President Saddam Hussein's address to the chiefs of state at the Third Summit Conference of Islamic states, January 25–28, 1981.

3. Statement of the Iraqi representative, S. Hammadi, to the United Nations secretary-general on October 15, 1980 (S/PV 22.50).

4. N. Mosaffa, M. Taramsari, A. Alem, B. Mostaghimi, (under the supervision of D. Momtaz), *Iraq's Aggression against Iran and the United Nations' Positions* (Tehran: Center for International Studies, 1987).

5. Statement of the representative of the Islamic Republic of Iran, S. Ardakani, to the Security Council on October 23, 1980 (S/PV 22.52).

6. See e.g., Security Council Resolution 479, September 28, 1980.

7. See Security Council Resolutions 522 (October 4, 1982), 582 (February 24, 1986), and 598 (July 20, 1987).

8. Hans Wemberg, *L'interdiction du recours a la force, le principe et les problemes qui se posent*, vol. 78 (La Haye: Recueil des Cours de Académie, 1951), 75.

9. Mosaffa et al., *Iraq's Aggression*, 59–60.

10. For the text of the treaty and protocol, see *A Review of the Imposed War by the Iraqi Regime upon the Islamic Republic of Iran* (Tehran: Legal Department of the Ministry of Foreign Affairs of Iran, February 1983).

11. The Iraqi News Agency, quoted in *Le Monde*, October 28, 1982.

12. Article 1 of the annex to the 1975 treaty.

13. Note no. 820/2/5 of May 27, 1978, of the embassies of Iraq and Iran.

14. Note no. 3472/18 of June 7, 1978, of the Iranian Ministry of Foreign Affairs.

15. Hubert Thierry et al., *Droit International Public* (Paris: Montchestien, 1975), 561; Article 3 (paragraph a) of the General Assembly Annex to Resolution 3314 on the definition of aggression.

16. Security Council Resolutions 522, 582, and 598.

17. Article 4 of the Protocol Defining Territorial Boundaries.

18. Jaroslav Zourek, "La notion de legitime défense en droit international," *Annuaire de l'Institut du Droit International*, Vol. 56 (1975), 50.

19. Joseph L. Kunz, "Individual and Collective Self-Defense in Article 51 of the Charter of the United Nations," *American Journal of International Law* 41 (1947): 876.

20. Zourek, "Legitime défense," 51.

21. Roger Pinto, *Le Droit des Relations Internationales* (Paris: Payot, 1972), 264.

22. Letter of the Iraqi foreign minister to the Security Council of the United Nations, October 24, 1980 (S/14236).

23. S. Calogeropoulos-Stratis, "Le recours à la force dans la société internationale," *Librairie Générale de Droit et de Jurispurdence* (Paris and Lausanne: Loisirs et Pedagogie, 1986), 46–47.

24. See League of Nations, Resolution 27 (September 1927), Nuremberg Declaration on Relations and Cooperation between States in Accordance with the United Nations Charter and General Assembly Resolution 2625, dated October 24, 1970.

25. Article 5 (2) of the annex to General Assembly Resolution 3314.

26. Article 19 of the International Law Commission proposal on the state responsibility. See the *Annals of ILC* 1 (1976): 56.

27. Ibid., 58.

28. Jacques Dehaussy, "Travaux de la Commission du Droit International," *Annuaire Français du Droit International*, ed. Centre National de la Recherche Scientifique (CNRS) (1985), 612. See recent work of the ILC on the responsibility of states.

29. Report of the Security Council of the United Nations to the 37th Session of the General Assembly.

30. Observations of Charles Chaumont in response to the report and questionnaire of Jaroslav Zourek, dated August 1, 1972, in *Annuaire de L'Institut du Droit International* 56 (1975): 76.

14

The Problem of Retaliation in Modern Warfare from the Point of View of Fiqh

HAMID ALGAR

Although Islam realistically treats warfare as a permanently recurring feature of human existence, it regards war as an exceptional and intrinsically undesirable state. The rank of the *ghazi* and still more that of the martyr are honorable ones, but the honor derives from the purpose to which the fighting is devoted—the elevation of God's word and the removal of injustice and disorder[1]—not from the act of fighting itself. As jurists have expressed it, war is intrinsically a type of *fasad*, a disturbance of the natural order, and it acquires its acceptability from factors extrinsic to itself; it is "good because of the goodness of other than itself" (*hasan ala husni ghayrihi*). Put differently, war is the attempt to repel a greater evil by means of a lesser one. As the Qur'an (2:191) says, gross disorder and corruption are worse than fighting (*al-fitnatu ashaddu min al-qatl*).

Given this concept of legitimate warfare in Islam, it follows that methods of fighting must be adopted that are consonant with its purpose and that wanton destruction and killing are to be avoided. Although the Prophet of Islam described himself as simultaneously the Prophet of Mercy and the Prophet of Battle,[2] the former attribute clearly has priority over the latter; mercy must therefore both limit and underlie the conduct of war. Earlier prophets had in some cases called for the annihilation of their enemies,[3] but the Prophet Muhammad, in view of the particular nature of his mission, adopted a more discriminating mode of war against the rejecters of revelation. According to a tradition found in both Shi'a and Sunni collections, he would issue the following instructions to the leaders of military expeditions: "Fight in the name of God and in the path of God, and in accordance with the religion of the Messenger of God. Do not cheat, do not break trust, do not mutilate. Do not cut trees unless compelled to do so, and do not kill enfeebled old people, children and women."[4]

The Qur'anic injunction, "Fight against the leaders of unbelief" (9:12), is obviously not to be considered in a restrictive sense. Taken together with the tradition just quoted, it suggests that the Muslim combatant should aim exclusively at destroying the organized existence of *Kufr*, not at eliminating indiscriminately all those under its sway. The military ethics of the Prophet were given further expression by Abu Bakr when he gave instructions to Usama on the eve of his campaign against Palestine. In addition to the prohibitions enunciated by the Prophet, Abu Bakr forbade the slaughter of animals, except for food, and the molestation of hermits and recluses.[5] Similar instructions were given to the Muslim forces by Commander of the Faithful 'Ali b. Abi Talib.[6]

In accordance with all these precedents, the different schools of Islamic law have sought to confine the losses and hardships of war to the actual combatants, explicitly protecting not only children, women, the aged and infirm, and religious recluses, but also merchants, traders, and peasants uninvolved in the fighting, as well as neutrals living in the zone of combat.[7] Even in classical times, however, it was not always possible to maintain rigorously the distinction between combatants and noncombatants and to protect the latter from harm. The Prophet himself engaged in and permitted others to engage in night attacks, even though such attacks might result in death or injury to noncombatants.[8]

The Ja'fari *faqih* (jurist) ash-Shahid al-Awwal, however, regards night attacks as *makruh* (undesirable), citing as an additional reason that "it is at night that the gates of heaven are opened and patience and mercy descend."[9] It is possible, nevertheless, that noncombatants might engage in battle or contribute substantially to the fight against the Muslims and thereby forfeit the inviolability to which they would otherwise be entitled. Thus, at the Battle of Hunayn, the Prophet permitted the killing of Durayd ibn as-Simma, a centenarian who had advised the enemy on strategy.[10] Some scholars, notably those of the Hanafi school, therefore conclude that all those potentially capable of fighting (i.e., able-bodied men) may be killed whether or not they are fighting, and all those potentially incapable of fighting must not be killed unless they actually fight or substantially contribute to the fighting.[11]

Another circumstance in which the unintended killing of noncombatants and other protected categories may excusably take place consists of attacks on the enemy from a distance at which combatants cannot be fully distinguished from noncombatants. The justifying precedent for such cases is provided by the siege of Ta'if in the eighth year after the Hijra, when the Prophet permitted the use of the *manjaniq* (mangonel) against the city.[12] Clearly, it is impossible to tell precisely where the missile cast by a *manjaniq* will fall or who will be killed and injured by it.

A further problematic situation discussed in the *fiqh* (jurisprudence) provisions on warfare is the enemy's use of a human shield (*turs*) of noncombatants or, in some cases, of Muslim prisoners or civilians. The principal Hanafi authority on matters of war and peace, Muhammad ash-Shaybani, regards it as permissible to attack an enemy protected by a human shield but stipulates that as much care as possible should be taken to avoid hitting the unfortunate persons placed in front of the enemy. If such care is taken, neither the individual Muslim soldier nor the Muslim state is liable to pay compensation for the death of a Muslim forming part of the enemy *turs*.[13] Ghazali, representing the viewpoint of Shafi'i *fiqh*, concurs. He cites the principle of *istislah*, i.e., the securing of an important interest of the Muslim community through the sacrifice of a lesser interest, in this case the lives of those making up the human shield.[14] Ash-Shahid al-Awwal agrees that attacking an enemy protected by a *turs* is permissible but specifies that the *bayt al-mal* should pay compensation to the heirs of Muslims unintentionally killed under such circumstances.[15] Among the classical *fuqaha*, only al-Awza'i regards it as impermissible to fire on a *turs* including Muslims. He cites in support of his view the Qur'an (48:25): "Were it not for believing men and believing women unknown to you whom you might have trampled and on whose account a crime would have accrued to you without your knowledge." This verse was revealed in explanation of the delay in the conquest of Mecca.[16]

All these cases in which otherwise protected persons may legitimately and excusably come under attack arise from the inevitable complexities and confusion of war. A different set of problems arises when the enemy, flouting or not recognizing any form of ethical restraint in warfare, deliberately attacks the noncombatant population of the Islamic state, choosing it as a primary target. Is it then permissible for the Muslims to retaliate in kind? To the best of my knowledge, there is no discussion of this problem in the classical sources of *fiqh*, in large part, no doubt, because mass attacks on civilian populations have been a direct outcome of modern developments in military technology. The contemporary Indian scholar, Muhammad Hamidullah, completely rules out retaliation under such circumstances because it would fail to punish the instigator or agent of the attacks on Muslim civilians and instead bring harm to those uninvolved in the war or only marginally involved in it. In support of this view he cites the phrase "No soul shall bear the burden of another" (*la taziru waziratun wizra ukhra*), which occurs five times in the Qur'an.[17] It may be objected that the context in which this phrase occurs is always that of man's individual accountability before God, not that of dealings among men. However, it is indubitably a principle of Islamic justice that one person should not be made to suffer for the misdeeds of another. The principle of *qisas* (retaliation for killing or the infliction of bodily harm) operates precisely on the basis of individual, not collective, responsibility.

It is said that the Prophet once permitted the mutilation of the enemy dead by way of retaliation against the *mushrikin* for their mutilation of the Muslim dead.[18] This cannot be taken, however, as a general justifying precedent for permitting otherwise forbidden acts on a retaliatory basis. The particular act concerned the bodies of dead combatants, not the persons of living noncombatants. Islamic law recognizes the possibility of an agreed exchange of hostages with the non-Muslim enemy, but even if the Muslim hostages are killed by the enemy, the enemy hostages held by the Muslims cannot be killed in retaliation. A clear and succinct statement by Imam Ja'far as-Sadiq instructs that "envoys and hostages are not to be killed,"[19] a strong suggestion that noncombatants as a class are not to be subjected deliberately to harm by way of retaliation.

In modern warfare, however, the use of certain weaponry, i.e., long-range missiles, bombs, poisonous gases, napalm, etc., predictably results in mass death for the civilian population. If the Muslim state renounces all recourse to such weapons, it may be placing itself at a permanent disadvantage vis-à-vis the enemy. It finds itself confronted with an ethical dilemma: whether to resort to the same methods as the enemy and thereby infringe established restrictions, or to expose its own population to unanswered assaults by the enemy. Inasmuch as this is a qualitatively new problem, only vaguely analogous situations are discussed in traditional *fiqh*. Both Hanafi and Ja'fari *fiqh* regard it as permissible to unleash at the enemy arrows and lances, the tips of which had been dipped in poison, while Malikis considered this either *haram* or *makruh*.[20]

Attacking the enemy with flame-bearing projectiles seems to have been deemed generally permissible.[21] Smoking out an enemy from a subterranean retreat (a process known as *tadkhin*) was regarded as permissible by Hanafi *fiqh* but only as a last resort.[22] The military or pseudomilitary use of poison gas appears to be an innovation of the twentieth century. However, a manuscript by an anonymous Hanafi *faqih* of unknown date suggests that it is permissible to use poisonous gas against military targets; he speaks of "foul, deadly odors (*ar-rawa'ih al-muntina al-qatila*) for the destruction of citadels."[23]

"Total warfare" is no doubt a relatively recent phenomenon, involving the indiscriminate devastation of the enemy's territory and the slaughter of its population. But even in earlier times it was not possible to restrict fighting to the primary military target, often identified in the literature of *fiqh* as citadels (*husun*). Shafi'i *fiqh* thus stresses that when attacking a city, the Muslim army should concentrate its attacks on the citadel. If the fighting spills over into residential areas, it is permissible for the Muslims to fight on while seeking to minimize harm to the noncombatant population.[24]

By general agreement, the flooding and burning of citadels (and, by analogy, ships) is permitted even if the resulting destruction cannot be restricted to the primary target and results in the death of noncombatants.[25] Again, denying the enemy its water supply or making it unusable by poisoning or pollution obviously affects the entire population of a given area, not just the combatants. It is nonetheless permitted, although designated as *makruh* in Ja'fari *fiqh*.[26] However, none of these cases is strictly comparable to the situation that arises when the enemy of the Muslim state resorts to mass destruction and refuses to desist unless answered in kind.

Another factor relating to retaliation and not considered in traditional *fiqh* (except tangentially, perhaps, under the heading of *baghy* [rebellion against legitimate rule]) is the existence of a nominally Muslim regime, ruling over Muslims, that attacks an Islamic state. Are the rulings concerning warfare against non-Muslim enemies applicable to this situation, or does the desire to liberate Muslims ruled by the Islamic pretender impose certain special criteria?

The questions raised here do not exhaust the range of problems associated with warfare in the present age that call for regulation through an expansion and reworking of *fiqh*. There is the grave problem of nuclear weapons: may the Islamic state acquire, construct, deploy, and make use of them? As a nonspecialist in the area, I can only call attention to the urgent need for a contemporary Islamic code of military ethics. This need is second only to the acquisition by the Muslims of an autonomous defensive capacity. The Islamic Republic of Iran, with its proud record of resistance to aggression, remains a principal focus of hope with respect to both needs.

Notes

1. See the Qur'an, 2:193, 4:75, and 22:39–40.
2. Reported in the *sunan* of at-Tirmidhi (*sunan* is the name of a collection of traditions of the Prophet).
3. See the prayer of Noah, in the Qur'an (71:26): "And Noah said: 'O my Lord! Leave not of the unbelievers a single one on earth.' "
4. Text in Sahih Muslim, and, with slight variations in wording, in Muhammad Jawad Maghniya, *Fiqh al-Imam Ja'far as-Sadiq* (Qum: n.p., n.d.), 2:272.
5. Tabari, *Tarikh* (Leiden), 1882–85, 3:160.
6. Maghniya, *Fiqh al-Imam*, 272–73.
7. The provisions of Sunni *fiqh* are summarized by Muhammad Hamidullah in *The Muslim Conduct of State*, 7th ed. (Lahore: n.p., 1977), 205–7. For Ja'fari

fiqh, see ash-Shahid at-Thani, *al-Lum'at ad-Dimishqiya* (Qum: n.p., 1387/1967), 2:386–88. It may be worth noting that the great Hanafi *faqih* Muhammad ash-Shaybani regarded the inviolability of monks as conditional on their absolute seclusion from the surrounding community (see Muhammad b. Ahmad as-Sarakhsi, *Sharh Kitab as-siyar al-Kabir*, vol. 4, ed. Abd al-'Aziz Ahmad [Cairo: n.p., 1971], 1436), and that of peasants as recommended, but not obligatory (ibid., 1443).

8. Ibid., 1468.

9. *ash-Shahid at-Thani*, 394.

10. Ibn Hisham, *Sira*, ed. Mustafa as-Saqqa et al. (Cairo: n.p., n.d.), 2:453. See also ash-Shahid at-Thani, 393.

11. as-Sarakhsi, *Sharh*, 1429; al-Kasani, *Bada'i' as'Sana'i'* (Cairo: n.p., n.d.), 7:101.

12. Ibn Hisham, *Sira*, 483.

13. as-Sarakhsi, *Sharh*, 1429; al-Kasani, *Bada'i'*, 1447, 1474.

14. al-Ghazali, *al-Mustasfa fi'l-Fiqh* (Cairo: n.p., n.d.), 1:141.

15. ash-Shahid at-Thani, 2:393–94.

16. Quoted in Majid Khadduri, *War and Peace in the Law of Islam* (Baltimore: n.p., 1955), 106.

17. Hamidullah, *Muslim Conduct of State*, 208.

18. al-Waqidi, *Kitab al-maghazi* (Calcutta: n.p., 1956), 284.

19. Maghniya, *Fiqh al-Imam*, 272.

20. as-Sarakhsi, *Sharh*, 1475; ash-Shahid at-Thani, 392; Abu'Abdillah Muhammad al-Hattab, *Mawahib al-Jalil li Sharh Mukhtasar Khalil* (Tripoli: n.p., n.d.), 3:352.

21. as-Sarakhsi, *Sharh*, 1469. Killing the enemy with the thrust of a sword or a lance is preferable, however.

22. Ibid., 1472–73.

23. Quoted in Hamidullah, *Muslim Conduct of State*, 226.

24. Khadduri, *War and Peace*, 107.

25. as-Sarakhsi, *Sharh*, 1467; ash-Shahid at-Thani, 393.

26. ash-Shahid at-Thani, 393.

15

Morale vs. Technology: The Power of Iran in the Persian Gulf War

JAMES A. BILL

I prefer a thousand strokes of the sword to dying in bed—Imam Ali

Fighting an invading Iraqi army in a lonely battle, Iran's tenacious and courageous performance in the Persian Gulf war of the 1980s confounded many outside observers and analysts. Iraq enjoyed the support of both superpowers. It had access to expensive modern military matériel supplied primarily by the Soviet Union and France. It was provided with huge financial resources from the plentiful reserves of neighboring oil-rich countries such as Saudi Arabia and Kuwait. And it received technical assistance from some Arab states, such as Egypt, Jordan, and Morocco. In addition to these factors, the Iraqi invasion caught Iran by surprise, and throughout the conflict the Islamic Republic was confronted with the difficult task of institutionalizing a revolution. For these reasons and others, many analysts predicted an easy and early Iraqi victory.

Yet Iraq was unable to defeat Iran, and it took ninty-five months before Iran would even agree to a cease-fire. Between 1982 and 1987, Iranian forces took the offensive in the war. They drove the Iraqi invaders out of most Iranian territory while carrying out counterattacks that resulted in Iranian occupation of limited but significant sections of Iraqi soil. Although Iraqi counterattacks in 1988 resulted in that country's recapture of most of the territory it had lost earlier, it is significant that it took the Iraqis eight long, hard years to drive Iran to a cease-fire. The massive Iraqi campaign of unprecedented missile and air attacks on both military and civilian targets and extensive use of chemical agents and poisonous gases in the spring of 1988 finally convinced Iranian leaders that the military option had to give way to diplomacy. I shall seek to analyze the reasons for Iran's success in defending itself for so long against the overwhelming firepower and military capacity of the Iraqis.

The Persian Gulf War Summarized

On September 22, 1980, Iraqi troops invaded Iran along a 400-mile front, while Iraqi aircraft carried out strikes against a dozen Iranian airfields. When the Iraqis struck, Iran was already an embattled country and its revolution was seriously threatened by both internal and external forces. The economy was unsteady and fragile; significant elements among Kurdish tribesmen were in revolt in the northwest; and counter-revolutionary forces were committing punishing acts of terrorism and sabotage in Tehran and elsewhere. At the same time, the United States and its allies in the international arena were applying strong pressures on the government because of Iran's detention of American hostages.

Although there had been skirmishes along the border and both sides had been engaging in provocative radio broadcasts beamed into one another's country, there is little doubt that Iraq invaded Iran and was by any standard of international law the aggressor. Much has been made of the tensions over the Shatt al-Arab (Arvand) waterway, the religious disagreements between Sunni and Shi'a regimes, and longtime Persian-Arab ethnic differences, but the real cause of the war was Iraq's ambition to gain hegemony in the Persian Gulf. Saddam Hussein's regime sought political domination of the region. A second but related goal of the invasion and one of special interest to the traditional governments in the region was to destroy the Iranian revolution, which was viewed as a disruptive threat to the political status quo in these countries.

Despite the surprise attack, Iran responded quickly and poured reinforcements into the southwest, where badly outnumbered and ill-equipped soldiers, police, and citizens were fighting a desperate war of defense. After a month of brutal hand-to-hand fighting and very heavy casualties, the city of Khorramshahr fell to the invaders. This was the only major Iranian city to fall to the Iraqis, and in May 1982 it was retaken by Iranian forces. After mobilizing and consolidating their forces and slowing down the invasion, the Iranians counterattacked in the fall of 1981 and spring of 1982. In two major battles fought in the area of Dezful in March and April 1982 and in Khorramshahr in April and May 1982, the Iranian troops won important victories, driving the Iraqis off most Iranian soil.[1]

Between 1983 and 1988, Iran attempted to take the offensive, seeking to drive through to Iraqi soil and hoping for a breakthrough that would destroy the regime of Saddam Hussein in Baghdad. Although mass attacks on fixed positions were only moderately successful, Iran did take the oil-rich Majnun Islands in February 1984 and the southern port city of Fao in February 1986. In January 1987, Iran narrowly missed breaking through to Basra. Notwithstanding these dramatic offensives, Iran settled down to probing, pushing, and pressuring the Iraqi lines.

Iraq, in turn, pursued a two-pronged strategy. First, it sought to break Iran's spirit and capacity to resist through massive missile, air, and gas attacks on both military and civilian targets. Major examples of this multifaceted tactic occurred in the spring of 1985 and again in the spring of 1988. In February and March 1985, Iraq threw all its might at Iran. This "war of the cities" involved Iraqi air attacks on forty Iranian cities, SCUD and FROG missile attacks on populated centers in western Iran, chemical and gas attacks in selected areas along the front, increased strikes against Kharg Island, attacks on Persian Gulf shipping, and a declaration that the air over Iran was to be treated as a war zone and that Iraqi war planes reserved the right to shoot down any aircraft in this airspace. These moves failed badly as the Iranian people responded to the punishment by rallying around their leaders and increasing their determination to fight the invaders to the bitter end.

In 1988, the Iraqis resuscitated their strategy of "war on the cities" and, escalating it dramatically, unleashed 160 Soviet-supplied SCUD-B missiles, outfitted with booster rockets, directly into Tehran. At the same time, they increased their air attacks and resorted to the devastating use of poisonous chemical gases on the northwestern Kurdish front, killing thousands of Kurdish civilians. This new escalation was accompanied by international pressures on Iran, including a large number of U.S. warships in the Persian Gulf itself. American clashes with the Iranian navy added a new dimension to the Iraqi war effort and brought Iran and America to the brink of serious international conflict.

This was all part of the second Iraqi tactic, to internationalize the war. Saddam Hussein had consistently sought to draw foreign superpowers, especially the United States, into the war. By 1988 he had partially succeeded in accomplishing this goal. The 1988 "war of the cities" was a larger, more devastating version of 1985 and caused more pain and suffering. It did not, however, fundamentally alter Iran's position about the war. After hundreds of thousands of deaths and casualties, Iran steadfastly refused to admit defeat.

Iran indicated its willingness to consider a cease-fire only if the international community set up a mechanism whereby Iraq would be declared the aggressor. After nearly eight years of conflict and casualties, Iran's leadership felt that to agree to anything less would be to sell out its own people. United Nations Resolution 598, passed in July 1988, held some hope that this could be done but emphasized that the cease-fire must take place before guilt for beginning the war could be ascertained. Iran eventually accepted this position even though it had little reason for confidence in the UN. Where had the United Nations been in September 1980 when Iran had been attacked and its territory occupied by Iraq? In fact, only two Security Council resolutions had been passed before Iran began to turn the war around, and neither had assessed blame for the war nor demanded that Iraq retreat to its prewar boundaries. It was, in fact, not until December 9, 1991, that the UN, in a report by the secretary-general to the Security Council, finally and formally declared Iraq the aggressor.

The Objective and Subjective Dimensions of Iranian Power

From the onset of the gulf war in 1980, Iraq enjoyed a massive superiority over Iran in military equipment, matériel, technology, and sophisticated intelligence-gathering techniques. Through the attrition of warfare, the unbalanced nature of this equation tilted even further in the Iraqi direction. By 1988, Iraq had great superiority in such important tools of war as aircraft, missiles, battle tanks, and heavy artillery. Furthermore, Iran was much more isolated in the international community than was Iraq. Most daunting to the Iranian position was the ironic fact that both superpowers, the Soviet Union and the United States, in varying degrees, supported Iraq in the war. The Soviets maintained an especially close relationship with the Iraqis, providing them with an estimated 60 percent of their military equipment. Besides aircraft such as the MIG 21, MIG 23, and the MIG 29, the Soviets sold Iraq thousands of devastating SCUD and FROG surface-to-surface missiles. Soviet advisors worked with Iraqi military officials on a regular basis. The Soviet Union was the major external power that stood behind the Iraqis.

Although the United States officially declared neutrality concerning the war, it tilted noticeably toward Iraq. In 1982, the United States removed Iraq from its list of countries considered supportive of international terrorism. High-level U.S. officials began to visit Baghdad in late 1983, and the United States subsequently extended Iraq approximately $2 billion in commodity credits. Beginning in 1984, it became widely known that Iraq was benefiting from intelligence supplied through American sources. Saddam Hussein himself flatly stated in May 1984 that Iraq had the use of intelligence provided by AWACS flown by American pilots based in Saudi Arabia. On November 26, 1984, the United States publicly restored diplomatic relations with Iraq. When Iraqi-fired Exocet missiles struck the frigate USS *Stark* on May 17, 1987, killing thirty-seven American sailors, the Reagan administration quickly accepted the official Iraqi statement that the attack was inadvertent. President Reagan afterwards stated curiously that "Iran is the real villain in the piece," and his administration issued a series of sharp warnings to Iran. Finally in 1988, American warships clashed with the Iranian navy, seriously crippling that nation's naval forces.

Yet, despite the superiority of the Iraqi military arsenal and the varying support of both world superpowers, Iraq was unable to win a clear-cut military victory over Iran. This was because of the power position of the Islamic Republic of Iran. The position can be analyzed from two perspectives, the objective bases of power and the subjective bases of power.

Although Iraq maintained a decided edge along the objective dimensions of power because of its deeper arsenal of weapons and matériel and its more varied and extensive access to financial resources, Iran was not without objective strengths of its own. The most significant of these was Iran's population of over 50 million, a population more than three times that of Iraq. In fact, Iran had a population twice that of all the other Persian Gulf states combined. In addition, Iran had one of the highest birth rates in the world. Between 1978 and 1988, its population increased from 38 million to over 50 million people, an increase of 12 million, more than half the size of the entire population of Iraq. Every year of the war 422,000 male Iranians reached the conscription age of eighteen; in Iraq the figure was 161,000.[2] Human resources are at least as important as material/technological resources in warfare, and in this regard Iran was clearly superior.

During the war, the various Iranian armed forces acquired a great deal of costly on-the-job training. Despite inevitable mistakes and tactical errors, the quality of the Iranian military improved with time. Both the Revolutionary Guards (*Sepah-i Pasdaran*) and the regular army steadily acquired important traits of professionalism and competence. Furthermore, the Iranian military had "gone a long way in shedding its former negative image among broad sections of the population. It has gradually acquired increased legitimacy as a genuine national institution in the public eye."[3] In Iran, the military forces were an integral part of the population and reflected the intelligence and skills of the Iranians. This improvement in manpower and professionalism helped ameliorate the overwhelming Iraqi edge in the actual tools and weapons of modern warfare.

One further objective basis of national power was Iran's geographic position. It was one-third larger than Iraq, and its capital city, Tehran, was situated much further from the military front than was Baghdad, the capital of Iraq. If necessary, Iranian forces could retreat indefinitely into the vast expanses of its northeastern province of Khorasan. Superior Iraqi military technology could compensate only partially for this natural reality. Despite these facts of population size, professionalism, and geography, Iran required something more in order to explain its dogged resistance and relative success in repulsing and confronting an invading neighbor supported by the most powerful nations in the world. This added factor involves the subjective dimensions of power.

The Power of Morale and the Principles of Jihad and *Shahadat*

The Iranian fighting forces exhibited a dedication and commitment to their task that enabled Iran to overcome many of Iraq's material and technological advantages. In struggling to defend their country, their religion, their leader, and their revolution, the Iranian people repeatedly indicated their willingness to make the ultimate sacrifice, to die if necessary. In this cultural context, dying power can at times be more potent a force than killing power. In the words of Hojjat ol-Islam Seyyid Ali Khamene'i when addressing the UN General Assembly in September 1987, this is the doctrine of "blood overcoming the sword."

The essence of the high morale that infused the Iranian war effort is contained in the words *jihad* and *shahadat*. The sacred struggle itself is known as jihad, a word poorly understood in the West but one that is instinctively understood by all practicing Muslims. Jihad (often translated as Holy War), which means a struggle against all evil and oppression, is a powerful force in promoting group solidarity and esprit within the community. In the words of the late Ayatollah Murtaza Mutahhari, jihad is both the "garment of piety" and the "impenetrable armor of God." Mutahhari went on to state: "A Muslim community equipped with the spirit of jihad is not vulnerable to enemy assaults. Jihad is the reliable shield of God. The armor is the defensive covering worn during fighting, but the shield is taken in hand to foil the enemy's strokes and thrusts. A shield is meant to prevent a blow, and armor is meant to neutralize its effect. . . . God will clothe with a garment of humiliation a person who refrains from jihad because he dislikes it. The people who lose the spirit of fighting and resisting the forces of evil are doomed to humiliation, disgrace, bad luck and helplessness . . . . The Muslim community is a community of power and force. Islam is a religion of power."[4]

In the view of the leaders and citizens of the Islamic Republic of Iran, the war against Iraq, a war referred to as the "Imposed War" (*jang-i tahmili*), was indeed a jihad. In one of his better-known lectures, Ayatollah Khomeini stated that "those who fight in jihad, against the external enemy never fear superior numbers, for the Prophet said that he would never turn back even if all the Arabs united against him. His cause was the cause of God, and the cause of God can never be defeated, nor is there any turning back from it."[5] The same clearly applied to an enemy armed with superior weapons and supported by superior external forces. It was within this context of jihad that the Iranian forces fought the Persian Gulf war.

The holy struggle of jihad is closely linked to the concept of shahadat, which is best translated as martyrdom. In the jihad that pits the believing Muslim against the forces of evil, oppression, and aggression, the ultimate weapon is that of the *shahid*, the martyr who dies in defense of a just cause. According to Ayatollah Mutahhari, shahadat is "the death of a person who, in spite of being fully conscious of the risks involved, willingly faces them for the sake of a sacred cause, or, as the Qur'an says, '*fi Sabil Allah*' (in the way of God)."[6] Shahadat has two basic elements: the life is sacrificed for a sacred cause, and the sacrifice is made consciously.[7] According to Ayatollah Mutahhari, "The shahid can be compared to a candle whose job it is to burn out and get extinguished in order to shed light for the benefit of others. The *shuhada* (martyrs) are the candles of society. They burn themselves out and illuminate society. If they do not shed their light, no organization can shine. . . . Had they not shed their light on the darkness of despotism and suppression, humanity would have made no progress."[8]

As one who dies in the cause of God, the shahid has little fear and is completely dedicated to his or her cause. The Islamic belief system, at the center of which lie these concepts of jihad and shahadat, carries enormous consequences for the morale and esprit of the Islamic Republic of Iran. The system inculcates a powerful form of courage and fearlessness that are so critical to success on the field of battle. General George C. Marshall, both a great soldier and an eminent statesman, once stated that "you can have all the matériel in the world, but without morale it is largely ineffective." He also wrote that "it is not enough to fight, it is the spirit which we bring to the fight that decides the issue. It is morale that wins the victory."

Western observers have failed to understand the Iranian dedication to their cause for they often lack knowledge of the political and religious culture of Shi'i Islam. What is in fact a complete commitment and a willingness to sacrifice for the community is viewed in the West as "irrational behavior" or "fanaticism." Furthermore, many external military observers predicted either rapid Iraqi victory or immediate Iranian defeat based on studies that focused exclusively on objective indices that tallied numbers of tanks, planes, missiles, etc. In so doing, they overlooked such critical subjective factors as morale, esprit, and élan. Not all Western observers were so negligent in their analysis. In an unusual article studying the Iran-Iraq war in late 1984, two perceptive American military observers wrote that the Iraqi leaders were learning "one of the primal truths of war: that morale casts a long shadow over all other aspects of fighting power." And they concluded by stating, "Having misplaced their faith in the machinery of war, the Iraqis have rediscovered the truth of the oriental aphorism that the fiercest serpent may be overcome by a swarm of ants."[9]

The powerful thrust of Islamic ideology that built the morale of the Iranian combatants was buttressed by the nation's strong support for the Islamic Republic. The fact that a million and a half Iranians suffered casualties in the war demonstrated that the revolution still maintained a broad base of popular support. The leaders of the Islamic Republic recognized the *mustaza'fin* (oppressed masses) as their major constituency and sought to meet the demands of the masses before all others. It was from the masses that the government recruited the young people who fought and died for the revolution on the western front. In the words of Ayatollah Khomeini, "To which class of society do these heroic fighters of the battlefield belong? Do you find even one person among all of them who is related to persons who have large capital or had some power in the past? If you find one, we will give you a prize.

But you won't."[10] In referring to the credibility and power of the poor, Ayatollah Khomeini stated that "it was Hazrat-i Ali who said that his shoes were more valuable than a position in government."[11] The special Islamic morale that energized revolutionary Iran was closely intertwined with the strong support that the leadership then maintained among the masses of Iranian people.

Iran refused to respond predictably to external pressures and to the physical and economic punishment meted out by the Iraqi military complex. The more pressure that Iraq seemed to apply and the more devastation it delivered, the more the Iranian people rallied in support of their government and its wartime policy. There were exceptions, of course, but both Iraqi "war of the cities" campaigns, for example, generally resulted in increasing Iranian resistance and determination to continue the conflict.

As long as the Islamic Republic of Iran remains a Shi'a state, the foundation of which rests on Islamic principles, it is unlikely that its position on military defense will change without a substantial change in the international environment in which the particular war is fought. Even the disappearance of particular personalities and changes in particular governments within Iran are not likely to alter Iran's basic commitment to defend its interests fiercely.

When Saddam Hussein, swept up by personal ambition and dreams of domination of the Persian Gulf, ordered his military forces to attack Iran in September 1980, he committed a monumental error. Instead of fighting a war, he found himself fighting a revolution fired by religious faith and supported by the Iranian people. The revolution is a fact of life. It will not be destroyed nor will it disappear. Too many Iranians have sacrificed and died to promote it, protect it, and sustain it. The related Islamic principles of jihad and shahadat remain at the center of the belief system that buttresses the new order.

Throughout the 1980s, Iran fought Iraq to a standstill—a lesson that cannot have been lost on other nations that might wish to see the revolution turned back. What military punishment can other nation-states inflict on Iran that Iraq had not already done? It is time for other important nation-states to approach Iran in diplomatic, nonconfrontational ways. Iran's revolution must be recognized and respected and its independence and autonomy honored. Policies based on threats, intimidation, and confrontation are doomed to fail; this is the cardinal lesson of the Iran-Iraq war.

Iran, on the other hand, cannot stand forever in confrontation with the international system of which it is an integral part. The Islamic Republic has proven its impressive capacity to wage jihad against outside aggression and has demonstrated the sacred power of shahadat. It has an obligation to itself to explain its revolution to the outside world better and to signal its own interest in creative diplomacy. It must develop an increased capacity to care for its own people who suffered so greatly in implementing the revolution and in defending their country.

In August 1990, Iran watched as the Iraqi archenemy they had fought for eight years suddenly invaded neighboring Kuwait, initiating an international conflagration that overwhelmed the Persian Gulf. The same countries, including the United States, the Soviet Union, and France, that had solidly backed Saddam Hussein against Iran now turned on their old client. Although Iran stood firmly alongside the American-led international coalition forces that defeated Saddam's military, the leaders of the Islamic Republic realized that, in the end, Iran's survival and independence as a nation-state depended ultimately on its own power, both military and spiritual. This was the major lesson that Iran learned at a terrible cost from the Persian Gulf war of the 1980s.

Notes

1. For elaboration, see William F. Hickman's fine monograph *Ravaged and Reborn: The Iranian Army,* 1982 (Washington, D.C.: The Brookings Institution, 1982). For two unusually valuable analyses of the Iran-Iraq war, see Gholam H. Razi, "The Effectiveness of Resort to Military Force: The Case of Iran and Iraq," *Conflict Quarterly* (Summer 1985): 44–57, and Robert C. Johansen and Michael G. Renner, "Limiting Conflict in the Gulf," *Third World Quarterly* (October 1985): 803–38.

2. These data have been calculated by Dilip Hiro.

3. Nikola B. Schahgaldian, *The Iranian Military under the Islamic Republic* (Santa Monica, Calif.: The Rand Corp., 1987), 36.

4. Murtiza Mutahhari, "Shahid," in *Jihad and Shahadat: Struggle and Martyrdom in Islam,* ed. Mehdi Abedi and Gary Legenhausen (Houston, Tex.: Institute for Research and Islamic Studies, 1986), 131. For Ayatollah Mutahhari's detailed

analysis of Islam and politics more generally, see his *Bakhsh Darbarah-yi Marja'iy-yat va Ruhaniyyat* (Discussions Concerning Supreme Religious Leadership and Islamic Clericalism) (Tehran, 1341/1963).

5. Khomeini, "Lectures on Surat al-Fatiha," in *Islam and Revolution: Writings and Declarations of Iman Khomeini*, trans. Hamid Algar (Berkeley, Calif.: Mizan Press, 1981), 387.

6. Mutahhari, "Shahid," 126.

7. Ibid.

8. Ibid.

9. David Evans and Richard Company, "Military Strategy: The Lessons of Conflict," *Atlantic* (November 1984), 26–34.

10. Quoted in *Tehran Times*, February 10, 1982, p. 6.

11. Ibid.

16

Aggression in Historical Perspective

RICHARD W. BULLIET

In my discussion of aggression in a historical context, I will deal with three kinds of aggression, or understandings of the concept of aggression, all of which are relevant in greater or lesser measure to the war between Iran and Iraq.

The first kind of aggression—*straightforward aggression undertaken for conquest*—we associate mostly with ancient and medieval history. Whether we read an Assyrian inscription from Nineveh, Jovaini's chronicle of the invasion of Genghis Khan, or the story of Nadir Shah's march on Delhi, the historical accounts typically devote little space to justifying the conquest legally or morally. It is the conqueror's heroic greatness that justifies it. In modern times, out-and-out wars of conquest have become so abhorrent to civilized opinion that leaders who engage in such aggression are frequently considered insane. Such was the case with Adolf Hitler, and in the nineteenth century that was the common European judgment of Napoleon. Avoiding the charge of being a madman is one of the reasons that modern leaders usually weave a cloak of legal justification around their attacks.

Ultimately, history and the world will arrive at a judgment concerning the beginning of the war between Iraq and Iran. Many factors will have to be weighed, but at least one will point to the war as an attempt at conquest resulting from personal love of power as great as that of the conquerors of the past. From the earliest hours of the war, the name given to the war in Iraq and in Iraqi literature circulated abroad was

Saddam's Qadisiyya. I have not yet found any parallel to this extraordinary naming of a war for a head of state. Perhaps the best comparison is the ancient Roman practice of conferring on a victorious general an honorary title taken from the name of the country he conquered. Scipio, for example, was called Scipio Africanus after conquering Carthage in Tunisia, but the Romans at least waited until the conquest had been achieved. Vaingloriously taking personal credit for invading a neighboring country, killing its people, and destroying its cities betokens a ruling personality that truly has delusions of grandeur on a par with those of past conquerors.

The second type of aggression—which, too, will ultimately figure into history's judgment of the Iran-Iraq war—we can call *the just war*, and ancient Rome is a reasonable place to examine it. In the early days of the republic, Rome's neighbors worshipped the same pantheon of gods as the Romans did. Wars of aggression were begun in a distinctive manner. The Senate sent a delegation of special priests, called *fetiales*, to the border of the state Rome wished to attack. The priests threw a magical spear into enemy territory and stated in loud voices that the victim state had committed some offense for which it must atone. The atonement was essentially a nonnegotiable demand or ultimatum that the Romans knew the enemy would refuse. It made no difference whether there was anyone on the other side of the border to hear the priests' challenge; they were addressing the gods to make sure that the gods did not think that Rome was attacking unjustly and thus decide to assist the enemy. When the priests returned to Rome, they reported to the Senate that the enemy had refused the ultimatum and that any attack the Senate chose to launch would be considered just in the eyes of the gods.

The importance of the gods in a "just" war carried over into the ceremony held after victory was achieved. In triumph the victorious general led his troops through the city, riding in a chariot and wearing special clothes. His face was painted with red lead like that of the statue of Jupiter on the Capitoline hill. Roman historians also tell us that a slave would run beside the chariot intoning, "Remember, you are not a god. Remember, you are not a god." As Rome grew, it abandoned these religious ceremonies, but Roman leaders continued to rely on legal pretexts for war that would make their aggression seem just in the eyes of the gods and of the people. Some Romans argued that in building their giant empire they never fought any war except in defense.

The later history of diplomacy and warfare among European states was strongly influenced by Roman practices. To make a war seem civilized, it had to appear "just," no matter how flimsy the reason put forward. This was not simply a diplomatic nicety. It continued to carry with it the belief that under certain circumstances the gods, or later the Christian God, would look on aggression against a neighboring state with favor and not exact retribution for the killing that such an attack would precipitate.

From this background arose a concept of aggression that is still powerful today. An attack on a neighbor is only defined as aggression if it lacks a justification, a plausible pretext that can serve to immunize the aggressor from the wrath of the gods and the opprobrium of world opinion. That assumption is the reason for recurring arguments among diplomats, rulers, and historians as to who is to blame for starting a particular war.

In every war one side initiates military action, but the attacker may avoid the label of aggressor if the pretext or provocation for the aggression appears to justify it. Did U.S. sanctions against Japan provoke and therefore justify Japan's attack on the American fleet at Pearl Harbor? Did the Egyptian request for the United Nations force to depart from Sinai, and its subsequent closing of the Strait of Tiran, justify the Israeli attack on Egypt in 1967? Did Iranian behavior and alleged treaty violation along the border with Iraq justify Iraq's attack on Iran in 1980? For the dead American sailors at Pearl Harbor, the dead Egyptian airmen at their bases outside Cairo, or the dead Iranians in Abadan, such questions are pointless, but it is right and proper for such issues to be debated openly. Whenever possible, an international consensus should be reached, because any hope for future world order and world peace depends on the existence of universally recognized moral standards of international behavior. I do not believe that Iraq's assault on Iran will ultimately be judged by world opinion to have been justified, but that final determination will be made only after both sides have had the opportunity to be heard. The sooner the process of naming the aggressor begins, the better.

Both of these types of aggression—straightforward, undisguised conquest and aggression in the name of "justice"—are relevant to the Iran-Iraq war. The first is pertinent because of the indications that Saddam Hussein attacked Iran out of personal megalomania and lust for power and glory. The second is applicable because Iraq's legalistic claims that its attack was justified must be heard and sustained or refuted in the court of world opinion.

The third type of aggression is less well recognized but in this context more profound than the first two. This aggression is carried out to destroy an ideology or a culture that the aggressor considers inferior but dangerous. Aggression of this type is occasionally attested to in early times. When the Romans invaded barbarian Britain, for example, they did not bother with priests and gods and justifications. But in recent centuries this type of aggression has been most commonly associated with European imperialism.

Twentieth-century ideologies of the left and right, communism and capitalism, developed within the political context of European history. Indeed, they developed within the context of that rather small portion of the male population of Europe that was sufficiently literate and politicized in the nineteenth century to operate within the intellectual milieu of politics. Today, most people who write and think about politics use these ideologies of the left and right as touchstones for analyzing and defining political activity everywhere in the world.

It is extraordinary that the political discourse of one small social stratum in one small part of the world has become amplified so that it is heard worldwide and drowns out almost all other sounds. There are obviously many reasons for this peculiar development. One reason that cannot be ignored is the centuries-long support of European imperialist powers for any political movement anywhere in the world that has had an objective of uprooting non-European ideologies. The Spaniards and other European settlers in the New World destroyed the kingdoms, cultures, and religions of the indigenous Indian peoples. The slave traders and slave purchasers of the European colonies wreaked destruction on the indigenous political formations of Africa. European adventurers backed by small bands of soldiers, and what amounted to a political hunting license from one or another European monarch, seized power from local rulers in India, Southeast Asia, and the Pacific islands.

These acts of aggression were not comparable to the exploits of empire builders such as Genghis Khan or Tamerlane. Greed more than pure lust for power and glory was the governing motivation. Nor did the perpetrators of these acts pay much attention to pretexts and justifications. Their foes were non-Christians and, in their eyes, barbarians, so it made little difference whether their kingdoms and cultures survived. A distinctive variation in this pattern of imperialism marked the European relationship with the Islamic Middle East, where direct invasion was limited to North Africa. The Europeans had known the Middle East for centuries. They had known it as a lucrative market and as a source of valuable trade goods, and they had known it as the original home of a religion that was similar to Christianity, but, in their view, dangerously and unacceptably different. The ideal Middle East, in the eyes of the European imperialists, would be economically open and at the same time ideologically powerless or subservient. If this ideal could be achieved without invasion, so much the better.

As it happened, internal political and social developments in the Islamic Middle East had produced, by the eighteenth century, a situation in which governments were comparatively weak and incompetent. At that time, social leadership and personal honor resided more with local religious figures and the pious men of substance who looked up to them than with the soldiers and officials of the government. Under these circumstances, there arose an unspoken collaboration between the imperialist states of Europe, represented by their ambassadors, and the ruling elites of the Middle Eastern states. Both the Europeans and the Middle Eastern rulers wanted to promote economic development and international trade and to reduce or eliminate the role of the Islamic religious leaders.

Between 1800 and 1970 this common goal that Europe, and later America, shared with the Middle Eastern ruling elites overturned the existing relationship between government and religion. In this relationship, established religious figures sanctioned government but also demanded that it abide by legally established norms of conduct. At the same time, government recognized the primacy and importance of religion in guiding the morals and actions of the population, including government servants. The new relationship was marked by an antireligious attitude derived from the anticlericalism of the most extreme moments of the French Revolution. Using various elements of European political ideology as intellectual foundations, but preserving an elite domination by soldiers and pashas inherited from the Mamluks, Ottomans, and Qajars, the new states of the Middle East suppressed religion in political life and destroyed or undermined its legal and educational supports. Today's neo-Mamluk states differ from the old Mamluks most profoundly in their discarding of Islam as a political ideology in favor of the European ideologies of right and left.

It may appear that I have strayed from the topic of aggression, but I do not think so. Although the process has been slow and usually nonviolent, at least in the conventional military sense, the destruction of the Islamically based ideology and society of the Middle East by European imperialism in collaboration with the neo-Mamluk governments of the area constituted an act of aggression. This aggression is of the same order as those spoken of earlier in which, without conscience or justice, European imperialists destroyed various non-European states and cultures around the world.

Currently, the Islamic political movement is the only potent and supranational political ideology in the world that does not have its roots in Europe. As a consequence, non-Muslims have a difficult time understanding it, or rather, seeing past their own stereotypes to observe it well. The same self-centered sense of obvious and unchallengeable superiority that led the earlier imperialists, with no pretext of justification, to destroy the civilizations of Africa, Asia, and the Americas prompted the United States, the Soviet Union, and many European countries to view the Islamic revolution as a danger that must be checked and discredited.

The international community may come to recognize that Saddam Hussein was legally the aggressor in the Iran-Iraq war and condemn the element of megalomania that prompted him to launch his country and Iran into disaster. However, it is unlikely that governments devoted to the political ideologies derived from European history will abandon their aggressive attitude toward the newly reformulated political ideology of Islam. The Islamic Republic of Iran will continue to loom as an unknown and threatening presence in world affairs, not so much because of its own characteristics but because of European intolerance for any fundamentally different political ideology.

One may hope, of course, that time and tolerance will diminish these aggressive feelings toward Iran and the Islamic revolution. Countries such as Japan and Korea, whose prosperity has won them worldwide economic respect and a measure of ideological autonomy, may serve as intermediaries to help countries with a European heritage realize that European ideological hegemony is no longer essential to a peaceful and productive modern world. More crucial will be the gradual growth among the world's Muslims, despite neo-Mamluk claims that ending the Iran-Iraq war signaled the end of the Islamic revolution, of the political ideology of Islam as a viable way of living in the modern world. Eventually Islam will be accepted, but the way will be slow and difficult. The war imposed on Iran by Iraqi aggression may be over but passive ideological aggression against the Islamic revolution remains.

The Need for Modification and Development of the Laws of War in Modern International Law

SAEID MIRZAEE YENGEJEH

Rules and principles relating to laws of war develop on the basis of the conduct of states and combatant forces in time of war, and as a result of their repetition they become binding customs. Many rules and conventional laws of war have been formulated after specific wars and from the experience gained in those wars. For example, the Paris Declaration of 1856 concerning naval warfare was issued after the end of Crimean War.

Aroused by the wounded of the Crimean war, Henry Dunate, a Swiss humanitarian, proposed the formation of an organization that would be trusted by belligerent states and that would protect the wounded of war. The International Red Cross was formed as a result of his initiative and played a major role in the adoption of the Geneva Convention of 1864, which committed the signatory states to care for those wounded in war. The Red Cross also played an important role in formulating and adopting Geneva conventions and protocols. The 1925 Geneva Convention prohibiting the use of chemical weapons was ratified in the wake of the experiences gained from World War I, in which such weapons were used. The 1949 conventions concerning easing the conditions of the wounded and sick, treatment of prisoners of war, and protection of civilians in time of war were formulated after considering the circumstances of World War II.[1]

The Iran-Iraq war provides experiences that can be utilized for further developing and modifying international laws of war. During this war, in addition to violating customary principles and rules of warfare, Iraq, the aggressor state, used measures resulting from technological developments and changes in the methods of conducting wars, for which no explicit and clear provisions exist. Below I present cases and analyses of Iraq's conduct, examining actions for which no provision has thus far been envisaged in international laws of war. Thus, I attempt to show that the laws and regulations of war need to be modified and extended.

In international relations, belligerent states are not free to choose any means with which to conduct a war. Throughout the eight years of war with Iran, the Iraqi regime repeatedly violated the principles and rules of international laws of war, e.g., it used chemical weapons and attacked residential areas. In addition, Iraq resorted to acts that contravene the spirit and purposes of laws of war: threatening international airlines, attacking commercial shipping in international waters, and striking nuclear power plants and oil platforms. Iraq's aggressive behavior had the characteristics of war crimes.[2] However, because of technological advances, and thus the extension of methods of warfare for such attacks that were not possible in the past, there are no clear and explicit provision in laws of war. It behooves the international community to develop and formulate rules for such cases now.

Threats to International Civil Aviation and Attacks on Passenger Airliners

In a note (no. 9016) addressed to international airlines, dated March 17, 1985, Iraq declared that because of the operations of its warplanes over Iranian airspace it would not ensure the safety of international flights there. Consequently, international flights to Iran from their regular routes in western Iran ceased. Iraqi warplanes threatened or attacked passenger planes on a number of occasions.

- On May 4, 1982, Iraqi air force jets shot down an Algerian airliner carrying Ben Yahya, the Algerian foreign minister, after it entered

Iranian airspace near the border of Turkey. The Algerian foreign minister and his party died.

- On February 20, 1986, two Iraqi jet fighters shot down an aircraft belonging to an Iranian airline en route from Tehran to Ahvaz, causing the deaths of its forty-two passengers.
- On December 30, 1985, a Turkish Airlines plane, which was to return a high-level Turkish economic delegation from Tehran to Ankara, was attacked by Iraqi jet fighters. The aircraft was forced to change course and land at the city of Van in east Turkey. It received instructions to continue the flight to Tehran but was again attacked by Iraqi planes and forced to return.
- On March 28 and 29, 1986, an airliner belonging to the Islamic Republic of Iran was hit by rockets fired by Iraqi jet fighters, and the plane's body was heavily damaged.
- In the evening of October 15, 1986, intruding Iraqi planes attacked a civilian plane of the Islamic Republic of Iran at Shiraz airport while the passengers were boarding; thirty people were killed.
- On October 30, 1986, the special plane of the advisor to the emir of Kuwait, en route from Turkey to Tehran, was pursued by Iraqi jet fighters in northwest Iran.

By threatening international air lanes and attacking passenger airliners, the Iraqi regime caused the death and injury of innocent persons and losses to neutral states. Iraq's illegal actions contravened two principles of the laws of war, namely, protection of civilians and the rights of neutral states. Furthermore, its actions were tantamount to disregard for its international obligations in accordance with the Chicago Convention of 1944 on the security of international air transport, the safety and regulation of flights, and the safety of airplane passengers and crews.[3] The breach of this obligation by any state is a flagrant violation of international law and entails responsibility for its perpetrators.

The issuance of note 9016 by Iraq contravened paragraph 1 of Article 3 in Annex 15 of the Chicago Convention, because this paragraph says that "no contracting state is permitted to issue a note about the territory of another contracting state." The threat to international civil aviation posed by the Iraqi regime was included in the agenda of the special meeting of the council of the International Civil Aviation Organization (ICAO) in April 1985. The council adopted a resolution on

April 23, 1985, calling on Iran and Iraq to guarantee the safety of flights and to take practical measures for the safety of passenger planes.

The secretary-general of ICAO, in accordance with a mandate from its council, requested that Iraq withdraw or cancel its note of March 17. Iraq responded that because the war between the two countries was not over, Iraqi war planes would continue to use Iranian airspace and the note was issued merely to inform airlines about military operations and thereby prevent probable mishaps for passengers. Thus, Iraq disregarded the ICAO Council resolution of April 23 and refused to cancel the threatening note. The council also adopted a resolution in December of the same year, reaffirming its call for the cancellation of Iraq's note, and the call was further confirmed by the sixth session of the ICAO's General Assembly. However, these moves did not change Iraq's position.

Threatening and Attacking International Shipping by Iraq

The Iraqi regime issued note 100/82, declaring that a naval blockade would be in force for some Iranian ports and would attack neutral ships entering and leaving these ports. From that time until May 1988, Iraqi planes attacked 315 ships in the Persian Gulf. Of this number, 183 were oil tankers; the rest were commercial and other kinds of ships. These attacks left 400 dead and 500 injured.

A review of laws of war, whether they derive from custom or treaty, shows that to ensure that neutral states observe neutrality, two rights have been recognized for the belligerent states. The opposing states may impose a naval blockade on their enemies and may visit and search commercial neutral ships.[4] From the standpoint of international law, a naval blockade involves preventing third states from reaching the enemy's armed forces and stopping the enemy's trade by blockading its ports and shores.[5] Naval blockades of the ports and shores of the enemy have a long historical precedence, but the formulation of rules on naval blockades began with the Paris Declaration of 1856. There are legal principles that should be observed by belligerent states when setting up naval blockades.

- Advance notice should be given to the enemy and other states of the intention to impose a naval blockade of enemy ports and coasts.
- A naval blockade should be solely against ports and coasts of the enemy.
- In order to make other states observe a naval blockade, the blockader state should have adequate strength to close entrance and exit routes to the coasts and ports of the enemy, and issuing a notice to this effect does not suffice. There is no set rule regarding the number of ships required for a naval blockade and its supervision; it depends on the case.

Although the effectiveness of naval blockades has been reduced to some extent because of changes in the techniques, methods, and scope of warfare, the rules of naval blockades stipulated in the Paris Declaration of 1856 remain valid. Some regulations pertaining to naval blockades were included in the London Declaration of 1907, but this declaration was not ratified by the signatory states.

The search and visit of neutral commercial ships is another right that has been recognized for belligerent states by customary international law. The reason behind such a custom was that the declaration of neutrality by a state does not necessarily mean it is truly neutral. In fact, there is often a difference between states' official positions and what they actually do. In recognition of this, international custom and practice permit belligerent states to search merchant ships of neutral states outside the enemy's territorial waters. This ensures that neutral states observe principles of neutrality, e.g., it stops the transportation of contraband goods to the enemy or assistance to enemy ships. If in the course of the visit and search the warships of belligerent states discover that contraband goods destined for the enemy are part of the ship's cargo, they have the right to seize the goods or, under certain circumstances, capture the ship carrying the contraband goods.[6]

This principle of international laws of war has been formally recognized in international regulations and declarations, including the Paris Declaration of 1856 and the London Declaration of 1909. There are numerous judicial pronouncements regarding such a principle in international custom.[7] To regulate the conduct of war and show respect for the rights of neutral states, certain criteria have been formulated in this regard.

After the navy of the Islamic Republic of Iran, in the middle of Iranian year 1363 (1984–85), started to search merchant ships suspected of carrying contraband goods to Iraq or with a final destination of Iraq, many states acknowledged such practices in war. (For example, the United Kingdom and the United States issued separate statements declaring that if there is sufficient cause to suspect neutral ships of carrying war matériel, then such ships could be searched.)[8]

In accordance with laws of naval warfare, the warships of belligerent states may attack and sink merchant neutral ships only under certain limited circumstances. If merchant ships of neutral states put up armed resistance against the warships of belligerent states, they may be attacked and sunk. Furthermore, if the warships of belligerent states discover, in the course of their search, that a neutral ship is carrying a considerable quantity of contraband goods to a destination on enemy soil, they can seize the ship and divert it toward their ports. If the circumstances do not allow directing the ship to the port, sinking the ship is recognized to be permissible. If sinking is to take place, some measures should be taken beforehand. For example, all persons on board must be evacuated and transferred to another ship. The question of the principle of international law on which Iraq's attacks on merchant ships and oil tankers is based needs to be clarified.

Naval blockades should be carried out by ships and in an effective manner. The Iraqi regime lost its naval force at the beginning of the war and thus did not possess the necessary fleet to carry out its blockade. By targeting ships and oil tankers by air, Iraq resorted to actions with no basis or foundation in international laws of war and neutrality.[9] Oppenheim states that a "naval blockade is historically a phenomenon specifically involving naval forces and a naval blockade solely by air cannot exist." Such attacks are carried out without identifying ships and their cargoes and without any advance notice or evacuation of crew and persons on board, causing heavy casualties and losses. They also inflict heavy losses on neutral states and their nationals and pollute the sea and the environment.[10]

Air attacks on ships run counter to the principle of free navigation in international waters. The international community has condemned attacks on merchant ships in international waters and has called for an end to such attacks.[11] The United Nations also reaffirmed the right to free navigation in international waters and called on Iran and Iraq to stop these attacks. As an example, in its resolution of October 31, 1983, the Security Council underlined the right of free navigation in international waters and told Iran and Iraq to cease attacks on sea lanes, navigable waterways, ports, and terminals and installations situated on the coast and at ports with direct or indirect access to the sea.[12] Security Council Resolution 552 of June 1, 1984, also asked all states to respect the right of free navigation in conformity with norms of international law and demanded that attacks be stopped on ships en route to ports of coastal states that were not parties to the conflict.[13]

Iraq's attacks on merchant ships had become possible as a result of technological advancements and consequent changes in methods of warfare. Thus, there is a critical need for the international community to take new measures to crystallize the purposes of war laws, with a view to banning such attacks. As pointed out earlier, in its resolutions 540 and 552 the United Nations recognized the need for such an action by the international community.

Attacks on Oil Platforms in the Persian Gulf

In February 1982, Iraq fired ten missiles at oil well number 3 in the Nowrooz oil field, causing oil wells 2, 3, and 4 to gush with oil. As a result, one of the oil wells caught fire. Three thousand barrels of oil poured into the waters of the Persian Gulf daily. The total volume of oil streaming into the Persian Gulf was estimated at 250,000 barrels. It spread over a vast area of the Persian Gulf, inflicting much damage not only on the Islamic Republic of Iran but also on other coastal states and on the marine environment. There are harmful effects from gushing oil.

- The sudden outflow of oil, which spread over a vast area of the Persian Gulf, caused much damage to the marine environment, killing marine animals on a great scale.
- The oil spillage threatened all coastal installations of the littoral states

on the southern coast of the Persian Gulf. Some of these installations, such as the desalination plants, are vital for the regional states.

- Because in some areas the thickness of the oil spread over the Persian Gulf reached two feet, international shipping lanes were endangered because many ships use sea water for cooling. Thus, the Iraqi regime violated principles of international law and the obligations it had undertaken.

In accordance with the Kuwait Convention on Protection of the Marine Environment and its binding protocols, Iraq had agreed to take all necessary measures to prevent or reduce pollution in the marine environment.[14] The Iraqi government also agreed in accordance with the protocol on regional cooperation against pollution arising from oil and other harmful materials, to take necessary and effective measures to protect the coastlines and interests of one or more contracting states against the harmful effects of oil and other materials in the marine environment.[15] In attacking oil installations of the Nowrooz wells, Iraq acted against its obligations under the Kuwait Convention. Furthermore, by refusing to cooperate in stopping oil spillage from these wells, Iraq ignored the obligations arising from the signing of the protocol annexed to the Kuwait Convention. During the regional session that was held in Kuwait for this purpose, Iraq refused to give any assurances that it would not attack these oil wells while experts were working on them. Fortunately for Iraq, these violations had no precedence as no such attacks took place in previous wars, so their prohibition was not envisaged in laws of war. To prevent these breaches from recurring, it is necessary that the international community clearly define rules on the prohibition of such attacks.

Attack on the Bushehr Nuclear Power Plant

In the course of the war, Iraq repeatedly attacked the Bushehr nuclear power plant.[16] The attacks were reported to, and registered with, the International Atomic Energy Agency (IAEA). As a result of these attacks, a number of experts at the power plant were killed or wounded and considerable damage was inflicted on its concrete wall. Because of the danger of radiation, the international community took some steps toward prohibiting attacks on these types of installations. Paragraph 3 of Article 35 of the first Geneva Protocol of 1977 annexed to the general conventions of 1949 bans the use of methods or weapons that cause excessive and durable damage on the natural environment or are likely to cause such damage. Also, in accordance with paragraph 1 of Article 56, "Attacks on such installations as dams . . . and atomic power plants, even when such targets are military targets, are prohibited."

In addition, the resolutions adopted by the IAEA ban attacks on nuclear power plants. For example, in the first paragraph of Resolution 407, adopted by the IAEA, all armed attacks on nuclear installations that are used for peaceful purposes should be explicitly and promptly banned. Resolution 444 of the general conference of the IAEA considers all threats or armed attacks on peaceful nuclear installations as violations of the charter of the United Nations, international law, and the principles of the constitution of the IAEA. The Iraqi attacks on the Bushehr nuclear plant occurred when such regulations were in place. Therefore, it is indeed appropriate for the international community to resort to serious measures to ban such attacks. The preparation and drawing up of a protocol similar to the 1925 Geneva protocol banning the use of chemical weapons can be an appropriate step in this direction.

Conclusion

During the eight-year war with Iran, Iraq initiated many attacks that contravened the spirit of laws of war. Some of the violations were novel and were not covered by formal law as they had been made possible only because of recent technological advances. The conferences that have been held to formulate and codify laws of war have never before been asked to deal with such cases; consequently there are no clear and explicit regulations that are pertinent to them. Based on the experience gained from the Iran-Iraq war, and to prevent repetition of these crimes in future wars and protect future generations from such atrocities, the international community must formulate and codify restrictive regulations for these new cases. This is essential, considering the prevailing international climate and the policies of superpowers aimed at creating tension and waging proxy wars in different parts of the world in order to reach their goals. The possibility of another imposed war, similar to that imposed on Iran, cannot be ruled out.

Notes

1. From the early nineteenth century, treaties and conventions were concluded and adopted that codified rules and regulations of war. These rules basically deal with the area of combat, the weapons that may be used in war, humanitarian considerations, protection of civilian property, protection of civilian life, and prevention of the extension of war to neutral states.

2. War crimes generally include offenses committed by the armed forces, including the heads of state, and entail punishment for the perpetrators. Most authorities believe that there are four categories of war crimes: violations of laws and customs of war; hostile military actions against civilian populations; espionage, destruction, and treason in time of war; and all kinds of plunder of property. Paragraph B of Article 6 of the Nuremberg Charter considers the second category as punishable crimes in international law.

3. Article 44 of the Chicago Convention, while enumerating the objectives of the organization, emphasizes that international civil aviation shall be carried out throughout the world in an orderly and safe manner and that the safety of flights for international aviation shall be promoted.

4. "Naval blockade" means naval blockade in time of war, which is different from naval blockade in time of peace and also from economic blockade.

5. For more information on "naval blockade," see L. Oppenheim, *International Law* (London: Longmans, 1965), 2:767–97.

6. For more information on the control of traffic and visit and search of ships by warships of belligerent states, see Mostafa Forootan, "Neutrality and Search of Merchant Ships," *Foreign Policy Magazine* (in Persian), 2, no. 1 (Winter 1984): 87–104.

7. The judgments of the U.S.-British Arbitration Tribunal in the Wanderer Case issued in 1921 and of the Hague Tribunal in the Cartage Case in 1913 confirm the existence of such a principle in international laws of war.

8. *New York Times*, January 14, 1986.

9. Oppenheim, *International Law*, 781.

10. According to *Kayhan* (Persian daily newspaper) of May 24, 1988, as a result of Iraqi attacks on oil tankers near Larak Island on May 14, 1988, oil spilled into the sea on a large scale, causing the death of millions of shrimp. A large number of oysters, crustaceans and mollusks were also destroyed, and other kinds

of marine animals were endangered. According to this report, except for 100 kilometers of Bandar Abbas shorelines, the water of the Straits of Hormuz was completely polluted by oily materials.

11. Resolution 540 of October 31, 1984.

12. After a long silence, the UN Security Council began to consider the problem of attacks on ships at the request of Bahrain, Kuwait, Oman, Saudi Arabia, and the United Arab Emirates. But, despite Iraq's admission of launching such attacks, the council refused to mention Iraq by name as a violator of international norms.

13. The Kuwait Convention on Cooperation for the Protection of the Marine Environment was signed in 1987 by authorized representatives of Iran, Bahrain, Qatar, UAE, Oman, Saudi Arabia, Iraq, and Kuwait.

14. Paragraph A of Article 3 of the Kuwait Convention.

15. Paragraph A of Article 3 of the protocol on regional cooperation against pollution resulting from oil and other harmful materials in emergency cases, annexed to the Kuwait Convention.

16. Iraqi planes attacked the Bushehr Nuclear Power Plant on February 12 and March 4, 1983. Between April 15 and November 20, 1987, the plant was attacked by Iraq on a number of occasions.

Contributors

ABDOLRAHMAN ALEM is assistant professor of political science at Tehran University.

HAMID ALGAR is professor of history at the University of California, Berkeley.

BAHMAN BAKTIARI is assistant professor of political science at the University of Maine.

JAMES A. BILL is professor of government and director of the Reves Center for International Studies at the College of William and Mary.

RICHARD W. BULLIET is professor of history at Columbia University.

ELIZABETH GAMLEN is a Ph.D. candidate in the Department of Peace Studies at the University of Bradford.

MEHDI HOJJAT is director of the Organization for Preservation of Cultural Heritage, Iran.

LAITH KUBBA is an Iraqi writer and political activist residing in London.

KEITH MCLACHLAN is director of the Geopolitics and International Boundaries Research Centre, School of Oriental and African Studies, University of London.

MOHIADDIN MESBAHI is assistant professor of international relations at Florida International University.

DJAMCHID MOMTAZ is professor of international law at Tehran University.

FARHANG RAJAEE teaches politics in Iran and is a senior research fellow at the Cultural Studies and Research Institute in Tehran.

PAUL ROGERS is professor of conflict analysis at the University of Bradford.

A. REZA SHEIKHOLESLAMI is Soudavar Chair of Persian Studies at the University of Oxford.

S. TAHERI SHEMIRANI is a career diplomat with the Iranian Foreign Ministry.

PAUL TAVERNIER is professor of law at Rouen University.

IBRAHIM ANVARI TEHRANI is a career diplomat with the Iranian Foreign Ministry.

SAEID MIRZAEE YENGEJEH is legal counsellor in the Mission of Iran to the United Nations.

Index

Library of Congress Cataloging-in-Publication Data

The Iran-Iraq war / edited by Farhang Rajaee.
p. cm.
Includes index.
ISBN 0-8130-1176-0 (cloth).—ISBN 0-8130-1177-9 (paper)
1. Iraq-Iran War, 1980-1988—Congresses. I. Rajaee, Farhang, 1952- .
DS318.85.I692 1993 92-33379
955.05'4—dc20 CIP